INSTRUCTIONAL MATERIALS

An Introduction for Teachers

LOUIS SHORES
DEAN OF THE LIBRARY SCHOOL
FLORIDA STATE UNIVERSITY

THE RONALD PRESS COMPANY · NEW YORK

37.3078
Sh78

Library of Congress Catalog Card Number: 60–6145

PREFACE

This book has been written as an introductory textbook for prospective teachers enrolled in the growing number of courses in instructional materials being offered by teacher-education institutions. It is also intended as a guide for teachers in service.

The underlying assumption of the book is that the trend away from the concept "library" and "audio-visual center" in our schools will continue and that increasingly the trend will be toward a unified Materials Center. Whether this resource center continues to be called a school library or not is less important than the fact that the school library is steadily assuming responsibility for the whole range of instructional materials and that the teacher must know how he can effectively use all these materials to increase his effectiveness in the classroom.

In this book all major types and subtypes of instructional materials used by teachers are identified. The extent to which each type is discussed is necessarily limited by the requirements of the introductory survey-type course for which the book is intended. For each type there is included a definition, an estimate of potential, some historical background, criteria and sources for selection, representative examples, and suggestions for utilization.

The first chapter provides an introduction to the organization of a Materials Center. Each of the next eleven chapters is devoted to a major area of materials. The final chapter, which takes up some of the details of Materials Center management, provides the initial stepping stone for those students who may choose to take additional courses leading to the position of librarian, coordinator, or materials specialist. This final chapter should also help those teachers in service whose

iii

77891

interest spurs them to assume responsibility for instructional materials leadership in a school without a trained librarian. The Appendix is a full list of the teaching tools cited throughout the book.

Acknowledgments for assistance in the preparation of this text are due all of my colleagues in the Library School of Florida State University and in the public schools of Florida, who have fashioned a new concept and pattern for instructional materials in the schools. Special acknowledgments are due Dr. Lloyd W. King, Past Executive Secretary, The American Textbook Publishers' Institute, who read and criticized very helpfully the chapters on textbooks and reference books; Professors Henry Becker and David E. Christensen of the Geography Department, Florida State University, for their criticism of the chapter on place media; Dr. Otis McBride, Professor William Quinly, and Miss Mary Alice Hunt of the Library School of Florida State University, for help with the chapters on still projections and motion pictures, recordings, and pictures, respectively; Dr. John G. Church, for reading and testing the manuscript in his class; and J. J. Shores of the *Toledo Blade*, for copyreading and "tasting."

Finally, my wife—with infinite patience—read, criticized, typed, and retyped the manuscript many times.

LOUIS SHORES

Tallahassee, Florida
January, 1960

CONTENTS

INSTRUCTIONAL
MATERIALS

1

INTRODUCTION

The unfavorable ratio of teachers to students constitutes a major factor in the current crisis in education. While pupil enrollment is on the increase, teacher supply continues behind the need. This quantitative imbalance cannot but cause a qualitative disturbance. Extension of school opportunities to all children inevitably widens the span of individual differences. The fact that there are too few teachers and too many pupils confronts the teaching profession with an almost impossible responsibility. Quantitatively, the solution is the employment of more teachers; qualitatively, the re-enforcement of teacher effort with an adequate selection of teaching tools and the preparation of teachers for use of those tools.

In the professional literature these teaching tools are now called Instructional Materials. They include the whole range of media through which teachers and pupils communicate. Since education is fundamentally communication between teacher and pupil, the importance of Instructional Materials is evident.

An Instructional Material may be defined as any medium of communication used by teacher and pupil to advance learning. Under this definition, all teaching tools are Instructional Materials. Library books, audio-visual aids, television and radio, glass slides, filmstrips, flat pictures and maps, real objects, and community resources are some of the classes of teaching tools of extreme importance to education.

Without them, and without adequate knowledge of their use, the present teaching force of the nation is no match for the overwhelming challenge of mounting individual differences in the pupil population. With an adequate selection of Instructional Materials one teacher can be as ten in the struggle to make universal education, for the first time in world history, a reality.

Parable of the Book. In a certain high school physics class Paul had trouble understanding the textbook. There was nothing basically wrong with the book. It was aimed at the background of the average eleventh or twelfth grader. But Paul was not average. He liked literature and history, but he suffered terribly in mathematics and shop. In his high school there was increasing emphasis on doing things with your hands. Paul wanted to make things, but he was not mechanically inclined. He liked to sit quietly in the library for hours and read. He knew he would fail in physics unless something like the miracles he read about happened soon.

The current subject was magnetism. He had read the chapter through desperately, not once but twice. As far as Paul was concerned, the author wrote in a foreign language. As Paul sat meditating his certain death in one of his subjects, he had an idea of his own. He walked to the 530 section of the library shelves and selected six physics books at random. He located the magnetism section in each book and read them in succession.

The first section was as difficult as his textbook. The second was no more helpful. But the third gave more history and biography and Paul's interest was aroused. The fourth went into the theory of molecules and their arrangement, and Paul's imagination began to stir. In the fifth he found a statement that conflicted with something the textbook writer had speculated about. By the time Paul had finished reading the sixth section he felt he had begun to understand something about magnetism.

Following through with his library experience, Paul next read two encyclopedia articles on the subject. His interest was now high. He discovered there was a film in the school library on magnetism. Also he bought himself a small magnet and a compass.

What happened in that physics class the next day was inevitable. When Paul was called on by the teacher, he arose and spoke for five minutes on the subject of magnetism. He gave its history and theory, and then described its applications in modern life. At one point he discussed differences in opinion among the authorities, citing sources, and ended with a demonstration of compass and magnet, and a report on the existence of the film.

The awe of teacher and fellow pupils was unrestrained. Paul had earned his "A." But, more important, he had discovered for himself the power of using varied materials in learning.

Parable of the Film. The sixth grade was interested in paper. Some discussion of how it is made was included in the textbook. But not even the teacher was too sure of the process. So Miss Vesprille sent her pupils in groups to the library, where some of them read encyclopedia articles and reported faithfully. Others brought examples of various kinds of paper. One pupil discovered a series of pictures about the process of paper-making. But no one in the class had any real comprehension of the methods and procedures used in paper manufacture.

On the following Wednesday the teacher took the class to the nearest paper mill. She believed that nothing could equal this personal experience. At the paper mill, she was sure, the whole class would begin to understand at last how wood is converted into pulp and then into wrapping or writing material.

The school journey was reasonably successful. Of the thirty-one pupils, at least six—the most aggressive and mechanically minded—were always right up front, peering into the vats, asking questions, and handling anything they were permitted to touch—and sometimes objects marked "Hands Off." But Miss Vesprille noted with concern that the rest of the class struggled to look in between and over the heads of the six to catch furtive glances before the group moved on. About five of the youngsters never got near enough to know what was going on and, toward the end of the tour, compensated for this by facetiously making up stories about things and persons they saw. Miss Vesprille's review in class the following day confirmed her estimate of the limited success of the school journey.

But she had one more teaching tool. From the school system's central film library she had ordered a 16-mm motion picture on paper-making. The room was darkened, and the film was projected.

Today's teacher has the choice of a variety of teaching materials. *Courtesy Curriculum Library, University of Wisconsin.*

There was no doubt from the first moment the showing began. All of the pulping and chemical processes came to life slowly and deliberately. From any point in the room every device and substance was clearly visible. Changes that took place almost invisibly at the mill became perfectly visible through camera close-ups and slow-downs of the motion. All at once both the class and the teacher understood why the motion picture was the supreme medium for explaining complex processes.

The Dynamics of Instructional Materials

Teaching is essentially an act of communicating to the one who is learning. In good teaching, communication is both informative and inspiring. The informing is largely sensory; the inspiring, usually extrasensory. What has concerned the teacher from the beginning of education has been how to communicate the accumulated experience of the human race to each new generation.

For centuries the principal medium of communication between teacher and pupil was the spoken word. This medium has in no sense diminished in importance, but it has increasingly been supplemented by other media.

In the beginning, the teacher's words were copied by the pupil. With the invention of printing, much of the copying was replaced by the textbook. As textbooks became more plentiful and less expensive, they assumed the role of dominant medium in the school. Well into the nineteenth century, schools accepted the proposition that a single textbook for each grade or subject was all the material that teacher and pupil needed to carry on successful learning.

Recognition of individual differences stimulated further supplements to oral teaching, copying, and the single textbook. A plethora of printing suggested immediately that, among the thousands of books, magazines, pamphlets, and broadsides, there might be found a sufficient number of different approaches to match the individual needs of children. Out of the psychological concept of individual differences and the material production of print was born the school library, fathered by Horace Mann as a means of improving the teacher's communication with his pupils.

By the beginning of the twentieth century, other media began to augment the printed word. The picture, an ancient means of communication, was reintroduced into the classroom in new proportions and forms. Comenius had shown the way as early as the seventeenth century with his illustrated textbook, *Orbis Pictus*. By the nineteenth century, technology started a series of inventions that led to ever-easier picture reproduction in black and white, color, and three dimensions. Cartoons brought story, drama, and humor to the medium and sped the acceptance of the flat picture as a teaching tool.

The still was followed by the motion picture. In succession, developments brought color, sound, three dimensions, and an ever-widening screen that included techniques with multiple cameras, projectors, speakers, sound tapes, and the peripheral vision of simulated reality.

In the world of sound, the phonograph record went through a series of improvements leading to long-playing records and to stereophonic achievements that produced the highest fidelity yet known. Tape recordings supplemented disks and provided a more economical means for individual communication. The phenomenon of radio became, almost immediately upon its commercial development, an educational accessory surpassed in teaching power only by the potential of television.

Despite the proliferation of media available for classroom use, two obstacles prevent their utilization in learning. One of the barriers is budgetary. Financial provision for the procurement of all kinds of Instructional Materials is still inadequate, although great strides have been made in several states.

The other obstacle is teacher education. Until recently very little attention was given to teacher preparation in the use of the whole range of Instructional Materials. Even now in many teacher education programs, Instructional Materials are "integrated" into methods courses, where more often than not materials are considered incidentally rather than intrinsically; or they are presented fractionally in a separate course on children's literature, library science, or audiovisual aids. Like the six blind men and the elephant, teachers who are products of these separate courses enter their profession with one-sided commitments to a single class of materials.

For example, it is not uncommon to hear this statement from the teacher who has had only a course in children's literature: "Reading is still 95 per cent of all education. Therefore books are the only instructional materials essential for learning."

And from the teacher who has had only a course in audio-visual education, something like this may be heard: "Everybody knows how to read. Why bother about teaching the use of books? What teachers need to know is how to teach with the motion picture."

From the teacher who has had a single course in library science, one might hear this statement: "It is a good idea to *supplement* books with films, recordings, maps, globes, and other nonbook materials."

All three of these teachers are certainly ahead of the teacher who has had no preparation in the selection and use of any major class of Instructional Materials. But better still would be an introduction to the whole range of Instructional Materials now available. Such an introduction is increasingly replacing the separate courses in audio-visual aids, library science, and children's literature accepted for teacher certification. Such an introduction, all-inclusive and up-to-date, is presented in this text.

The New Battle of the Books

One of the dilemmas that confronts the teacher in search of more effective media for communication with his pupils is the contending appeals of the various classes of Instructional Materials. The advocates of the textbook insist that all a good teacher needs to supplement his own classroom efforts is a single textbook, although some of them will go so far as to admit the addition of a workbook or a supplementary text. The importance of the textbook in learning is incontrovertible. It represents an important and fundamental class of Instructional Materials. But its value can be reinforced by the use of a great variety of supplementary materials.

Chief among the supplements are what are known as library materials. These are not only books, but also magazines, pamphlets, documents, and broadsides. In addition—

in most school libraries—there are pictures, maps, globes, bulletin boards, exhibits of science, art, and other objects and specimens. And some libraries include glass slides, film-strips, disk recordings, and 16-mm motion pictures. The supplements in the last two categories are as often called audio-visual since they are library materials.

"Visual education" was the term first used for teaching which stressed visual rather than verbal methods. The principal media of visual education were still and motion pictures. When sound came to movies and the use of radio became widespread, the term "audio-visual education," or "audio-visual instruction," came into use. Audio-visual education is defined as a way of learning—that is, learning through media that communicate primarily through the senses of sight and hearing, but also through the senses of touch, taste, and smell.

The term "audio-visual" is also used to identify classes of materials or teaching aids. The exact classes of school materials called "audio-visual" and those termed "library" are not clearly distinguished by the professional literature of either librarianship or audio-visual instruction. Books are universally accepted as representing library materials and films as representing audio-visual. Beyond that, classes of materials are included as either library or audio-visual, depending upon the philosophies of the librarians and audio-visualists concerned. Since pictures, maps, charts, globes, bulletin boards, exhibits, disk recordings, and several other categories of school materials are claimed by the professional literatures of both librarianship and audio-visual instruction, there is a noticeable trend in schools to refer to all of these classes of teaching tools as Instructional Materials. Similarly, because it becomes increasingly more difficult for teachers and pupils to determine which classes of materials should be housed in the school library and which in the school's audio-visual center, there is a marked trend to combine or at least to correlate all of the school's Instructional Materials resources into a Materials Center.

THE MATERIALS CENTER

"Materials Center" can be defined as both a concept and an administrative unit. It is the unit—in a school system, building, or classroom—devoted to the selection, procurement, housing, organization, and dissemination of Instruc-

The Materials Center integrates a variety of materials. *Courtesy Southern Illinois University.*

tional Materials for the improvement of learning and instruction. Substitution of the term "materials center" for "school library" and "audio-visual center" has both its opponents and proponents. Librarians would understandably regret the passing of the term "library," which has come to mean so much through the ages, just as audio-visual specialists would regret a tendency to absorb their special interest under the general term "library." Proponents of the term "materials center" contend that it represents best the present opportunity for both camps to merge their interests in a unified system.

Echelons of Service

As the idea for a Materials Center develops, three echelons of service emerge. The middle echelon, or *building level,* is the one most commonly associated with the term. This is found in most high schools as the school library, which has gradually expanded its collection to include audio-visual as well as printed materials. In the elementary school and in many of the new high school buildings the library or Materials Center has been planned from the start to house the full range of Instructional Materials.

At the county or city *school-system level,* the Materials Center is the directing, supervising, or co-ordinating unit for the over-all Instructional Materials program. The Materials Center for the system may procure materials such as motion pictures too expensive to duplicate in the individual schools, a professional library for the teachers, and collections intended to supplement periodically heavy demands within the individual buildings. The Center also frequently processes all materials acquired by the schools and maintains a central inventory of all the Instructional Materials and equipment owned by the system.

The ultimate consumers are at the *classroom level*—the teacher and his pupils. Good teaching today calls for a classroom that is essentially a Materials Center. The basic difference between the classroom and building echelons, however, is in scope of selection and permanence of housing. A good classroom Materials Center is characterized by a frequent change of materials. Most of the books, pictures, disks, films, charts, and other media found in the classroom are related to the unit under study there. When the unit is completed, these materials are returned to the building Materials Center. Because of the great variety of Instructional Materials now used in a classroom, architects are increasingly planning for what the National Education Association has described as the "3-D classroom," wired for listening, lighted for reading, and darkened for viewing.

The Materials Center can, therefore, be seen as a school-wide Instructional Materials program that parallels the organization of the school system itself. Necessary to its functioning are adequately prepared personnel at every level. A director or supervisor of Instructional Materials is needed at the system level for over-all planning. Librarians or building-level co-ordinators are required in each of the schools to work directly with teachers and pupils. But fundamental to a successful Instructional Materials program are teachers at the classroom level who know Instructional Materials well enough to use them intelligently in their teaching. This knowledge includes a familiarity with the potentials and limitations of the various classes of materials and an understanding of methods of procurement, organization, and distribution. It consists further of some skill in the handling of the materials and of the equipment that accompanies some of them. In particular, this knowledge necessitates sufficient competence to enable the teacher to select and utilize Instructional Materials for a given subject area and age level.

Content of a Materials Center

The Instructional Materials found in a good Materials Center at the classroom, building, or system level must meet requirements for a variety of ages, grades, and subjects and assume a variety of formats. The usual groupings of Instructional Materials as to age and grade are:

Elementary—Kindergarten through sixth grade
Junior High—Seventh through ninth grades
Senior High—Tenth through twelfth grades

Most lists of Instructional Materials recognize these groupings. Some lists are more specialized or more refined. For example, there are lists of materials especially for preschool use. There are other lists for primary grades one through four. And there are young-adult lists for grades twelve through fourteen. One booklist, the *Children's Catalog*, employs a grade-by-grade grouping.

What must be remembered always is that no solid line can be drawn between grades and between ages. Within each grade and chronological year there may be a range of as much as six years of reading, viewing, and listening ability. Consequently, any appraisal of Instructional Materials should consider a specific age or grade as constituting only a median.

Materials may be distinguished much more clearly by the elements of format and subject.

Format Classification of Materials

An exhaustive listing by format of the various kinds of materials found in our schools would produce a list of nearly a hundred categories. The word "format" is used here to mean the physical make-up of a particular Instructional Material. The following classification of Instructional Materials by format is a guide to the contents of a Materials Center:

A. *Print Materials*
   1. Textbooks
   2. Reference Books
   3. Reading Books
   4. Serials
B. *Graphic Materials*
   1. Place Media
   2. Pictures
   3. Objects
   4. Community Resources
C. *Projected Materials*
   1. Stills
   2. Motion Pictures
   3. Miniatures
D. *Transmissions*
   1. Disk Recordings
   2. Tape Recordings
   3. Radio and Transcriptions
   4. Television and Kinescopes

There are numerous subclasses. Many of these will be described as each of the major classes of format is examined in the following chapters. All of these formats require some distinctive labeling, handling, and housing in most Materials Centers.

Subject Classification of Materials

Despite reclassifications in some academic and special libraries that have embraced the Library of Congress System, about 95 per cent of all American libraries and nearly 100 per cent of all American school libraries use the Dewey Decimal Classification System (1–1).* Any library classification aims to bring materials on similar subjects together. The Dewey Decimal Classification System, devised by Melvil Dewey and professionally referred to as "DC," divides all knowledge as found in books and other materials into ten broad classes:

000	General Works (for materials including two or more of the subjects)	400	Linguistics
		500	Pure Science
		600	Applied Science
100	Philosophy, Esthetics	700	Arts and Recreation
200	Religion	800	Literature
300	Social Sciences, Sociology	900	History

Each of these ten classes of knowledge is divided into nine divisions of that subject (see pages 16–17). For example, 500, Pure Science, has the following divisions:

510	Mathematics	550	Geology
520	Astronomy	560	Paleontology
530	Physics	570	Biology
540	Chemistry, Crystallography, Mineralogy	580	Botany
		590	Zoology

Continuing with the decimal plan, each of these divisions is further subdivided into nine sections. For example, 510, Mathematics, has these divisions:

511	Arithmetic	516	Analytic Geometry
512	Algebra	517	Calculus
513	Geometry	518	Special Functions
514	Trigonometry	519	Probabilities
515	Descriptive Geometry		

In turn, Arithmetic, for example, is further divided into subsections—511.1 Systems of Arithmetic—and so on. These

* Throughout this book, the numbers enclosed in parentheses refer to entries in the "List of Tools Cited" (Appendix, pp. 365–89).

General Scheme of Classification *

DIVISIONS

000	General Works
010	Bibliographical Science and Technique
020	Library Science
030	General Encyclopedias
040	General Collected Essays
050	General Periodicals
060	General Societies Museums
070	Journalism
080	Collected Works
090	Book Rarities

100	Philosophy Esthetics
110	Metaphysics
120	Metaphysical Theories
130	Fields of Psychology
140	Philosophic Systems
150	Psychology
160	Logic
170	Ethics
180	Oriental and Ancient Philosophy
190	Modern Philosophy

200	Religion
210	Natural Religion
220	Bible
230	Systematic or Doctrinal Theology
240	Devotional Theology
250	Pastoral Theology
260	Ecclesiastical Theology
270	Christian Church History
280	Christian Churches and Sects
290	Non-Christian Religions

300	Social Sciences Sociology
310	Statistics
320	Political Science
330	Economics
340	Law
350	Public Administration
360	Social Welfare
370	Education
380	Commerce
390	Customs

400	Linguistics
410	Comparative Linguistics
420	English Language
430	German Germanic Languages
440	French Provencal
450	Italian Rumanian
460	Spanish Portuguese
470	Latin Other Italic
480	Greek Hellenic Group
490	Other Languages

500	Pure Science
510	Mathematics
520	Astronomy
530	Physics
540	Chemistry Crystallography Mineralogy
550	Earth Sciences
560	Paleontology
570	Biological Sciences
580	Botany
590	Zoology

600	Applied Science
610	Medical Sciences
620	Engineering
630	Agriculture
640	Home Economics
650	Business and Business Methods
660	Chemical Technology Industrial Chemistry
670	Manufactures, Continued
680	Manufactures, Continued
690	Building Construction

700	Arts and Recreation
710	Landscape Architecture
720	Architecture
730	Sculpture
740	Drawing Decorative Art
750	Painting
760	Prints and Print Making
770	Photography
780	Music
790	Recreation

* From *Dewey Decimal Classification and Relative Index,* Standard (15th) Edition (Forest Press, Inc., 1952). Reprinted by permission.

800	Literature	880	Greek and Hellenic Group Literatures
810	American Literature	890	Literature of Other Languages
820	English Literature		
830	German and Other Germanic Literatures	**900**	**History**
840	French, Provencal, Catalan Literatures	910	Geography
		920	Biography
850	Italian, Rumanian, Romansch Literatures	930	Ancient World History
		940	European History
860	Spanish and Portuguese Literatures	950	History of Asia
		960	African History
870	Latin and Other Italic Literatures	970	North American History
		980	South American History
		990	History of Oceania

numbers are referred to professionally as "five eleven point one," etc., not "five eleven and one tenth," etc.

It is obvious from these enumerations that one principle of DC is "from the general to the particular." Thus, broad Pure Science, 500, narrows to 510, Mathematics, which narrows further to 511, Arithmetic, which narrows still further to 511.1, Systems of Arithmetic, and so on.

But there are other features of DC that have accounted for its universality as a library classification system. One of the principal characteristics of DC found in almost no other popular classification scheme is that of mnemonics, or aids to memory. For example, the history of a subject is always 09 (Pure Science 500, History of Science 509; Education 370, History of Education 370.9; Arithmetic 511, History of Arithmetic 511.09). The philosophy of a subject is always 01 (Philosophy of Education 370.1); the teaching of a subject is always 07 (Teaching of Science 507).

The convenience to the teacher of these mnemonics is considerable. For a book on the teaching of chemistry, he can walk directly to the shelf with 540.7 in mind.

There are many other features of value in DC, but these need not be mentioned here. Worth mentioning, however, is the fact that most school libraries vary DC in fiction and biography. The former is usually arranged alphabetically by author and under author by title without regard to the literature or nationality numbers. Biography is arranged alphabetically by the biographee, and under the biographee by author.

A selected list of other useful mnemonics for the teacher might include the following:

Mnemonic	History (940–970)	Geography (914–917)
Europe 4	940	914
England 42	942	914.2
France 44	944	914.4
Asia 5	950	915
Africa 6	960	916
North America 7	970	917
United States 73	973	917.3

Note that although England, for example, is always 2 (Literature 800, English Literature 820), 2 is not always England:

Mnemonic	Literature (810–840)		
	American (810–819)	English (820–829)	German (830–839)
Poetry 1	811	821	831
Drama 2	812	822	832
Fiction 3	813	823	833
Essays 4	814	824	834

Some libraries use in addition a *Cutter number*. This is an arbitrary number assigned to each author's last name. For example, the Cutter author number for Charles Dickens is D548 and therefore the full call number for his novels is 823 D548.

In the Materials Center books are universally arranged by DC. Periodicals usually are arranged by title. Some centers also arrange disk recordings, filmstrips, and films by DC. The *Educational Film Guide* offers DC classification, but as a rule film collections are not arranged by DC numbers.

Catalogs and Indexes to the Materials Center

Knowledge of the classification system saves the teacher's time by enabling him to go directly to the subject that concerns him at the moment. Even more specific are the various catalogs and indexes found in a good library. These can be divided into two types: those prepared by a library to locate materials within that library, and those printed by outside agencies to locate materials in any library.

Of the first type the teacher needs at once to distinguish among three kinds of records found in most libraries. Too many adult users shy away from the terms "accession record," "shelflist" and "card catalog" as if they were esoteric technicalities to be handled only gingerly by the layman. All three are simple and essential library tools.

Accession Record. The accession record is usually kept in a ledger. It lists all of the books in the library in the order in which the books came into the library. The very first book that came into the library was given the number 1; if to date 8,773 volumes have come into the library by purchase or gift, then the last accession number will be 8,773. This does not necessarily mean that there are that many volumes in the library. Some of them may have been lost or discarded, and their withdrawal will have been noted on the accession record. Other items of information found in the accession record are the author, title, publisher, date, source, and price of each book. For a long time insurance companies insisted on paying for losses only on the basis of accession records. A number of libraries now combine the accession record with the shelflist.

Shelflist. The shelflist is a file of 3x5-inch cards. It is usually kept behind the desk or in the workroom. But it is not arranged like the card catalog; the cards are in the exact order that books are found on the shelves. This makes the shelflist a sort of inventory record, and, indeed, the library takes its inventory each year by checking the book stock against the shelflist. But the shelflist can be extremely useful to the teacher at the beginning of a unit when he is checking to see what materials on his subject are available in the library.

Card Catalog. The card catalog is a 3x5 card file in which the cards are arranged alphabetically with authors, titles, and subjects in the same alphabetic sequence. Because this resembles a dictionary arrangement, this tool is often referred to as the "dictionary catalog."

There are a number of teacher aids in a card catalog if some of its intricacies can be mastered. Most catalogs have

---

Donnelly, Richard Joseph, 1919–
Active games and contests ₍by₎ Richard J. Donnelly, William G. Helms ₍and₎ Elmer D. Mitchell. 2d ed. New York, Ronald Press Co. ₍1958₎

672 p. illus. 24 cm.

"Earlier edition by Bernard S. Mason and Elmer D. Mitchell."

1. Play. 2. Games. ɪ. Title.

GV171.D6   796   58–5644 ‡

Library of Congress   ₍15₎

---

651   **Weeks, Bertha M**
How to file and index. Rev. ed., rev. printing.   Ronald 1956

306p illus

First published 1937. The 1956 edition is a revised printing of the 1951 edition; minor details have been brought up-to-date and the chapter on the transfer and final disposition of records has been partially rewritten

"The fundamentals of filing methods, with their practical application to particular types of business, such as a hospital, an engineering firm, an accountant's office, and a lawyer's office." Bkl.

1   Files and filing (Documents)   2 Indexing   ɪ Title   651

2-1-57   (W)   The H. W. Wilson Company

Printed catalog cards. Top: Library of Congress. Bottom: H. W. Wilson Company.

two kinds of cards: printed and typed. The printed cards are prepared either by the Library of Congress or by the H. W. Wilson Company, which also publishes such indexes as the *Readers' Guide*. Some publishers are now printing cards to accompany the books they publish. The typed cards are prepared by the library staff, usually for books for which there are no printed cards, but sometimes also because there are no funds for the purchase of printed cards or because central processing has shown that economy can be effected by producing the cards for all of the schools within the school system.

The three basic entries in a card catalog are author, title, and subject. Author cards are known as "main entries," because, if any variation exists on the cards, the fullest bibliographic information is always given on the author card. An author card is easily recognized by the author's name on the top line, and the card is filed by the author's last name.

If the title card is printed, it looks exactly like the author card except that the title has been typed above the author's name. This card is filed by the first significant word of the title. If the title card is typed, it is usually very brief, omitting most of the bibliographic information found on the author card.

The subject card is especially useful. Again, if it is printed, it looks just like the author card except that the subject is placed on the top line, either in red or in capital letters. The subjects are chosen from standard subject-heading lists, such as those prepared for the Library of Congress or adapted for smaller libraries. Some Materials Centers have developed their own subject-heading lists based on the units of the curriculum.

A noticeable trend is in the direction of filing together the cards for all kinds of materials. This is most helpful to the teacher. For example, if he is about to begin a unit on transportation, he can go to his Materials Center catalog and find under the subject heading TRANSPORTATION, cards not only for all of the books in the Materials Center that can contribute to the study of that unit, but for all of the films, filmstrips, tape and disk recordings, pictures, maps, globes, charts, and so on. Some Materials Centers use a different color card for each format, and others merely use a letter symbol to distinguish them.

Because the rules of filing in a card catalog sometimes vary from what is expected, it is well for the teacher to remember some of these variations. The rule "nothing comes before something" can be illustrated by the fact that New York precedes Newark in the catalog. Another rule—"persons, places, things"—means that cards will be arranged in that sequence. For example:

> Pontiac, Chief (person)
> Pontiac, Michigan (place)
> Pontiac automobile (thing)

There are other filing rules to be picked up with catalog use. National histories are arranged chronologically by period. The Mc's and Mac's among authors are arranged as if they were all Mac. Initials are filed as if they were spelled out—for example, N.E.A. under National Education Association.

Citation of Materials

Teachers are sometimes embarrassed to find that they cannot locate materials because of inadequate bibliographic information. Although the world of scholarship has not yet agreed on one standard bibliographic form for citing materials, there is a noticeable trend toward standardization in the work of UNESCO, the Modern Language Association, and other learned societies. Despite the lack of bibliographic agreement on such matters as capitalization, punctuation, sequence of items, roman or arabic numerals, and underlines or quotation marks, certain basic elements of bibliographic entry are common to all forms.

Every teacher should know that there are four primary elements in every bibliographic entry: (1) author, (2) title, (3) imprint (place, publisher, date), and (4) collation (pages and volumes, total number or inclusive). Some bibliographic forms refer to items (3) and (4) as "facts of publication." There are also certain secondary items needed only with some materials. Some of these are: (5) series, (6) price, (7) location, and (8) annotation. Formats other than books require additional or other items. Periodicals may require month and date in addition to the year as part of the imprint. Films require time and color and sound indications, and disk entries call for inclusion of revolutions per minute.

Sample citation forms for major classes of Instructional Materials are tabulated for ready reference on the facing page. The entry sequences are an adaptation of various forms. It must be emphasized that there is no unanimity on bibliographic form. Any style may be adopted by the teacher as long as it is consistently and systematically used.

Books. In citing books, bibliographic method favors author's last name first, followed by a comma and full forename if one, or initials if more than one. For example:

> Ley, Willy
> Shallcross, J. E.

In the case of women authors the first forename is always spelled out: Fisher, Dorothy C. Multiple authors may both be given if only two: Mahony, Bertha E. and Whitney, Elinor. If more than two, only the first is given, followed by the words "and others" or "*et al.*": Brinton, Crane, and others. Books written by a great many authors, no one of whom has major responsibility, may be entered under the title: for example, *Encyclopaedia Britannica.*

Following the author's name, a period, and three spaces, the title is entered, exactly as it appears on the title page of the book. Most styles favor underline rather than italics for the title. Although Library of Congress card form capitalizes only the initial letter of the first word and proper nouns, more common form favors capitalization of the initial letters of all significant words.

The imprint follows the title, a period, and three spaces. The order is place, publisher, date. Some forms omit place if it is New York, since most books are still published there. Publishers who are well known may be entered briefly, as, for example, Ronald rather than The Ronald Press Company, but care must be taken not to abbreviate a publisher's name if confusion with a similar name is possible; for example, only the name Barnes would not show whether A. S. Barnes & Co. or Barnes & Noble, Inc., is the publisher. The date should be taken from the title page if given there; if not, the last copyright date on the verso should be used. The parts of the imprint are separated from each other by a comma and single space.

Collation follows imprint, period, and three spaces and consists primarily of paging. When citing a whole book the number on the last numbered page is given: 341p. If a part of a book is cited, inclusive paging is given: p. 117–26.

Variations on the above can be found both in the Library of Congress form which appears on library catalog cards and in the University of Chicago Style Manual used in preparing many theses. The latter, for example, favors a colon between place and publisher and uses "pp." for paging.

Periodicals. Follow book order for author, but give the article title in quotes, underlining the name of the periodical. The date comes after the periodical title, a period, and three spaces and is followed by a period, three spaces, and the volume and pages. Both the Wilson indexes to periodicals and the Chicago Style Manual differ from this form, but in different ways.

Suggested: *Parent's Magazine.*   Sept. 1957.   v. 32, p. 50–51.

Wilson: Parent's Magazine   32:50–51 S '57

Chicago: *Parent's Magazine,* XXXII (September, 1957), 50–51.

Newspapers. Entry is usually under title or headline of the story, followed by the place and newspaper name, date, page, and column. When there is more than one section to the newspaper and its paging is not continuous, the section is cited in Roman numerals. The *New York Times Index* uses

Sample Citation Forms for Major Classes of Instructional Materials

	Entry Sequence	Example
Book	(1) Author. (2) Title. (3) Imprint. (4) Collation.	Ley, Willy. Space Stations. Poughkeepsie, N. Y., Guild Press, Inc., 1958. 44p. (or p. 27–29.)
Periodical	(1) Author. (2) Article title. (3) Periodical name. (4) Date. (5) Volume and page.	Hyde, Vance. "Style Her For Neatness." Parents' Magazine. Sept. 1957. v. 32, p. 50–51.
Newspaper	(1) Headline. (2) Place and newspaper name. (3) Date. (4) Page and column.	"Moon Rocket Try Expected Sunday." Tallahassee, Fla. Democrat. Aug. 13, 1958. p. 1, col. 2.
Map	(1) Editor, cartographer. (2) Title, format. (3) Imprint. (4) Size (cm or inches). (5) Color. (6) Series and catalog no. (7) Scale. (8) Projection. (9) Relief. (10) Special features.	Van Valkenburg, Samuel. Europa. (map) Chicago, Denoyer-Geppert, 1954. 133 x 108 cm. Color. 12 Rp. 1:4,750,000; 75 mi. to inch. Simple conic, true parallels 40° and 60°. Hypometric tints.
Slide	(1) Title, format (2) Imprint (3) Number, size.	Children of Mexico. (slides) Chicago, Society for Visual Education. 1954. 10 (2 x 2).
Filmstrip	(1) Title, format. (2) Imprint. (3) Frames. (4) Sound. (5) Color.	Prairie Dogs. (filmstrip) EBF, 1956. 53 fr. si with captions. Color.
Motion Picture	(1) Title, format. (2) Imprint. (3) Time. (4) Sound. (5) Color.	Television in Your Community. (film) Coronet, 1956. 11 min. sd. b. & w. or color.
Disk	(1) Composer/author/poet. (2) Title, format. (3) Imprint, catalog no. (4) Sides, size, rpm. (5) Series. (6) Performer. (7) Notes.	Beethoven, Ludwig van. Symphony No. 3, EROICA, op. 55, E flat major. (disk). Decca, 1956, DL 9865. 2 sides. 12 in. 33⅓ rpm. (Gold Label). Berlin Philharmonic Orchestra, Eugene Jochum, conductor. Recorded in Europe by Deutsche Grammophon; program notes by Wm. Flanagan.
Tape	(1) Composer/author/poet. (2) Title, format. (3) Imprint. (4) Time. (5) Series. (6) Performer. (7) Source.	Oppenheimer, Robert. Analogy in Science. (tape) American Psych. Assn., 1955 45 min. Sc 93. Kent State University.

II 1:2 for section two, page one, column two. However, in a bibliography that includes many formats this citation form might confuse page and volume, if, for example, Wilson and the *New York Times Index* forms were used.

Maps. A full map entry may include ten or more elements. Authorship will involve editor and cartographer. The title should be followed by format identification (map) as book, periodical, and other printed material entries seldom are. Other items not usually included for printed materials are size (given either in centimeters or inches), color, catalog number, scale in miles to the inch or in a ratio, projection with the true parallels indicated, and relief shown by contours, hachures, or tints. Although full bibliographic description of a map is useful especially to the geography and history teachers, it is possible to identify a map with only the four basic elements plus publisher's catalog number.

Slides. To the title and imprint must be added format (slides) and size and number of slides. The two principal sizes are 2 x 2 and 3¼ x 4. There are also transparencies as large as 10 x 10 used on the overhead projector.

Filmstrips. The suggested entry sequence introduces frames into the collation instead of pages, and adds the elements of sound and color. *Filmstrip Guide* and the Library of Congress catalog provide other bibliographic forms that may be adopted. Format should be indicated after the title.

Motion Pictures. The shorter term "film" may be used to designate format. In addition to sound and color, running time must be indicated in minutes. Since most motion pictures used in schools are 16 mm, size designation is not necessary unless the film is 8 mm or 35 mm.

Disks. The number of elements for a disk recording entry may be many. The author entry may involve composer, poet, and adapter. Imprint calls for producer's catalog number. Collation introduces the number of sides, which may be one or both sides of the record or an album running up to eight or ten sides. Since many record players now have variable speeds, any number of rpm (revolutions per minute) may be indicated, but three are most frequent—78, 33⅓, and 45. The most common sizes (diameters) are 12, 10, and 7 inches, although some 16-inch records are still in use. Such series designations as (Victor) Red Seal and (Decca) Gold Label may be helpful identifications. Performer—that is musician, reader, or lecturer—must be cited as well as author or composer.

Tapes. As for disks, a great many elements may be included for tapes. The *National Tape Recording Catalog* uses a comparatively simple entry form. Elements of time and source must be included. Inches per second (ips) are not needed in the entry form unless the school has a tape recorder of the old-fashioned type with only one speed. The most usual ips are 3¾ and 7. A simple time table can be based on:

IPS	Feet	Minutes
3¾	600	30
7½	1200	30

Tape recordings are usually acquired by sending blank tapes to be recorded at the library which has the master.

Other Formats. A great many other formats of Instructional Materials—such as pictures, government publications, models, community resources, and television programs—are considered in this book, but application of the principles of four basic bibliographic elements will enable the teacher to make a proper citation for either requesting or reporting on any type of material.

Printed Indexes and Catalogs

There are, in addition to the catalogs prepared by the library for its collection, many printed catalogs and indexes prepared by outside agencies, which are especially useful to the teacher in selecting materials for addition to the school collection. The development of an adequate library in the school is by no means solely the librarian's responsibility. In many schools a faculty library committee devotes itself meticulously to the task of working with the librarian to develop a good Materials Center with the resources available. This involves not only careful purchase, but alert discrimination among the many free or sponsored offerings now available to schools. Selection is a tremendous task. In view of the proliferation and the almost continuous production of various media, only the concerted effort of the faculty can accomplish intelligent selection.

A division of work among the teachers is the most expeditious procedure, with each faculty member assuming responsibility for checking the sources for materials in his subject area and grade level. A good practice is to maintain a "Want File" in the Materials Center on 3 x 5 order cards or slips, filed alphabetically by author. An example of such a card is shown in the illustration below.

Class No.	Author (surname first)			
Accession No.	Title			
No. of copies ordered				
Date ordered	Publisher			
Of	Edition or series	Year	Volumes	List Price
Date received	Requested by			
Date of bill	Notify	Address		
Cost per copy	Reviewed in			
L. C. card No.	Approved by			
GAYLORD 101-L PRINTED IN U.S.A	Libraries combining order and accession records may use the reverse of this card for recording symbols of branches, and other data.			

Order card. *Courtesy Gaylord Brothers, Inc.*

A carbon of all cards submitted by the teacher can be maintained by him to see what progress the library is making toward filling his wants. Since no school has all the money it

Huntington, Harriet E. 1909-
* Let's go to the desert; illus. with photographs by the author. Doubleday 1949
90p illus $2.75 (3-5) **574.5**
1 Adaptation (Biology) 2 Desert fauna
3 Desert flora (W)
"Plants and animals of the desert are pictured here in twenty-two fine photographs and simple text. An attractive and informative book which the author wrote for her own children." Horn book

Webber, Irma Eleanor (Schmidt) 1904-
* Anywhere in the world; the story of plant & animal adaptation. Scott, W.R. 1947
64p illus boards $2 (4-6) **574.5**
1 Adaptation (Biology) 2 Animals—
Habits and behavior 3 Botany (W)
"A young science book of real importance because in simple language it tells how plants and animals in different parts of the world are equipped to survive in a particular place. In the desert or in polar regions, in wet or dry climates, things that grow and animals that move about have become adapted to their individual environment. Only man has learned to live anywhere in the world. Attractive bright pictures and excellent type." Horn book

574.92 Marine biology

literature p195-99 **808.8**
In Johnson, E. comp. Anthology of children's literature p484-88 **808.8**
Many wives. Chrisman, A. B.
In Chrisman, A. B. Shen of the sea p115-28 **S C**

Maple sugar
Fiction
Frost, F. Maple sugar for Windy Foot (4-6) **Fic**
Paull, G. A. Pancakes for breakfast (1-3) **E**
Maple sugar for Windy Foot. Frost, F. M. **Fic**
Mara, daughter of the Nile. McGraw, E. J.

and how to find them: Preparation of specimens; Mounting specimens for keeps; Photomicrography is easy; Smoke in your eyes; Home-made micro-projectors; Still more fun with these accessories; Introduction to bacteriology
"Careful instructions and fairly simple language." Bkl.
Illustrated with photographs and diagrams

579 Biological and natural history collections

Brown, Vinson, 1912-
How to make a home nature museum; illus. by Don Greame Kelley. Little 1954
214p illus $2.50 (5-9) **579**
1 Collectors and collecting 2 Natural history (W)
"This handbook for the amateur collector on how to display and give meaning to a nature collection 'discusses space for and arrangement of the collection, collecting, classifying, mounting, and labeling specimens, collecting pictures and photographs, and making molds and models, drawings, charts, diagrams, and paintings.'

Marine biology
Lane, F. C. All about the sea (4-7) **551.4**
Reed, W. M. Sea for Sam (5-8) **551.4**
Zim, H. S. Seashores **574.92**

See also pages in the following books:
Hylander, C J. Out of doors in summer p107-29 (5-9) **574**
Sanderson, I. T. ed. Animal tales p183-95 (7-9) **591**
See also Biology; Marine fauna; Nature study
Marine fauna
Bronson, W. S. Children of the sea (6-8) **599**
Hausman, L. A. Beginner's guide to sea-

Grades 4-6

Adler, I. Time in your life **529**
Æsop. Fables of Aesop **398.2**
Alden, R. M. Why the chimes rang, and other stories **S C**
Angelo, V. Bells of Bleecker Street **Fic**
Bailey, C. S. Miss Hickory **Fic**
Barrie, Sir J. M. bart. Peter Pan in Kensington Gardens **Fic**
Becker, M. L. ed. Rainbow book of Bible stories **220.9**
Bendick, J. First book of automobiles **629.22**
Bennett, A. E. Little witch **Fic**
Beston, H. Henry Beston's Fairy tales **S C**
Bishop, C. H. All alone **Fic**
Bothwell, J. Little flute player **Fic**
Boulton, R. Traveling with the birds **598.2**
Bowie, W. R. Story of Jesus for young people **232.9**
Brenner, A. Boy who could do anything & other Mexican folk tales **398.2**
Bridges, W. Zoo pets **591**
Brindze, R. Gulf Stream **551.4**
Brindze, R. Story of gold **553**
Brink, C. R. Baby Island **Fic**
Brink, C. R. Family grandstand **Fic**

Dickens, C. Magic fish-bone **Fic**
Djurklou, N. G. friherre. Fairy tales from the Swedish **398.2**
Duvoisin, R. A. And there was America **973.1**
Duvoisin, R. A. Three sneezes, and other Swiss tales **398**
Eager, E. M. Half magic **Fic**
Earle, O. L. The octopus **594**
Edmonds, W. D. Matchlock gun **Fic**
Eells, E. S. Tales from the Amazon **398**
Eells, E. S. Tales of enchantment from Spain **398**
Elting, M. First book of Eskimos **919.8**
Elting, M. First book of Indians **970.1**
Elting, M. Ships at work **387**
Elting, M. Trucks at work **629.22**
Estes, E. Hundred dresses **Fic**
Estes, E. Middle Moffat **Fic**
Estes, E. The Moffats **Fic**
Estes, E. Rufus M **Fic**
Ewing, J. H. G. The brownies, and other stories **S C**
Farjeon, E. Eleanor Farjeon's Poems for children **821**
Farjeon, E. Mighty men **920**
Farjeon, E. Silver curlew **Fic**

Entries in *Children's Catalog,* showing classification by Dewey Decimal System, author and subject, and grade. *Courtesy H. W. Wilson Company.*

needs, it is desirable to mark the cards as to first, second, or third priority.

For each teacher to carry his load in this important phase of selection, it is desirable to establish a systematic checking habit. Checking can be fascinating and stimulating, and it is one of the best ways to keep up with a field. What to check will vary with the level and subject, but a few suggestions will be indicated here.

For books, teachers will find it useful to check both retrospective sources for overlooked titles and current lists for new materials. Among the retrospective sources, five lists— two for elementary and three for secondary areas—are of paramount importance. Elementary teachers should examine the *Children's Catalog* (1–2) and its annual supplements. Since these are arranged by decimal classification as well as by author and subject and by grade, it is possible to turn to the items specifically related to an area or unit. *A Basic Book Collection for Elementary Grades* (1–3) contains a collection of 1000 carefully chosen titles. It is jointly produced by committees of the N.E.A. Department of Classroom Teachers, the Association of Childhood Education International, the National Council of Teachers of English, the Association for Supervision and Curriculum Development, and the American Library Association.

The secondary teacher will want to examine the *Standard Catalog for High School Libraries* (1–4) and its supplements. This catalog is the counterpart of the *Children's Catalog*. Both are published by the H. W. Wilson Company. As a parallel to *A Basic Book Collection for Elementary Grades*, there are *Basic Book Collections* for junior high school (1–5) and for senior high school (1–6), all three published by the American Library Association.

For current books, *Publisher's Weekly* (1–7) is recommended. Each week it lists all of the books published during that week in the United States in a department called "The Weekly Record." Since "PW" is the official journal of the American book trade, it supplies also much current information about books in its articles and advertisements. A regular

WEEKLY RECORD

THIS LIST aims to be a complete and accurate record of American book publication in the week just preceding the date of issue. Publishers should send copies of all books in advance to assure entry simultaneous with publication. Books not received in advance will be listed as near publication date

ART: fine arts
BI: biography
BUS: business
DR: drama

AGATE, James, comp.
The English dramatic critics; an anthology, 1660-1932. 382p. S (Dramabk. D15) 58-11370 ['58] N.Y., Hill & Wang pap., 1.65

ALASKA—*the forty-ninth State—in pictures;* introd. by E. L. (Bob) Bartlett. 64p. il., maps O 58-13382 [c.'58] N.Y., Sterling Pub. Co. pap., 1.00
Photographs of the land, people, animals and industry of Alaska, that illustrate both modern changes and traditions preserved from the past.

ALBRECHT, Lillie Vanderveer   FIC
Hannah's Hessian; il. by Berkeley Williams. 109p. O 58-9009 [c.'58] N.Y., Hastings House 2.75
When little Hannah's father goes to fight in the Revolution, her poor family has difficulty surviving, until a friendly Hessian soldier helps them and helps Hannah in a very special way. Age 8-12

Walsh on "Adventures in Americana."

ANDERSON, Sherwood   BI
A story teller's story. 442p. D (Evergreen ed. E-109) 59 8887 [c.'24,'51] N.Y., Grove Press 3.00, pap., 1.95
Only the paperback book is an Evergreen edition. Also available in a specially bound limited edition of 100 numbered copies.

ANDERSON, Walt   DR
"Me, Candido!" a modern fable. 77p. diagrs. D [c.'50,'58] [N.Y.] Dramatists Play Service pap., 1.25
A play about a Puerto Rican waif sheltered by a Puerto Rican family in New York City.

ANDREYEV, Leonid Nikolaevich   ★FIC
(Leonid Nicholaevich Andreev)
The seven that were hanged, and other stories. 249p. S (Modern Lib. paperback P40) 58-6369 [c.'58] N.Y., Modern Lib. pap., .95
"The Seven That Were Hanged," "The Abyss," "Silence," "The Lie," "Lazarus," "Laughter," "Ben Tobit," "The Marseillaise," and "The Red Laugh."

Publisher's Weekly and a page from its "Weekly Record." *Courtesy R. R. Bowker Company.*

reading of *Publisher's Weekly* is a sure way to keep up with books.

More restricted current lists are the *Booklist* (1–8), published semimonthly most of the year and limited to the best books as selected by a committee of librarians. Various book reviews are helpful in checking, particularly the *Horn Book* (1–9) for elementary and the *Wilson Library Bulletin* (1–10) for secondary selection.

The Booklist. Courtesy R. R. Bowker Company.

Each of the other formats also has its retrospective and current checklists. For example, motion pictures are evaluated in the *Educational Film Guide*, filmstrips in the *Filmstrip Guide*, and tapes in the *National Tape Recording Catalog*. These will be considered in the chapters related to these types of material. There are also several effective selected lists of free materials—pamphlets, pictures, films, filmstrips. Film catalogs issued by state extension agencies and film libraries, and the catalogs of disk recording companies, will prove helpful for the rental of 16-mm motion pictures and for the purchase of phonograph records, respectively.

It is of course desirable to back up list-checking with previewing and reviewing of the materials themselves. This is
possible in a number of ways. At faculty selection meetings
reviews of books may be given based on access to individually owned copies or books borrowed from the public
library or local bookstore. Some films may be secured for
preview either from the state film library or from the producer. A faculty committee or the faculty as a whole can
determine on priorities, and such priorities should be subsequently supported by evidence of use.

Readings

AINSWORTH, IRENE. "Today's Library Becomes a Materials Center," *Library
    Journal,* LXXX (February 15, 1955), 473–75.
BRISTOW, W. H., and SIMON, LEONARD. "Resource Centers," *Review of Edu-
    cational Research,* XXVI (April, 1956), 184–96.
DURR, W. H. "What Is Your School's I.M. Quotient?" *National Education
    Association Journal,* XIII (October, 1953), 439.
FINN, J. D. "What Is Educational Efficiency?" *Education* (January, 1957),
    262–65.
HOBAN, C. F. *The Audio-Visual Way.* Tallahassee: Florida State Department
    of Education, 1948. Pp. 1–9.
LARSON, L. C. "Coordinate the A-V Way and the Library Way," *Educa-
    tional Screen,* XXXIV (June, 1955), 252 ff.
SHORES, LOUIS "Union Now: The A-V Way and the Library Way," *Edu-
    cational Screen,* XXXIV (March, 1955), 113 ff.

Part I

The World of Print

2

TEXTBOOKS

First among teaching tools is the textbook. No good school library or Materials Center fails to include a representative collection of textbooks. Usually they are labeled by the librarian with a "T" on their spines. This letter may or may not be followed by the DC number, depending whether or not textbooks are classified. Sometimes textbooks "in adoption" are separated from those "out of adoption." Always textbooks are cataloged at least briefly so as to be accessible for examination.

As the teacher considers the various classes of Instructional Materials at his disposal, he must inevitably begin with the textbook. Traditionally the "T" book has performed in the classroom as the great organizer. It has been a code of law on basic content. As common denominator, it has served to bind a class of pupils together and to the teacher. Through the textbook the teacher has been able to develop intensive reading effort and fundamental study habits among his pupils.

Any doubt that the textbook is here to stay can be easily dispelled. Classroom teachers in our nation's schools are using more textbooks today than ever before, and the number is increasing yearly. Over the last six decades the increase in textbook use has been continuous. In 1897 the national expenditure for textbooks was only $7.5 million. By 1913 the figure had more than doubled to $17.25 million, and by 1928 textbook expenditures were up to $49 million. The current school year will show more than $200 million spent on textbooks. Even with new techniques of teaching developing almost daily, and revolutions in the quantity and format of various Instructional Materials, more textbooks are being written and used every year.

THE AMERICAN TEXTBOOK

"A true textbook," according to the American Textbook Publishers Institute, "is one especially prepared for the use of pupil and teacher in a school or class, presenting a course of study in a single subject, or closely related subjects."

Because it is possible, also, to use as textbooks many books that are not especially so prepared, a broader definition representing a composite from several standard dictionaries is offered: A textbook is any book used by a teacher and students as a basis for content and organization of a course of study.

Accompanying the textbook in many cases is the workbook, a manual to guide the student's work. Usually this guidance comes in the form of questions to answer or activities to undertake. In short, a workbook usually performs functions complementary to those of a textbook. It provides (1) questions, problems, exercises, activities, based on the textbook; (2) instructions on how to do the assignments; and (3) a place for the pupil to record (by writing in the workbook) the work planned and done.

Textbooks and workbooks exist for virtually all of the subjects and grade levels found in the nation's schools.

Yesterday's Textbooks

There are three milestones in the history of U. S. textbooks. They are the *New England Primer,* circa 1687; Noah Webster's *American Spelling Book,* 1783; and the McGuffey *Eclectic Readers,* 1836–1857.

Before the publication of the *New England Primer* there was almost complete dependence in the colonies upon Great Britain for school textbooks. Among the earliest importations were three spellers. One of these was Coote's *English Schoolmaster* (London, 1596), which included some supplements in arithmetic, history, writing, prayers, psalms, and cate-

Textbook and related workbook. *Courtesy Florida State University.*

chism, and modestly stated that: "He that hath this book only, needeth to buy no other. . . ." Another was Nat Strong's *England's Perfect Schoolmaster* (1676), which promised that with it a "lad may be taught to read a chapter in the Bible in a quarter of a year's time." The most popular of the three spellers, however, was Dilworth's *A New Guide to the English Tongue* (reissued by Benjamin Franklin in 1747).

To these three from England must be added a fourth significant textbook imported from the continent. Comenius' *Orbis Pictus* (2-1), or "Visible World," though probably not the first illustrated textbook, as often claimed, nevertheless heralded visual education. It contained 150 copper cuts, one for every subject, plus an explanation in Latin and in English. For a century after its first appearance in 1658, *Orbis Pictus* was the most popular textbook in Europe and was translated into fourteen languages. Its popularity in colonial America was almost as great.

There were other importations. A few arithmetics, such as Cocker's (1677), Hodder's (1739), and Dilsworth's (1743), found their way into the New World's schoolrooms. But soon, as a result of economic and transportation problems, American ingenuity went to work on makeshifts and reprints. Of the former the most famous was the hornbook, which consisted of a single sheet of paper or parchment, usually 3 x 4 inches, fastened on a piece of board with a handle that looked very much like today's table-tennis paddle, and covered with a translucent sheet of horn, for protection "from the children's dirty little fingers." Thin strips of metal, usually brass, fastened both sheets, and the handle was pierced with a hole to which a string could be attached so that the child might wear it about his neck. At the top of the paper the alphabet, in capital and small letters, was printed, followed by the vowels, double lines of vowel-consonant combinations, the benediction, the Lord's Prayer, and sometimes the Roman numerals.

New England Primer. The birth date of the *New England Primer* (2-2) is uncertain. We know only that its compiler and first printer, Benjamin Harris, moved to Boston in 1686, set up his press, and began publishing America's first newspaper, *Public Occurrences*. We know also, that he opened

THE

N E W - E N G L A N D

PRIMER

I M P R O V E D

For the more eafy attaining the true reading of Englifh.

T O   W H I C H   I S   A D D E D

The Affembly of Divines, and Mr. COTTON's *Catechifm*.

B O S T O N :

Printed by E D W A R D D R A P E R, *at* his Printing-Office, in *Newbury-* Street, and *Sold* by J O H N B O Y L E in *Marlborough-Street*. 1777.

Title page of the *New England Primer. Courtesy American Textbook Publishers Institute.*

the Boston Coffee House and book shop and printed pamphlets and broadsides. In 1691, *The Almanack for the Year of the Christian Empire* announced: "There is now in the press . . . a second impression of the *New England Primer . . .*"

The idea for the primer was almost completely borrowed from Britain. At that time the word was applied to any children's elementary textbook that included the alphabet, syllable sounds, and various reading helps. Other material commonly included, mostly for the religious education of the young, were devotionals for the hours, the creed, the Lord's Prayer, the Ten Commandments, a few psalms, and simple instructions in Christian knowledge.

The *New England Primer* stayed with the pattern. It became a best seller. Every colonial home placed it alongside the Bible. By the time of Paul Revere's ride, two million copies had been sold. It was *the* textbook in those eighty years, imitated by an epidemic of "New York," "American," and "Columbian" primers.

The "Blueback." We won our war for independence and set about remaking a British colony into an American nation. In the process the first American textbook was born. Noah Webster was its father. A tall, lean, indefatigable school teacher, salesman, lawyer, author, publisher, promoter, and above all, 100 per cent American, he revolted against Dilworth's *New Guide to the English Tongue.* His patriotism was affronted by its teaching of British spelling and usage. He knew he could write a better textbook, and in 1783, at the age of 25, he tried. He went to his former teacher, who had in the meantime become president of Yale, and accepted his gruesome suggestion of a title for his speller: *The First Part of a Grammatical Institute of the English Language.* (The other parts were to be a grammar and a reader.) At his own risk and expense, Webster contracted with the Hartford firm of Hudson & Goodwin to print 5000 copies, but not until he had secured a Connecticut copyright, in itself a hazardous undertaking in those days. Thus, Webster embarked upon the multiple career of lexicographer, author, publisher, promoter, and salesman.

In 1817 he changed the title to *The American Spelling Book.* He had in the meantime carried his manuscript also to the president of Princeton, then to Trenton to lobby for a

New Jersey copyright law, and then in succession to New York, Pennsylvania, Massachusetts, and the Constitutional Convention itself, to advocate the kind of legal protection that would "promote the progress of science and useful arts by securing for limited time to authors and inventors the exclusive rights to their respective writings and discoveries." To Noah Webster a considerable debt is owed by authors for present-day copyright protection and royalties from books and other writings.

Such protection inevitably contributed to removing the extra hazard on his own speller. One printer paid $40,000 for a fourteen-year franchise to issue the book in his territory; another gave $3000 a year. In 1829 the book was revised and renamed the *Elementary Spelling Book* (2–3), and it was this issue that became affectionately known as the *"Old Blueback Speller."* It rose to an almost all-time record of best-sellerdom. First published in 1783, by 1785 it was selling at the rate of 500 copies a week. By 1818 the total sales had passed five million. In 1840 D. Appleton took over the publishing, and in 1880 he reported:

It has the largest sale of any book in the world except the Bible. We sell a million copies a year, and we have been selling it at that rate for forty years. We sell them in cases of 72 dozen, and they are bought by all the large dry goods and supply houses and furnished by them to every crossroad store.

Later the American Book Company took over its publication, and the president of that company wrote, in 1946: "And it is not yet dead. . . . 163 years after its first publication, we printed 5,000 copies of it."

Because of Webster, spelling became not only the most important school subject, but a national craze. Spelling bees rivaled corn-huskings as a competitive sport, and in school the spelling of the terms became almost as important as the subject being taught.

McGuffey Readers. The McGuffey *Readers* (2–4) surpassed even the "Blueback" in total sales—122 million for the former to 70 million for the latter. There were six of these readers: the first and second were published in 1836, the third and fourth in 1837, the fifth in 1844, and the sixth in 1857. There were also a primer and a speller. For two generations these *McGuffey Eclectic Readers* educated Americans. In 1931 a memorial was erected to McGuffey in his birthplace, West Finley Township, Pennsylvania. Five years later The American Book Company offered a further commemoration in the form of two volumes by Harvey C. Minnich, curator of the McGuffey Museum, Miami (Ohio) University, one a biography, and the other a collection: *Old Favorites from the McGuffey Readers, 1836–1936.*

William Holmes McGuffey, rural school teacher, professor of languages, and college president, had already published a treatise on "Methods of Reading" and planned a series of readers when he was approached by the Cincinnati firm of Truman & Smith, which was interested in publishing such a series. They offered him 10 per cent royalty on each reader until the author had received $1000 for each title; then the books were to become the publisher's absolute property. Considering the success of the readers, this was not much compensation. However, the publishers did give him bonuses and a pension.

The *Readers* themselves are characterized by high ethical tone, although an overemphasis on the sanctity of property has been pointed out by some critics. Promptness, goodness, kindness, honesty, and truthfulness are stressed throughout the now classic selections. Among the more famous of these are such children's favorites as "Mary's Lamb," "Waste Not, Want Not," "Twinkle, Twinkle, Little Star," "Washington's Little Hatchet," and "The Lame Dog." The last lesson of the First Reader sets forth the immortality of the soul under the title "We All Must Die." Whatever the historian in retrospect may think of the McGuffey *Readers,* their influence on the shaping of the American national mind cannot be discounted.

Today's Textbooks

Two aspects of today's textbook picture contribute perhaps most importantly to an understanding of selection and utilization by teachers. One of these is the American method of textbook production; the other the method of distribution.

Textbook Production. First it is important to understand that, in the United States, textbook production has been predominantly in the hands of private initiative. A number of large publishing houses have developed, and these have had a significant influence on education in America. In some states there has been an effort on the part of government to regulate, control, and in some instances take over the activities of textbook publishing.

Prior to 1830 textbook publishing, like most American enterprise of the period, was sporadic and erratic. Because it was a trial-and-error process, textbooks existed in quantities unrelated to need. A conglomeration of readers, grammars, histories, geographies, language books, and what-not appeared largely on hunches. The producers—printers and authors—were scattered everywhere. Because Webster had made his start there, Hartford was nearest to being a publishing center.

According to Will S. Monroe in his *Early American Textbooks*, the professional publisher made his appearance in 1843. He was Samuel Griswold Goodrich, better known as Peter Parley, author of sugar-coated ethical stories for children. In all, he published some 84 textbooks, including readers, primers, spellers, grammars, histories, geographies, and science books.

But probably the first true textbook firm was Truman & Smith, the same team that launched the McGuffey *Readers*. The influence of this firm took several directions. Largely because of an understanding of westward expansion and its implications for the textbook industry, they established themselves in Cincinnati. When the Federal Treasury surplus of 1836 was distributed among sixteen states, Truman & Smith exerted influence to see that a share of this windfall went to the schools for textbooks. Sensing correctly that the West, with its strongly nonsectarian feeling, would want less religious influence in its textbooks than New England, Truman

& Smith encouraged the inclusion of secular selections with a high ethical flavor. By surveying the field, anticipating need, and interpreting sales figures, Truman & Smith initiated the methods used by textbook firms today.

One of these firms was founded by Edwin Ginn in 1867, with the publication of Craik's *English of Shakespeare.* Another, D. C. Heath & Company, was born when the partners of Ginn & Company amicably separated, dividing the titles so that the entire modern language series went to the new firm of Heath in Boston, and Myer's History remained with Ginn.

By 1890 trust-making was part of the American business climate. It was therefore no surprise to see trust arrangements develop in the textbook industry. In that year, the textbook departments of four firms (D. Appleton; A. S. Barnes; Ivison, Blakeman & Taylor; and Van Antwerp, Bragg) decided to join together to form the American Book Company. During the next few years, this "Syndicate of Four," which became known as the Textbook Trust, took over the textbook business of nearly a dozen more companies and gained control of 93 per cent of the nation's schoolbook business. Fortunately, the pendulum swung back. Old companies reclaimed their textbook departments at the end of their contract, and new companies arose to restore the competition of private enterprise. Nevertheless, state departments of education continued to look at monopolistic tendencies with a jaundiced eye.

Increased competition brought dangerously cutthroat conditions. Extraordinary efforts were made to influence school purchasers. As a result, Edwin Ginn in 1902 renewed his plan of co-operation within the industry to regulate sales practices. This was not a new idea. The School Book Publishers Board of Trade was organized in 1870 to regulate selling practices. Seven years later *Publishers' Weekly* announced the death of this league of publishers. But the idea persisted, and resulted, first, in a series of textbook conferences, and then, in 1931, in the Thirtieth Yearbook of the National Society for the Study of Education, entitled *The*

Textbook in American Education. On the basis of the Year-book's recommendations, a committee was formed which brought educators and publishers together to study common problems.

Publishers, from their side, continued to seek answers to problems and finally appointed Dr. Paysen Smith, formerly commissioner of education in Maine and Massachusetts, to interview a cross section of the nation's educational leaders for a consensus on the textbook's place in today's schools. Dr. Smith concluded that the textbook is an indispensable tool for teacher and pupil, and an inadequate supply of suitable books is a major educational defect. For this reason, continuous review of textbook production in the light of school support, administration, requirements, and methods is imperative. Since textbook publishers are engaged in an important public service, they are justified in strengthening their enterprise. And Dr. Smith's findings led him to believe that the interests of both educators and publishers could be served by forming an association of the leading textbook publishers.

As a result of Dr. Smith's last recommendation, the American Textbook Publishers Institute was organized on July 1, 1942. The Institute aims to promote better understanding by the public of the place of textbooks in American education. It does this through various public relations programs and through co-operation with citizen groups, agencies, and professional associations. It provides a clearinghouse for new ideas and stimulates research on textbook teaching problems. Twenty-eight companies became charter members, and the membership has grown steadily. Lloyd W. King, formerly state superintendent of instruction in Missouri, was appointed executive secretary.

Textbook Distribution. In 1818, Philadelphia was the first city in the United States to make free textbooks available in the public schools. Massachusetts enacted the first free textbook law in 1884, and by 1900, twelve states had followed suit. By 1957, free elementary textbooks were provided by 36 states, or their political subdivisions, and the District of Columbia. Only two states make no provisions for free elementary textbooks; the others make partial provision. On the secondary level, 24 states provide free high school textbooks and 12 provide some books free. The trend is definitely in the direction of free instructional materials for all pupils. Such a trend emphasizes more strongly than ever the importance of textbook distribution by publishers and selection by educators.

At the core of the whole process of textbook procurement is the commitment to uniformity. In the beginning, when education was largely on an individual basis, each pupil was given an assignment in the book he happened to have. But as enrollments increased, the necessity for a uniform text became imperative. Such uniformity provided a basis for more systematic teaching and learning.

As individual schools became parts of school districts or county or city school systems, they turned to the central administration for textbook selection. In most instances the superintendent appointed a committee, or the local board of education itself made the selections, grade by grade and subject by subject. Then the state stepped into the picture to assume supervision and control over selections or adoptions in all its school systems. A rating committee is usually appointed by the state superintendent and the final authority placed with the state board of education.

There are both advantages and disadvantages to the system of state-wide textbook adoption. It does enable the child to move from school to school in the state without having to change textbooks each time. But objectors point out that the fierce competition among publishers may result in questionable efforts to secure adoptions. Some states, such as Texas, California and Kansas, have taken steps that have in some instances resulted in textbook publishing by the state. But by and large the adoption method is at the heart of the procurement and selection of textbooks.

State adoptions follow usually one of four selection patterns: (1) Under the "single" or "basal" list plan, the one book selected for each subject must be used exclusively by the schools. (2) The "co-basal" list plan gives the schools a choice between two books. (3) The "multiple" list plan provides a choice of one of three or more books adopted for each subject. (4) Finally, under the "approved" list plan, books are not formally adopted, but rather the schools are given a choice of any of the titles on the list. Adoption periods are for from six to eight years in some states, and for shorter periods in others. About half the states follow the state-wide adoption system; the remainder favor local adoptions.

In the usual procedure for what is known as "adoption" the state superintendent first appoints a textbook rating committee to pass on the merits of the various titles. Publishers' representatives are invited to appear before the committee and advocate their products. The committee examines the books and discusses them in detail before making its recommendations to the superintendent and to the state board of education, which may accept, reject, or modify the committee's recommendation. But what is of most concern to the teacher are the criteria used by the committee in selection.

EVALUATION

The quest for the perfect textbook is universal among those who teach. It is no less tantalizing to those who publish:

How to write the perfect textbook? You did say *perfect,* didn't you? Well. First of all, write it so simply that the dullest child can read it with ease, yet make it so scholarly that professors of subject matter will approve it. Organize it so ingeniously, so tightly, that each lesson applies what has been taught before and prepares for what is to follow, yet make your organization so adaptable, so flexible, that chapter five or chapter ten may be presented first to fit any local course of study. (American Textbook Publishers Institute, *Textbooks in Education,* 1949, p. ix)

This constant striving for the perfect teaching tool is nowhere better expressed than in the letter a textbook editor wrote to a teacher about the techniques of choosing a textbook (*Textbooks in Education,* 1949, pp. 85–92). He urges two general criteria: (1) Does the author's teaching aim *harmonize* with that of the teacher? (2) Is the author's aim, at least, *fulfilled?* You will want to read the editor's own words and extract for yourself the significance of his message. But there are fifteen specifics of utmost importance in this letter—seven for the teacher and eight for the pupil.

From the teacher's viewpoint: (1) First test the book on yourself. Be both pupil and teacher, and see how well the textbook you are evaluating does the job. (2) Then look at the author's teaching program. How good is it? (3) Next consider your classroom scene. How well does he visualize it? For, after all, the American classroom scene must include your own classroom situation. (4) You have day-by-day practical problems of procedure. Does the author understand them? For example, if he suggests class activities, are they practicable and workable in your environment? (5) If the author and teacher are to be a teaching team, they must support each other. How are these roles realized in this particular textbook, and does his part correlate with yours? (6) There is a matter of time and timing. How good is the author's sense of this problem? (7) Finally, as you look at the details, page by page, is each section, unit, and chapter driving toward the goal?

Now let us look at the book from the pupils' viewpoint. (1) Your pupils have backgrounds. How well has the author considered these? (2) You know the vocabulary range in your class. Will the book's words and style communicate with your students? (3) To what extent has the author personalized his message so that each pupil will feel it is directed to him? (4) Is there any condescension anywhere —any writing down? (5) What about visual aids? Cartoons, diagrams, maps, graphs, and charts, included because they really teach, can save many spoken and written words. (6) Then there is the matter of summary. Is there time to catch up and review? (7) Are the activities suggested practical for your pupils? (8) Finally, is special work provided that takes individual differences into account?

Using these fifteen points, the editor and publisher evaluate textbook manuscripts before they are accepted for publication.

Textbook Measuring Sticks

Since 1900 educators—like editors—have sought systematically to develop criteria for textbook evaluation. Among all of the studies there will be found a variety of approaches and measuring outlines. The number and sequence of major or "master" items in the different instruments vary considerably. But the agreement on fundamentals is so convincing that it is comparatively simple for every teacher to draw up an outline of his own, a measuring stick which he can apply to any textbook he wishes to evaluate for his own teaching purposes. Suggestions can be found in J. A. Clement's *Educational Significance of Analysis, Appraisal and Use of Textbooks in Junior and Senior High Schools* (Champaign, Ill.: Daniels Press, 1939). Two older professional books with good evaluation principles are A. L. Hallquest's *The Textbook: How to Use and Judge It* (Macmillan, 1918) and C. R. Maxwell's *Selection of Textbooks* (Houghton Mifflin, 1918). Reports of state textbook committees also contain criteria.

An eclectic evaluation sheet can be developed from all of the measuring sticks. First, the *content* of the textbook will indicate its relation to the course of study and the extent to which all of the parts are treated. Text samplings here and there will reveal outdated information, omissions, or overemphasis on relatively minor aspects.

Considerable attention must be paid to the *level* of treatment. One index is vocabulary, gauged by such measures as the Thorndike frequency word list, later described. Another factor is an estimation of reading difficulty, exposed by Gray and Leary—*What Makes a Book Readable?* (University of Chicago Press, 1935)—and by Flesch—*The Art of Readable Writing* (Harper, 1949). This factor covers such elements as the number of easy and difficult words, percentage of monosyllables, quantity of personal pronouns, average sentence length, number of prepositional phrases, number of simple sentences, and percentage of different words.

The *sequence* of subject matter, its organization and arrangement, is another criterion. Textbooks develop their content along different lines.

The *format*, or physical make-up, of the textbook is a critical consideration. This includes binding, paper, type, and illustrations. Physical aspects of type, leading (spacing between lines), and page size were investigated by Buckingham in "New Data on the Typography of Textbooks" (National Society for the Study of Education, *Thirtieth Yearbook*, Pt. II, 1931, pp. 93–126). Among other things he found that 12-point type (72 points equal one inch) with certain definite leading and page size was most readable, in the first grade at least. But this conclusion has been challenged. Considerably more investigation of format features as they affect pupil understanding is needed.

Other criteria for the evaluation of textbooks involve *authorship*. The integrity of the author and the publisher affects the quality of the product. It is desirable that the author's subject knowledge be fortified by teaching experience, either his own or a collaborator's. A publisher cannot escape evaluation on the basis of his previous publications.

Finally, the extent to which the book suggests other materials must be considered. Good *bibliographies* in textbooks can no longer always be limited to other readings. Viewings of pictures, films, filmstrips, and opaque and transparent projections are a part of multi-materials teaching. So also is listening to selected tapes and disks.

Evaluation Checklist for Textbooks

Content: Relation to course-of-study requirements
Level: Vocabulary and style
Sequence: Organization and arrangement of subject matter
Format: Illustrations, page make-up, paper, typography, binding
Authorship: Standards of author and publisher
Bibliographies: Quality of lists of supporting materials

UTILIZATION

"In America the textbook is the focus of class attention and the teacher functions as an aid and witness to its assimilation." So wrote W. S. Learned some years ago. But if that ever accurately represented the relation of the teacher to his basic tool, it can hardly be said to represent the modern concept of the place of any particular form of Instructional Material in education. On the contrary, the textbook is only one of many media through which teacher and pupil communicate with each other in an effort to carry forward the learning process.

It is important to understand that (1) the textbook has not been replaced by other teaching materials and (2) the textbook does not replace other kinds of materials. Effective teaching and learning utilize textbooks and other teaching materials in complementary combination. In such combination, textbooks can lead the learning effort, supported by a variety of other materials—library books, magazines, graphics, projected and sound media, and various community resources.

It is necessary to realize also that (1) textbooks establish the course of study and (2) textbooks do not and should not determine the curriculum. Realistically, curriculum and materials interact. For this reason, it is unwise to build a curriculum first, and then seek materials to implement it; nor is it desirable to develop a curriculum from a selected group of materials. Strong reliance upon Instructional Materials is inevitable, however, since most of the cumulative knowledge, thought, and action of the past and present are recorded in books, films, and recordings.

Functions of the Textbook

As an Instructional Material, the textbook has its own distinctive role; it acts as the course organizer. There is no conflict between "incidental" and "systematic" learning in the organized course of study. Textbooks help set classroom objectives and suggest related activities.

The table of contents of a textbook acts as guidepost for a term's work. Scope and sequence are contained within the adopted text, insuring coverage of the facts and concepts considered worthy by those who developed the course of study.

The textbook functions as a common denominator for a class of individual differences. Its influence is unifying—not regimenting. Through suggested readings and activities it charts diverse roads to the common goal.

Use of a textbook gives practice in intensive reading, a skill as important as reading extensively. Perhaps no other teaching tool places quite the emphasis on analytical reading that is essential in textbook study. This makes for a study habit that must be included in the educational development of every pupil.

These five functions—namely, to provide (1) course organization, (2) basic content, (3) a common denominator for a class composed of individual differences, (4) practice in intensive reading skill, and (5) opportunity to develop study habits—are performed best of all by the textbook. In the hands of the skillful teacher, the textbook not only aids learning but leads all of the other teaching media to perform their rightful parts in the perfecting of communication between teacher and pupils.

Teaching the Textbook

If the textbook is to perform as the fine tool it is, then it must be known to teacher and pupil. It cannot be taken for granted. Even in the lowest grades the teacher must allow time to examine the new textbook with the pupil. In the elementary grades the introductory examination will be relatively simple, but on the secondary level detailed attention to all the parts of a book should be given. There are at least ten fundamental elements that comprise most textbooks. Usually they are, in order of appearance, cover, title-page, copyright page, preface and/or introduction, table of contents, list of illustrations, text, special aids, appendix, and index.

The very first day that teacher and class meet their new textbook together, they should look at it closely. Begin with the *cover*. If title and author are given on both the front and on the spine, their degree of fullness should be noted. The fact that only the last name of the author appears, and perhaps an abbreviated title, should suggest that fuller information must be sought elsewhere.

The book's *title page* will soon provide fuller information. (If, in passing, a half-title is noted, then comparison of all four places can be made: cover, spine, half-title page, and title page). It can readily be seen that Jones' ARITHMETIC is not enough to distinguish this book from others that may be identified in the same way on the cover. For this reason, a book is best identified by its title page. On that page also will be found the publisher's full name, the place of publication, and possibly the date of publication.

If the date of publication is not on the title page, it can be found on the verso, or reverse side of that page. But even if the date is on the title page, a comparison can be made with the date on the verso, and the subject of copyright introduced. The significance of a series of dates in the copyright notice should be discussed. If the last copyright date is much earlier than the imprint date on the title page, this fact should be cited as a possible indication of outdated material or point of view.

In the *preface* or *introduction,* or both, the reader learns something about the purpose of the book. There the author often tells how he came to write the book, the area covered, and how the material is to be used, and acknowledges help he has received.

The *table of contents* is next. It is an organized aid to study providing an overview of the whole course and specific topics for each assignment. By reading the table of contents together in class, the pupils can see (1) how much relative space is given each division of the subject and (2) the sequence of these divisions. The teacher can also explain variations in order and emphasis he proposes to make during the term. In this way anticipation is created.

At this point it would be well to turn to the *index* for contrast. Comparison of the logical sequence of subjects in the table of contents with alphabetic order in the index should lead to a discussion of when each arrangement is more useful. The convenience of the index in ready reference should be illustrated, with special emphasis on how quickly a minor subject can be located there.

If there is a *list of illustrations,* this feature should be examined next. Differentiation among the most common types of illustrations should be made: maps, charts, diagrams, drawings, photographs, tables. If some types are not well represented in the textbook, examples of each type can be displayed by means of an opaque projector, or other books or separately printed illustrations can be exhibited.

The meaning of the word *appendix* may then be explained. Again, examples of features included may be opaque-projected. Bibliography, glossary, document, case study—all are worthy of definition and illustration, with particular attention to the specific contribution of each in a book.

Nor should a look at the *text* itself be neglected. Its organization by chapter titles, centered division heads, paragraph heads, and other subheads if any should be noted, and their contribution to the organizing of a student's study explained. Running heads at the top of each page should be cited, too, as aids to ready reference. The importance of captions and legends for illustrations and the difference between these two terms belong in this introduction to the textbook.

That the student will have a better appreciation for his textbook through such a first-day orientation there can be no doubt. Periodic review of these elements throughout the year will also be profitable.

Kinds of Textbooks

The good Materials Center shelves at least one copy of every adopted or approved textbook. In addition, it may also house a selection of textbooks not in adoption. It should be clearly understood that the Materials Center's basic responsibility for textbooks is the same as for any other class of

Instructional Materials: housing, organizing, and interpreting individual examples to assist teachers and pupils in learning. It is not the responsibility of the Materials Center to act as the clerical agency for distribution of textbooks to pupils. If the principal decides he does want the Materials Center to supervise this necessary task, then additional space and clerical assistance should be provided so that there is no encroachment on the important educative function the Materials Center must perform.

Textbooks are arranged in many ways in the Materials Center. In some cases shelving is by Dewey Decimal Classification with all other kinds of books. In other cases a separate Dewey Decimal arrangement is provided, with the letter "T" placed before the Dewey numbers in the card catalog and on the spine of the book.

Some Materials Centers arrange textbooks by themselves, grouping them much as in state adoption listings. Such an arrangement takes grade level into account first, and then subject. Following a somewhat similar pattern, a classification scheme for textbooks is here suggested, based somewhat on the organization of *Textbooks in Print*, the R. R. Bowker annual American Educational Catalog.

Classes of Textbooks

A. LANGUAGE ARTS (Dewey classes 400 and 800)
   1. *Readers,* both basal and supplementary, and reading skill books, remedial and phonetic
   2. *Spellers*
   3. *Language,* including composition, speech, and rhetoric books
   4. *Literature,* comprising anthologies

B. FINE ARTS (Dewey class 700, except division 790)
   1. *Art Appreciation*
   2. *Drawing*
   3. *Handicrafts*
   4. *History of Art*

C. SOCIAL STUDIES (Dewey classes 300 and 900 and the division 150)
   1. *Basic Curriculum*
   2. *History,* including American, state, ancient and medieval, modern European and English, Latin American, Canadian, and

world history, contemporary problems, and international relations
3. *Geography,* including maps
4. *Civics, Citizenship, Government*
5. *Economics*
6. *Sociology*
7. *Psychology*

D. SCIENCE AND MATHEMATICS (Dewey class 500)
  1. *Mathematics,* including arithmetic, general math, algebra, geometry, trigonometry, trade math
  2. *General Science* and physical science, astronomy, physics, chemistry, biological science, botany, zoology

E. HEALTH AND PHYSICAL EDUCATION (Dewey divisions 610 and 790)
  1. *Hygiene*
  2. *Recreation*
  3. *Driver Education*
  4. *Safety*

F. VOCATIONAL EDUCATION (Dewey class 600, largely)
  1. *Home Economics,* including child care and development, consumer problems, costume design (clothing and fashion), food and nutrition, homemaking, marriage and the family
  2. *Industrial Arts,* including automotive mechanics, aviation trades, building trades, drafting and mechanical drawing, electricity, printing, shop and metal trades, woodworking
  3. *Agriculture,* including crop, animal, dairy farming
  4. *Business,* including accounting and bookkeeping, advertising, business English, business law, business math, retailing and salesmanship, shorthand, typing

SOURCES OF TEXTBOOK INFORMATION

In July of 1872, *Publishers' Weekly,* journal of the American book trade, published a list of textbooks then in print, arranged by subject. Although this list had apparently been included in the publisher's own house organ, the *Literary Bulletin,* since 1869, the 1872 issue is recognized as the beginning of the annual list of textbooks known until recently as the *American Educational Catalog.* With the 85th annual edition in 1956, the title *Textbooks in Print* was adopted. This is the complete (or nearly so) list of textbooks that every teacher should know.

Arranged under headings comparable to those indicated in the foregoing list of classes of textbooks, reasonably full bibliographic information is given for each title and series, including author, title, series, publisher, price. Sometimes the date is also given. There is an author index with page reference to the entry, and there is a title and subject index which gives quarter-of-the-page reference.

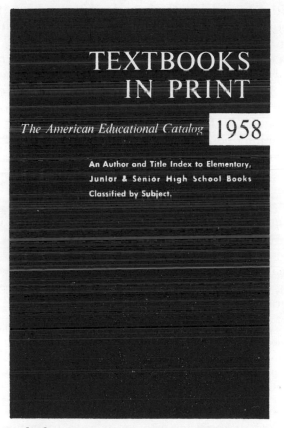

Textbooks in Print. Courtesy R. R. Bowker Company

New textbooks are mentioned and reviewed in some periodicals and professional journals, but no medium "reviews textbooks in the sense that trade books are reviewed as a regular feature in many magazines and in many newspapers" (From a letter to the author from Lloyd W. King, executive secretary of the American Textbook Publishers Institute). The best sources of evaluation are (1) professional journals dealing with the teaching of a specific subject or area, such as the *English Journal* of the National Council of Teachers of English or *Science Education* or *Social Studies,* and (2) the reports of the various state textbook rating committees, beginning of course with the one for your own state.

As an example of the latter, the *Report of the Florida State Textbook Rating Committee to the State Board of Education, Feb. 14, 1952* is cited. This was prepared by nine educators from Florida school systems. It includes a letter of transmittal which states five basic principles constantly kept in mind while reaching conclusions, followed by general statements of standards and criteria applied.

The adoptions are grouped under headings comparable to those found in *Textbooks in Print;* namely, "Readers," "Dictionary," "Science," "Mathematics," etc. Each adoption statement approximates a discriminating review, the committee stating its reasons, in educational terms, for the specific selection.

As an example, here are the committee's reasons for recommending the World Book Company's "Growth in Arithmetic" series, grades three through six:

1. The material is based on the child's experience background, hence lends itself to the interpretation of the individual's social environment.
2. Emphasis is placed on learning through understanding rather than by rote. There is adequate practice material to establish the mathematical concepts.
3. In the opinion of the Committee, this series of arithmetic, grades 3–6, correlates with and provides continuity with both the series recommended for adoption in grades 1 and 2 and the series now in use in grades 7 and 8.
4. In problem solving, the child is encouraged to seek the solution for himself. Hence, the children are permitted to seek all possible approaches to the solution of the problem. The child

therefore follows his own mental reasoning rather than a fixed textbook pattern.

5. There is adequate material for the development of computational skills.
6. The illustrations are clear, colorful, and are related to the contextual materials of the book.
7. The format of the book is desirable as to size, color variation, type, and arrangement.

Teachers consulting a textbook in the Materials Center. *Courtesy Appalachian State Teachers College.*

Any selection of textbooks is extremely difficult. The good Materials Center relies on several sources for its choice of titles. A first guide is the state list of adoptions. In some states the Materials Center will automatically be supplied with a complete set of the books in adoption.

Other aids to textbook selections are standard library indexes and bibliographies. Among these, the *Children's Catalog*, the *Standard Catalog for High School Libraries*, and the three "Basic Lists" introduced in Chapter 1 are helpful, although textbooks are not separated from other kinds of books in these sources.

Quite useful as selection aids are the indexes by Eloise Rue, *Subject Index to Readers* (2–6), first published in 1938, indexing 300 readers and 250 other books that include grammars, arithmetics, handicraft, story, and picture collections. Subsequently, subject indexes to books for primary grades and books for intermediate grades were indexed in separate volumes. The 1950 edition of the latter has been expanded to include some 1875 titles.

Textbooks are powerful teaching media. In the hands of the skilled teacher, the "T" book can prime the whole process of Instructional Materials teaching. As the great organizer, as the reading helper, as the common denominator for a class of individual differences, the textbook is worthy of careful study in itself by both teacher and pupil.

Readings

"A Model Plan for the Analysis and Improvement of Textbooks and Teaching Materials as Aids to International Understanding," in *A Handbook for the Improvement of Textbooks and Teaching Materials as Aids to International Understanding*. Paris: UNESCO, 1949. Pp. 69–90.

CARTWRIGHT, W. H. *How To Use a Textbook*. (How To Do It Series, No. 2.) Washington, D. C.: National Council for the Social Studies, 1950. 6pp.

CASS, J. M. *Textbooks and Learning*. New York: American Textbook Publishers Institute, 1956. 4pp.

CLEMENT, J. A., and DOLCH, E. W. "Textbooks." In MONROE, W. S., *Encyclopedia of Educational Research*, New York: The Macmillan Co., 1941. Pp. 1301–5.

LAUWERYS, J. A. *History Textbooks and International Understanding*. Paris: UNESCO, 1953. 82pp.

Report of the State Textbook Rating Committee to the State Board of Education, February 14, 1952. Tallahassee: 1952.

Textbooks Are Indispensable. New York: American Textbook Publishers Institute, n.d. 91pp.

Textbooks in Education. New York: American Textbook Publishers Institute, 1949. 139pp.

3

REFERENCE BOOKS

Reference books naturally complement the textbook. They define terms. They contain facts. They uncover statistics. They give the salient points about people, places, and things. In short, they answer the hundreds of questions that pop into pupils' minds if a subject arouses their interest at all. They also perform the necessary bibliographic function of sending the pupil on to additional Instructional Materials.

The "R" book is so called because in every library and Materials Center the big "R" precedes the Dewey number on the spine of the book and in the upper left-hand corner of the catalog card. It is differentiated from other books by the fact that, as a rule, it does not circulate.

The reference book is further differentiated from other kinds of teaching tools by the nature of its use. Although many books are intended to be read from cover to cover, the reference book is not. A dictionary, for example, is meant to be referred to for specific information. *Any book intended to be referred to for specific information is a reference book.*

All books are used for reference at times. A Shakespeare play consulted to locate a particular soliloquy is on that occasion a reference book, but its purpose is not for reference. The plays are intended to be read through.

In the Appendix there is a selected list of representative reference books that one might find in any school library. A review of this list before entering the library will arm any teacher sufficiently to walk among the "R" shelves with confidence.

The "R" Book's Potential

The "R" book has a unique potential. For the teacher to take advantage of that potential, he must know not only specific reference books, and their strengths and weaknesses, but also the functions peculiar to this class of teaching tool as a whole.

First, the reference book is a *fact-finder*. It is the tool the teacher must select from his collection to answer pupils' questions about specifics. Which is taller, the Empire State Building or the Eiffel Tower? Who invented the automobile? What does the word "reservation" mean in connection with Indians? Did drugstores sell more drugs or more confections last year? When was *Huckleberry Finn* written? How does a mongoose kill a cobra? And so on. For answers to definite questions like these, which may well arise at any time in a teaching unit, the reference book is invaluable.

But ready reference for fact-finding is not the only teaching possibility of the "R" book. A comparatively neglected function is the *overview*. At the outset of a new subject, no single teaching tool offers a better survey than a good encyclopedia article. Again and again students have found the way to a quicker understanding of a new subject is to read an encyclopedia article on that subject. Such reading has the added advantage of creating anticipation in the pupil as he sees the subject unfold more deliberately during the term.

But there are other teaching possibilities in the "R" book. It is an excellent *documenting device*. Pupils in search of support for a position on a social issue will find both sides presented objectively and opinions argued by authorities who cite chapter and line in documents. The "R" book is also a good *guide to reading*. At the end of each article or elsewhere in the book are bibliographies intended to send the reader on progressively to further information. Finally, the "R" book can be used as a *summarizer*. Its articles usually perform this function in a much less stereotyped fashion than some textbooks or motion pictures.

Evaluation of Reference Books

Of the six criteria most often applied in evaluating reference books for teaching purposes, *scope* is critical at three points: coverage, relevance, and recency. A good reference book article will cover the subject, relate it to standard units in school courses of study, and include developments as up-to-date as the last year. Checks on scope in all three of its aspects can be made by examining the copyright date, reading the editor's preface, and sampling articles on several key topics in any subject field.

Nearly as vital is the criterion of *treatment*, which involves *clarity* and *bias*. Although attempts to establish grade levels through vocabulary and other factors have not always been too successful in the case of school reference books, readability has become a basic requirement. One test of clarity that a teacher can make is to read a reference article on a subject about which he knows little or nothing and see if he understands it clearly. One of the better school encyclopedias once had an article on Egypt prepared by an outstanding Egyptologist. Although the content was impeccably accurate, judged by the highest standards of scholarship, it could not be understood by the young audience for whom it was intended. Not until the material had been rewritten several times by editors practiced in writing for children was it found to be clear and meaningful to the young people who read it.

The other element in treatment—bias—is aggravated by modern world tensions over censorship and the freedom to read what one wishes. Reputable reference books handle controversial subjects, usually, in one of two ways. An outstanding authority known for his objectivity is invited to write the article and summarize the arguments for both sides, or two authors representing opposing points of view are offered equal space to present their respective cases. To check bias, certain controversial subjects, such as the Reformation, Communism, or fluoridation of water can be examined.

A third criterion is *arrangement*. Since fact-finding is one of the principal uses for reference books, accessibility of information becomes a prime requisite. The contents of most "R" books are arranged alphabetically somewhere. There may be an index in the back, or in the front (as in the case of the *World Almanac*), or the entire work may be alphabetically arranged. But there are also other schemes. Geographical tools may be arranged by continent, country, state, and smaller divisions. History "R" books may also follow the geographic sequence or adopt a chronological one, beginning with ancient times and coming up to contemporary events.

Although the alphabetic arrangement appears simplest, it also presents hazards to the uninitiated. For example, not so long ago a teacher wrote in to complain she could find nothing on the subject of "phalanx" in the *Encyclopaedia Britannica*. What she had failed to understand was that the *Britannica* has two separate alphabetic arrangements, the first one for the articles in the 23 volumes and the other for the index in the 24th volume. There are 40,000 articles in the first alphabetic sequence, but there are 400,000 subjects listed in the second alphabetic sequence. Since "phalanx" is a comparatively small subject, its chances of rating a separate article in the *Britannica* are small—no better than 1 in 10.

Other hazards in the alphabetic arrangement result from variations in filing rules. Some reference books file Newark ahead of New York, on the basis that "a" precedes "y." Other sets follow library filing rules, which say "nothing comes before something," and New York has nothing after "w," whereas Newark has an "a." Initials cause trouble, too, some books treating them as if they were spelled out; in that case one has to know what the initials stand for. Such variations should not prove too difficult, provided pupils are alerted to these variations.

A fourth criterion in selecting a reference book is *format*, which means the physical make-up of the book. In format are included such elements as binding, which should be durable; paper, which should be opaque enough to prevent type from showing through the back of the page; type, which should be large enough, well spaced, readable, and aesthetically pleasing; and margins, which should be generous enough on the inside of the page to insure against "gutter reading" in case the book is rebound (in this case the gutter refers to the inside margins—the blank space between the two open pages).

To these elements of format must be added illustrations, of which there are many kinds. Line drawings can be reproduced successfully on almost any kind of paper, but half-tones cannot. A halftone is a reproduction of an illustration with continuous tones, such as a photograph or painting. Since many grades of relatively inexpensive paper will not reproduce halftones satisfactorily, illustrations of this type are often printed together on more highly finished paper bound into the book as an insert. In such books the illustrations may be some distance from the related text, and therefore not so satisfactory as a book which uses the more highly finished paper throughout so that halftones can be printed on the same page as the related text matter.

A somewhat similar problem is involved in the location of maps. Although many reference books place maps close to the pertinent text, others continue to assemble the maps in one place. The *Encyclopaedia Britannica* does the latter and the *Encyclopedia Americana* the former. There are good arguments for both decisions. Awareness of this difference in map locations makes for more intelligent selection and use of reference tools.

An increasing number of reference books are employing "bleed" illustrations. These are illustrations which extend into the margin to the edge of the page. A picture which runs off on all four margins is known as a full bleed; those which run off on one, two, or three margins are known as one-fourth, half, or three-fourths bleeds, respectively. Such illustrations are identified in the minds of some with *Life* magazine. But the *Britannica Book of the Year* and many other reference books have long featured bleeds.

Then there is the increasing use of color illustrations, which vary in quality. The halftone color process consists

MOTORBOAT RACING   459

to replace the voluntary British Film Production fund; (2) the National Film Finance corporation was empowered to continue its work of making loans for film production; (3) the exhibitors' quota regulations were to be continued.

The B.F.F.A. was established on July 1, 1957. Its duties, as defined in the act, were to administer the funds accruing from a levy on admission prices to British motion-picture theatres. The amount of these funds in the first year, which started in Oct. 1957, was expected to be £3,750,000, as against £2,250,000 which was raised in 1956–57 under the previous voluntary scheme. In subsequent years the agency was directed to raise an annual sum of between £2,000,000 and £5,000,000.

In 1957 the scale of the levy was from ½d. to 1¼d. on each admission according to the seat price. Admissions at 9d. and under were exempt. The money was paid out to makers of qualified British films, and to the all-industry Children's Film Foundation Ltd.

A matter of considerable interest to both the British and United States film industries was a conference held in July by the Centre Européen de Spectacle, at which it was announced that the French, western German and Italian film industries were considering the steps to be taken for their closer integration within the Common Market. Together these industries could provide a film market as large as the domestic United States one and, with freedom of trade between them, they could have an important, and not altogether helpful, effect on British and U.S. film exports.   (D. Cw.)

Canada.—The year 1957 marked an increase over 1956 in the volume of Canadian motion-picture production. Two Canadian-produced 26-min. dramatic entertainment film programs for television were released over the Canadian Broadcasting system network. The year also marked the beginning of industry-wide collective bargaining with the signing of an agreement by members of the Association of Motion Picture Producers and Laboratories of Canada and the Canadian Council of Authors and Artists, representing professional motion-picture talent.

Canadian production in the theatrical field consisted entirely of short subjects. Nontheatrical production for other than television release continued at about the same dollar volume as in 1956. A tabulation from the report of the Canadian government

Summary Statistics of Canadian Motion-Picture Production
(Private Industry)

Year	Salaries and wages	Gross revenue Production	Printing and laboratory
1953	$1,150,890	$1,592,779	$1,230,493
1954	1,549,233	2,106,131	1,456,405
1955	1,460,421	2,456,038	1,817,784
1956*	2,483,910	3,726,557	2,095,985

*Figures for 1956 include film laboratories with no affiliated motion-picture production facilities. They are not included in the figures for prior years.

bureau of statistics, covering Canadian motion-picture production by private industry for all purposes, is shown in the table.

Industry leaders estimated that the 1957 figures would show an increase of about 20% over 1956, resulting altogether from the increase in the amount of film production for television.
    (F. R. Cv.)

Motorboat Racing. The year 1957 saw a concentrated assault on almost every class record in all of the racing categories, with four one-mile standards being established for the inboard classes and three new records in the stock outboard classes. The racing outboards and the inboards both had six new five-mile competition marks put into the record books while the stock outboards broke old records five times for the five-mile distance. The unlimited hydroplanes also shattered all previous competition marks. However, the one-mile record of Stanley S. Sayres of 178.947 m.p.h. for propeller-driven craft remained untouched, though several attempts were made to raise this mark. On Nov. 7 on Lake Coniston, Eng., Donald Campbell established a new world water speed record of 239.07 m.p.h. in his jet-engined "Bluebird II," subject to official confirmation.

The unlimited hydroplane "Hawaii Kai III" of Seattle, Wash., owned by the former crew of the "Slo-mo-shun IV," headed by Mike Welsch and driven by Jack Regas, almost completely dominated the unlimited ranks, winning practically every major unlimited class trophy with the exception of the Gold cup which was again won by Willard Rhodes' "Miss Thriftway" of Seattle, driven by Bill Muncey. Among the trophies won by the "Hawaii Kai III" were the Silver cup at Detroit, Mich., the President's

START OF THE ORANGE BOWL REGATTA at Miami Beach, Fla., a nine-hour endurance race for all classes of motorboats. The race was held Dec. 31, 1956

A bleed illustration from the *Britannica Book of the Year. Courtesy Encyclopaedia Britannica, Inc.*

of combining red, yellow, blue, and black in the right proportions to secure all the shades and colors desired. Examples of brilliant coloring in a reference book can be found in *Collier's Encyclopedia* or in *Compton's Pictured Encyclopedia*, or in any of the other good sets. Color overlays have been used in *American Peoples' Encyclopedia* to show the human anatomy.

CONTRIBUTORS

A.J.R. Anne J. Richter
Book Editor, R. R. Bowker Co., New York
City CALDECOTT MEDAL, NEWBERY MEDAL

A.J.S. Arthur J. Schaefer, Ph.B.
Vice-President for Development and Public
Relations, DePaul University, Chicago, Ill.
DEPAUL UNIVERSITY

A.Ke. Alexander Key
Author, *With Daniel Boone on the Caroliny Trail.* BOONE, DANIEL

A.Ko. Arthur Koehler, M.S.
Author; Wood Technologist and Consultant.
BUILDING MATERIALS Articles

A.Lai. Alexander Laing, M.A.
Author; Educational Services Adviser, Dartmouth College Library, Hanover, N. H.
BRIDGE; CANAL; SHIP; and Related Articles

A.Lau. Alexander Laurie, B.S., M.A.
Professor Emeritus of Horticulture, Ohio
State University, Columbus.
HORTICULTURE Articles

A.L.B. Alfred LeRoy Burt, M.A.
Professor Emeritus of History, University of
Minnesota; Author, *A Short History of Canada for Americans; The Old Province of Quebec; The*

A.N. Allan Nevins, A.M., LL.D., Litt. D.,L.H.D.
Professor of American History, Columbia
University; Chairman, Advisory Board,
American Heritage Magazine; Author, *Grover Cleveland* and *Hamilton Fish* (Pulitzer Prizes,
1933 and 1937); and Other Books.
EISENHOWER, DWIGHT D.; TRUMAN, HARRY S.

A.N.J. A. N. Jorgensen, Ph.D., LL.D.
President, University of Connecticut, Storrs.
CONNECTICUT, UNIVERSITY OF

A.Pab. A. Pabst, Ph.D.
Professor of Mineralogy, University of California, Berkeley.
MINERAL, and Related Articles

A.Parr. Albert Parry, Ph.D.
Chairman, Department of Russian Studies;
Professor of Russian Civilization and Language, Colgate University, Hamilton, N. Y.
SOVIET and BALKAN LEADERS Biographies

A.Pe. A. Persien
Formerly, General Secretary-Treasurer, International Hodcarriers', Building and Common Laborers' Union of America.
HODCARRIERS', BUILDING AND COMMON LABORERS' UNION OF AMERICA, INTERNATIONAL

A.M.Ba. Alfred M. Bailey, B.A., D.Sc., D.P.S.
Director, The Denver Museum of Natural
History, Colorado.
MARSH and WADING BIRDS Articles

A.M.Bu. Arthur M. Buswell, Ph.D.
Research Professor, University of Illinois.
SANITARY ENGINEERING Articles

A-M.M. Auguste-M. Morisset, M.L.S., J.C.L.
Librarian and Director of the Library School,
University of Ottawa, Canada.
OTTAWA, UNIVERSITY OF

A.M.Mu. Arthur M. Murphy, Ph.D.
President, Saint Mary College, Xavier, Kan.
SAINT MARY COLLEGE

versity, Kingston, Ont.
MANITOBA and Related Articles;
BRITISH COLUMBIA CITIES Articles

A.R.We. Abdel Ross Wentz, Ph.D., D.D., LL.D., Th.D.
Professor Emeritus of Church History, Gettysburg Seminary (Pa.) REFORMATION Articles

A.R.Wi. A. R. Wildhagen, M.A.
Assistant to Director, Public Information
Office, University of Illinois, Urbana.
ILLINOIS, UNIVERSITY OF

A.S.,Jr. Arthur Schlesinger, Jr., A.B., LL.D., Litt.D.
Professor of History, Harvard University;
Author, *The Age of Jackson* (Pulitzer Prize,
1945), and Other Books. STEVENSON, ADLAI E.

World Book Encyclopedia page showing list of contributors. *Courtesy Field Enterprises, Inc.*

A fifth criterion for evaluation and selection of reference books concerns *authority*. No tool is stronger than its producers. It is expected that an established publisher with a reputation for integrity and quality will tend to produce a better tool than will a firm unknown in the reference field.

Major encyclopedia sets are issued by subscription book publishers who sell their products directly to the consumer, often through house-to-house canvass. Many other reference books are produced by trade publishers, and some are the products of textbook publishers.

The list of editors and contributors, usually placed at the beginning of a volume, indicates the authority behind the work. Scholars of reliable reputation lend assurance that information will be objective, documented, up-to-date. Editorial staffs composed of competent writers insure readability.

Evaluation Checklist For Reference Books

Scope: Are coverage, relevancy to course of study and recency adequate?

Treatment: Readable at what level? Free from bias on controversial subjects?

Arrangement: Alphabetic, chronologic, geographic, or other?

Format: Is the binding durable, the paper opaque, the type clear? Are the illustrations closely related to the text?

Authority: Are the publishers, editors, contributors estimable?

Bibliographies: Are they graded? Are Instructional Materials other than books listed?

The sixth and final criterion for evaluating reference books concerns the extent to which the tool in hand relates itself to other materials. In other words, are there good *bibliographies?* Are there lists of other Instructional Materials that will carry the reader forward in his study from the point where the reference book leaves off? Increasingly good school reference books are relating their bibliographies to the student's learning need rather than to the scholar's documentation. A good example of this type of educational-bibliographic approach is found in the 20th volume of *Collier's Encyclopedia*. Also, reference books are beginning to include films, tapes, and other kinds of Instructional Materials in their lists.

Kinds of Reference Books

Among the 10,000 reference titles in the world, there are many classes and types. Some are more useful for research, others for education. Of the latter a small but significant number are of specific value in schools. The principal types of school reference books include (1) bibliographies, (2) indexes, (3) encyclopedias, (4) dictionaries, (5) yearbooks and almanacs, (6) biographical dictionaries, and (7) geographical references. There are also special reference books related to the major subject areas, such as the language arts, social sciences, natural sciences, fine and practical arts, and religion and ethics.

The following survey of reference books considers the principal types in approximately the Dewey Decimal order in which they are found on the shelves in the average school library or Materials Center. In the Appendix there is a representative but necessarily highly selected list of reference books suitable for schools, from kindergarten through grade twelve. Aids for selecting more reference titles are included in the discussion of bibliographies.

BIBLIOGRAPHIES

A bibliography is a list of Instructional Materials relating to one or more subjects. Some of the more common types are (1) selection aids, (2) national and trade bibliographies, (3) format lists, and (4) subject lists.

Reference Selection Aids

Among the selection aids are several that help the teacher select "R" books. Three basic ones, all published by the American Library Association, list and evaluate standard and new reference books.

Shores' *Basic Reference Sources* (3–1), based on the author's previous *Basic Reference Books,* describes some 81 types and 270 examples of general reference works, selected for their usefulness in school, public, college, and special libraries. It is intended as a textbook for librarians.

Winchell's *Guide to Reference Books* (3–2) is an annotated list of about 5500 reference books classified by type and subject. Supplements, the first of which (1950–1952) added 1000 titles, provide a current selection aid.

For reviews of current reference books, the A.L.A. *Subscription Books Bulletin* (1–8) is distinctive for its fearless exposure of shoddy works. A jury of reference librarians evaluates each reference title, or major revision, as it appears, closing its review with the italicized words "Not recommended" in the case of an undeserving work. Up to September, 1956, this journal was issued separately as a quarterly, but since then its frequency has been increased through a merging with the A.L.A. semimonthly *Booklist,* and the new publication is known as the *Booklist and Subscription Books Bulletin.* Although previous emphasis was on the review of subscription books—books sold directly by the publisher to the consumer—trade and even textbook publishers' reference titles are now critically evaluated.

General Selection Aids

The *Booklist* itself, which has been a librarian's book-buying guide since 1905, undertakes semimonthly to select and annotate from the current publishers' output those titles that seem best suited for the patrons of small and medium-sized libraries. The sections on books for children and young people are particularly useful to teachers. Annotations give a good idea of the content of each book and compare the book with comparable ones available.

For a core collection of school materials, there are five basic bibliographies. Two of these are published by the H. W. Wilson Company (New York), the world's largest index publishers. The first is the *Children's Catalog* (1–2), which in its ninth edition listed more than 3000 titles recommended by a representative group of librarians and children's literature specialists. It is an easy catalog to use. Part One is arranged by the Dewey Decimal Classification, listing the books approximately in the order in which they appear on the shelves of a library. Part Two is even simpler, because it is alphabetic, with authors, titles, subjects, and "analytics" of books, all in one sequence. The analytic feature is especially valuable for teachers, because even if only part of a book is devoted to the subject on which a teacher wants help, that part is listed under the subject heading. For example, E. B. Jordan's play "The Lost Hour" can be found in Schauffler's *Days We Celebrate* v. 2, p. 15–24, under Holidays. A third part of the *Children's Catalog* is a graded list for kindergarten through grade eight.

The other Wilson aid is the *Standard Catalog for High School Libraries* (1–4). It has almost the same arrangement as the *Children's Catalog*, except that the nearly 5000 titles are selected basically for grades nine through twelve, and the alphabetic list precedes the Dewey classified arrangement. Both Wilson catalogs star a small number of titles for first purchase and give full bibliographic detail.

Three other core lists are sponsored by the American Library Association. The first of these, prepared by a joint committee from the National Education Association, Association for Childhood Education, and National Council of Teachers of English, lists and annotates by subject more than 1000 titles suitable for kindergarten through grade eight, with grade level indicated. A magazine selection is also helpful. A second list does the same job for the junior high school, and the third selects more than 1500 titles for small and medium-sized high schools.

It is not so important for the teacher to memorize the features of these five book selection aids as to recall these tools on appropriate occasions. These occasions may occur at the beginning of a unit, or on the day the librarian requests suggestions for spending wisely the sum of money allocated for library books. In the first instance, a quick check in one or more of these aids of the titles under the desired subject will help the teacher enter the Materials Center with clear purpose. In the second instance, the teacher can actively participate as a full partner in selection and can support his own judgment with the composite judgments of experts in the field.

National and Trade Bibliography

Every civilized nation has what it calls its chain of national bibliography—chronological links that undertake to list all the books published in that country during any given period. Systematically our bibliographers, like those of other nations, have sought to list all titles ever issued from the time of the first printing press.

Cumulative Book Index. Courtesy H. W. Wilson Company.

For example, *Publishers' Weekly* lists every book published in the United States during the week, in a department called the "Weekly Record." A teacher can thus check information on any very recent books through this source. Librarians generally feel that the best way to keep up with books is to read *Publishers' Weekly* regularly.

The fullest current world list of books in the English language is the *Cumulative Book Index* (3–3), known as *CBI*. It is now issued monthly except August, and accumulated into semiannual, annual, biennial, and five-year volumes. All books published in the English language during these periods, both in the United States and in other parts of the world, are arranged in dictionary form—by author, title, and subject. This is the tool to use if you are seeking full information on a book, including the author's full name, exact title, publisher's name and address, paging, and price. The *CBI* is found in many of the larger high school libraries and certainly will have a place in the Materials Center for the school system.

A bibliographic tool found usually in the public library or in the school system's central Materials Center is the *Publishers' Trade List Annual* (3–4). It is primarily an annual collection of American publishers' catalogs, arranged alphabetically by publisher, with a separate author-title index called *Books in Print*. The value of this tool lies in the fact that often one can recall only the publisher of a book and not the author or title; in that case *PTLA* will help.

Format and Subject Lists

All of the bibliographies described thus far have not been limited by subject or format. But there are lists of films, filmstrips, disk recordings, tapes, magazines, pamphlets, and so on. An example of a format bibliography is the list of *Selected United States Government Publications* (5–13), which can be obtained free of charge from the Superintendent of Documents at the United States Government Printing Office, Washington, D.C.

The *Vertical File Index* (3–6), formerly known as the *Vertical File Service Catalog*, is an "annotated subject list of pamphlets, booklets, brochures, leaflets, circulars, folders, maps, posters, charts, mimeographed bulletins, and other inexpensive material . . . ," issued monthly, with annual cumulations in December.

Then there are lists of materials in specified subject fields in the language arts, social studies, sciences, and vocational subjects. Examples of these can be found in the quarterly *Bibliographic Index* (3–7), which indexes more than 1000 periodicals regularly for such subject lists. Usually these subject lists can be found on the shelves under RO16 with the subject number following the decimal. Thus, a subject bibliography on the social studies would take the 3 from 300, the class number for social sciences, and appear as RO16.3.

INDEXES

Like bibliographies, indexes are a class of reference tools that send you on to other sources of information. An index is a systematic list of references to the contents of any single material or group of Instructional Materials. Usually indexes are arranged alphabetically by author, title, and subject, but they may also be arranged geographically or chronologically.

Book Indexes

One important type of index analyzes the contents of books—especially those books, such as readers and collections of essays, which contain miscellaneous subjects.

Because she felt that a great many important readings were locked inside the many readers not necessarily in adoption in a particular school system, Eloise Rue in 1938 produced her *Subject Index to Readers.* This was subsequently revised in 1943 under the title *Subject Index to Books for Primary Grades* (2–6). Here is a teacher's "R" book which analyzes some 430 readers and 250 other books, such as picture books, song books, and easy books, for subjects of interest to little children. In 1946 a first supplement was added, indexing 225 titles published from 1942 through early 1946. In 1950 the second edition of her *Subject Index to Books for Intermediate Grades* appeared, in which some 1800 text and trade books were analyzed under about 6500 subject heads with grade-level indications. Here are two real aids to unit planning.

On the high school and adult level, the *Essay and General Literature Index* (3–8) performs a comparable service. It indexes 100,000 essays by subject in its several volumes and continuing service. For example, the foundation volume, which indexes some 2144 volumes published from 1900 to 1933 lists no fewer than 40,000 essays on various subjects. There are three seven-year supplements and continuing semi-annual and cumulated volumes that reveal good essays on politics, government, history, art, science, education, religion, and other subjects. A notable feature is the analysis of authors, including a list not only of each author's works, but also of works about him and criticisms of his work.

Periodical Indexes

Because periodicals present the same problems as readers and collections of essays, there are also numerous periodical indexes. The best known of these is the *Readers' Guide to Periodical Literature*. The large *Readers' Guide* (3–9) indexes selections in over 100 popular American and Canadian periodicals such as *Life, Newsweek, Saturday Evening Post* in dictionary fashion, by author, subject, and title when necessary. The smaller *Abridged Readers' Guide* indexes only about one-fourth as many magazines, but most of these are more nearly related to school interests.

Features about the two worth remembering are cumulation and price, characteristics of many of the H. W. Wilson publications. The *Readers' Guide* is issued every two weeks. If these issues were not cumulated, it would mean that at the end of a year it would be necessary to consult no fewer than 26 alphabets to locate an article on a subject published some time during the past twelve months; at the end of five years there would be some 130 separate alphabets to consult. But by the Wilson cumulative device, succeeding issues of the *Readers' Guide* integrate the previous alphabets into the new one.

When Wilson announces the cost of an index will be on the "Service Basis," it means libraries will be charged in proportion to the use made of the index. Thus if a library is subscribing to only about half of the periodicals indexed in the *Readers' Guide,* it is obviously making less use of the index than the library subscribing to all of the indexed magazines, and therefore pays proportionately less.

In addition to the *Readers' Guide,* Wilson issues many other indexes. The *Cumulative Book Index* and such other bibliographies as the *Children's Catalog* and the *Standard Catalog for High School Libraries* have already been mentioned. Other periodical indexes include the *International Index* and the *Education Index.* The *Book Review Digest* (3–10) indexes about 80 American and English review periodicals. Under the author of each book reviewed there is a brief annotation of the book, followed by excerpts from the leading reviews. For each excerpt, the length of the full review in number of words is indicated, and a plus or minus sign is used to represent favorable or unfavorable comment.

ENCYCLOPEDIAS

The good encyclopedia, intelligently used, can fortify the teacher's lesson plan. It has within it all of the knowledge significant to mankind—authoritatively summarized, intelligently organized, often artistically presented. Into this major Instructional Material there has often been poured a quantity of human, economic, educational, aesthetic, and institutional resources seldom found in any other medium.

Most encyclopedias are produced by so-called subscription book publishers—publishers who sell their products through their own agents direct to the consumer. For the major sets a permanent editorial staff is maintained, and hundreds or thousands of contributors are employed to write articles. Talented artists devote their energies to extending the printed word by means of line drawings and halftones. Color is used aesthetically, sometimes lavishly, in an effort to lure the reader to knowledge. Indexers and bibliographers analyze the content of the set and send users on to other sources for further information. Directing the whole enterprise is an editor-in-chief assisted by advisory editors who are experts on curriculum, library, children's literature, and the various subjects.

Encyclopedia Features

In the expert teacher's hand, the encyclopedia becomes a teaching tool of varied opportunity. It is the fact-finder extraordinary, through its planned arrangement and detailed index. It provides overview and background, verbal and pictorial, for any teaching unit. In the last few years school encyclopedias have turned to the picture with abandon and have gained the applause of the visual-minded educators.

A high degree of creativity is employed in the planning of encyclopedia illustrations. For example, the editors of one school encyclopedia were confronted with this problem: children know a giraffe's neck is long, but how long? These editors knew that when New York children were asked how large a cow is it was discovered that the only size cow they had ever seen was the one on the label of a condensed milk can. There was the challenge. Somehow all the important animals of the world had to be brought together to pose for the children so that at a glance it could be seen which was larger, the giraffe or the cow, the horse or the rhinoceros, the dog or the coyote. One of the editors hit upon the idea of having a museum arrange stuffed animals in a huge panorama that was photographed and printed in the book.

The encyclopedia acts also as a guide to pupil interests. Whereas encyclopedias once represented the scholar's so-called circle of knowledge, the modern school set is more nearly guided in subject selection and space allocation by the advice of curriculum experts and psychologists of childhood and adolescence. Consequently, the teacher can look to the content of an encyclopedia as an aid in lesson planning.

With regard to accessibility of information in an encyclopedia, it is important for the teacher to understand arrangement patterns. Most encyclopedias are arranged alphabetically by subject; several important works are not. Among the adult one-volume encyclopedias, for example, the *Lincoln Library of Essential Information* classifies its content by broad areas; so also do such children's sets as the *Book of Knowledge* and *Our Wonderful World*. All of these provide

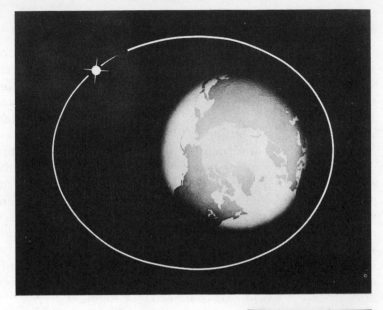

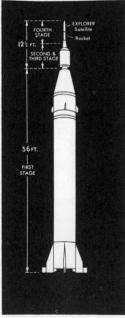

New developments, such as space exploration, are promptly illustrated in encyclopedias. *Courtesy Collier's Encyclopedia.*

alphabetical indexes, but their major sequence of articles follows a logical or psychological arrangement rather than a dictionary one.

Among the sets that are alphabetically arranged there are at least two patterns. According to one of these, long articles with big chunks of knowledge are presented, and a detailed alphabetical index lists the smaller topics. An example of this pattern has already been discussed in connection with the "phalanx" situation in the *Britannica*. Among the school encyclopedias, *Compton's* also favors the large-subject pattern. The *World Book* tends to favor the small-subject pattern. With this arrangement, separate articles for ampere, dynamo, ohm, and watt, might be found in addition to the general article on electricity. In a work using the large-subject pattern, the single article on electricity might cover all of the smaller topics, and it would therefore be necessary to go to the analytical alphabetical index to locate information on the ampere. In order to establish the relationships among the smaller topics and their relationship to the larger subject, the *World Book* uses a synthetic classified index. For comparison, contrast the *World Book's* "Reading and Study Guide" (volume 19) with the *Britannica's* index (volume 24).

Compton's has innovated a device in its index that deserves careful understanding by the teacher because of its ready-reference potential. Known as the "Fact-Index," it differs from most indexes in two respects: a portion of it is in the back of every volume, and, in addition to page references, brief facts are given. This means that in the A volume, for example, the Fact-Index part acts as a "guide to all volumes for subjects beginning with A." It means also that the Fact-Index not only refers to articles which provide information on a subject, but also itself answers the question briefly.

Compton's is responsible for another innovation now almost universally adopted by alphabetically arranged school encyclopedias: placement of all of the articles beginning with one letter in one volume. This is known as the whole-letter volume, and, although it makes for different thicknesses among the volumes in the set, it also produces greater

BIOGRAPHY

Montesquieu, Baron de, M—5218
Rabelais, François, R—6730
Sainte-Beuve, Charles, S—7146

Others

Brandes, Georg, B—962
Dowden, Edward, D—2071
Juvenal, J—4089
Lessing, Gotthold E., L—4378
Nordau, Max S., N—5707
Papini, Giovanni, P—6087
Plutarch, P—6426

EXPLORERS AND DISCOVERERS

See also *Geographers*

Peary, Robert E., P—6161
Pike, Zebulon M., P—6335
Schwatka, Frederick, S—7260
Smith, Jedediah S., S—7508
Stanley, Henry M., Sir, S—7692
Waldeck, Theodore J., W—8562
Walker, Joseph R., C—1137

British

Baffin, William, B—603
Burton, Richard F., Sir, B—1077
Cook, James, C—1705
Drake, Francis, Sir, D—2077
Franklin, John, Sir, F—2751
Frobisher, Martin, Sir, F—2791
Gilbert, Humphrey, Sir, G—2993
Gosnold, Bartholomew, G—3069
Hearne, Samuel, H—3341
Hudson, Henry, H—3563
Livingstone, David, L—4540
Park, Mungo, P—6118
Parry, William E., Sir, P—6128
Puget, Peter, P—6661
Raleigh, Walter, Sir, R—6793
Ross, James C., Sir, R—7053
Scott, Robert F., S—7285
Shackleton, Ernest H., Sir, S—7363
Speke, John H., S—7638
Vancouver, George, V—8431

Canadian

Iberville, Sieur d', I—3613
Joliet, Louis, J—4052
Mackenzie, Alex., Sir, M—4676

Vespucci, Amerigo, V—8481

Portuguese

Cabral, Pedro Á., C—1105
Dias, Bartholomeu, D—1979
Gama, Vasco da, G—2854

BIOGRAPHY

Henry the Navigator, H—3387
Magellan, Ferdinand, M—4703

Scandinavian

Amundsen, Roald, A—274
Andrée, Salomon, A—287
Bering, Vitus, B—753
Ericson, Leif, E—2373
Eric the Red, E—2373
Hedin, Sven A., H—3361
Nansen, Fridtjof, N—5388
Nordenskjöld, Nils Adolf Erik, Baron, N—5707
Rasmussen, Knud J., R—6803

Spanish

Alvarado, Pedro de, A—248
Balboa, Vasco N. de, B—609
Cabeza de Vaca, Álvar N., C—1101
Coronado, Francisco Vásquez, C—1743
Cortes, Hernando, C—1748
De Soto, Hernando, D—1964
Jiménez de Quesada, Gonzalo, J—4034
Narváez, Pánfilo de, N—5401

Aiken, Conrad P., A—105
*Alcott, Louisa M., A—205
Aldrich, Bess Streeter, A—207
*Aldrich, Thomas B., A—207
*Alger, Horatio, A—224
*Allee, Marjorie Hill, A—230
*Allen, Hervey, A—231

A page from a classified encyclopedia index, the *World Book Encyclopedia*. *Courtesy Field Enterprises, Inc.*

ease in article location. Contrast the single guide letters on *Compton's* or *World Book* with the split-letter guides (ABA-AMO) on such adult encyclopedias as the *Americana* and *Britannica*.

A serious problem in encyclopedias is keeping the information up to date. The major sets now practice continuous rather than periodic revision. Under the latter plan a set was completely revised once every ten or more years. Continuous revision calls for a permanent editorial staff which reads, reviews, revises, rewrites, deletes, and adds continually. It is estimated that 5 per cent of the text and illustrations, (on an average) in the major sets is changed with each yearly reprinting. In terms of selection, this means that school sets should be replaced at least every five years, if not more often. Hard use will dictate more frequent replacement than content change requires. By staggering the purchases, it is possible to have at least one set with the current year's imprint in the Materials Center or in a classroom.

With most sets, continuous revision is now supplemented by yearbooks. While these annuals do nothing to keep the set itself up to date, they do keep the owner of the set informed of current happenings. All major adult sets issue an annual arranged alphabetically, like the encyclopedia. Of the school sets, *World Book, Book of Knowledge,* and *Compton's* offer yearbooks.

Classes of Encyclopedias

Today's encyclopedias may be grouped as follows: school alphabetic, school classified, adult multi-volume and adult one-volume.

School encyclopedias. Among the school alphabetic sets, *Compton's* (3–11) and *World Book* (3–12) have already been compared on arrangement patterns. These two sets are epitomes of their respective encyclopedia patterns. *Compton's,* for example, has long been known for its readable style and its special attention to dramatic, colorful, and pertinent illustrations. Its charts and pictorial maps have introduced a fresh visual dimension into verbal tools. *World Book,* by its compact and well-organized writing, has tended to approach most nearly the adult encyclopedia style. Its illustrations are plentiful and selected for their support of the text. Both of these sets have earned places of first importance in all learning from kindergarten through high school.

Other good school alphabetic encyclopedias include *American Educator* (3–14) and *Britannica Junior* (3–13). The former is based on the first edition of the *World Book,* and the latter on a set named *Weedon's Modern Encyclopedia.* Both have been continuously revised for so long that they are far removed from their predecessors. *Britannica Junior* (3–13) is published "with the advice and consultation of the faculties of the University of Chicago and the University Laboratory School" and is aimed at elementary and junior high levels. The first volume is a ready reference index with the *Compton* fact feature, and volume 15 includes an atlas. The *American Educator* (3–14) is a short-article, small-subject type of encyclopedia, with no index but with many good illustrations.

One of the oldest and perhaps best-known school classified encyclopedias is the *Book of Knowledge* (3–15). Its 20 volumes include some 18 departments, such as The Earth, Science, Animal Life, Men and Women, Fine Arts; the 20th volume is an index with some 40,000 entries. An advantage in this type of arrangement is that, for self-education, continual and related reading can be encouraged with minimum recourse to index or cross reference. A disadvantage is that for ready reference, the index must always be consulted in order to find the desired information. A new classified set is *Our Wonderful World* (3–16) which follows a thematic organization. Basically the set is a profusely illustrated anthology of selections from books, magazines, and pamphlets, with citations of the sources. The *Oxford Junior Encyclopedia* (3–17), a British children's set of which an American edition is in preparation, is a cross between the alphabetical and the classified arrangement. Each of its twelve volumes is devoted to one broad area—for example, Natural History, Communications, Farming and Fisheries—and each is arranged alphabetically. A 13th volume provides a general index.

Adult Encyclopedias. There is a place for adult encyclopedias in the intermediate grades, as well as in junior and senior high school. The *Encyclopedia Americana's* clever ad showing the pony-tailed, teen-age girl under the caption "Naturally I use an adult encyclopedia" is in fact supported by even fifth and sixth grade youngsters who, unlike Johnny, can read and are looking for something that spurs them on.

Of the adult encyclopedias, four major sets and two one-volume works are essential teacher tools. All of them can be used with varying degrees of success as early as the intermediate grades to challenge and stimulate bright pupils and average youngsters with an advanced interest in a hobby subject. It goes without saying that the teacher himself will find much enrichment for his own preparation in these encyclopedias.

Collier's Encyclopedia (3–21) provides an excellent example of transition from school level to adult level. Its format is attractive—the black, red, and gold binding; the paper; the profuse illustrations both in black and white and color; and the make-up. A graded bibliography under some 125 headings, concentrated in the last volume, represents a departure from the usual list of references after each volume.

American Peoples' Encyclopedia (3–18), marketed through Sears, Roebuck and Company, presents adult information readably and compactly, so high school students can use the set effectively. One of the innovations in illustration is the use of transparency overlays, such as the one for human anatomy which contributes to an understanding of the relationships of the various organs.

The *Encyclopedia Americana* (3–19), the oldest continuously published American encyclopedia, is distinguished by its coverage of American cities and towns and its long, almost volume-length articles on various countries. A feature of note is its summaries under each century. Increasing attention to the needs of high school students has made the *Americana* a reference source of note in the school library.

The set almost synonymous with the word encyclopedia is the *Britannica*. Originally English and now owned and edited in the United States, the *Britannica* has steadily sought to make its great store of knowledge understandable by lay readers. Distinguished for its notable contributors, its high scholarship, its comprehensiveness, and its tremendous index of over 500,000 entries, the *Encyclopaedia Britannica* has a program of continuous revision for relating its storehouse of information progressively to the needs and abilities of the lay reader.

Although naturally less comprehensive than the sets, the one-volume encyclopedias are handy for quick fact-finding.

The *Columbia Encyclopedia* (3–22), with its 70,000 subjects, presents compactly many sought-after answers to school questions. Among its features are biblical names, towns and cities, and a number of short definitive articles. The other most frequently found one-volume encyclopedia in libraries is the *Lincoln Library of Essential Information* (3–23). Unlike *Columbia*, which is alphabetically arranged, subjects in the *Lincoln Library* are classified into twelve major divisions. Among its features are the tables, outlines, glossaries, chronologies, test questions, and classified biographies. Prepared originally for teachers by a teacher, the *Lincoln Library* offers help to all teachers and to many pupils.

ANNUALS AND ALMANACS

Annuals

To supplement their encyclopedias, publishers of all the major sets now issue yearbooks which summarize the significant developments of the last completed year. Subjects are arranged alphabetically, and usually a calendar of events, necrology, and issues that have concerned the world are included.

The *Compton Yearbook* (3–24), newest of these supplements, was launched in 1958. Unique in its arrangement is the division of the main text into nine principal topics, each one of which is then arranged alphabetically by subtopics. A general index lists all of the subjects alphabetically.

World Book Encyclopedia Annual Supplement (3–25), paperbound and punched for loose-leaf binding, follows a straight alphabetical sequence of subjects. A cumulative index to previous years aids ready reference. *World Topics Yearbook* (3–26) is the successor to a quarterly issued by the *American Educator Encyclopedia* prior to 1956, and supplements also another United Educators' publication, *Wonderland of Knowledge*. *Book of Knowledge Annual* (3–27) is like the other supplements only in its alphabetical arrangement and calendar. Its articles and illustrations are distinctive and are more markedly an augmentation of the encyclopedia material.

Only *Britannica Junior* issues no yearbook of its own. It offers its subscribers the "senior's annual," *Britannica Book of the Year* (3–28), a supplement that is quite different in make-up from its parent set. For example, in contrast to the *Encyclopaedia Britannica's* conservative page make-up, the *Britannica Book of the Year* displays many bleed photos, modern type and headings, and a page organization that invites reading. Featured are extensive chronology, major articles on subjects of current interest, and a cumulative index.

Americana Annual (3–29) features chronologies and a cumulative index and probably resembles its parent set more than does any other yearbook. Features of *American Peoples' Encyclopedia Yearbook* (3–30) are the attention to biography, to "names in the news," and to the listing of heads of government agencies. *Collier's Yearbook* (3–31) has each year presented major articles on controversial issues often debated by adversaries, in addition to the regular yearbook summary of developments arranged alphabetically by topic.

Almanacs and Other Yearbooks

Separate from encyclopedias and useful for current facts and figures are the almanacs. These were, years ago, calendar books with weather predictions for the farmer. But today the almanac has become a miscellany of facts and figures.

Best known and perhaps most comprehensive of the American examples is the *World Almanac* (3–32), distinguished by the index in the front of the book. Facts and figures are given on subjects from politics to sports, including business, government, transportation, family, education, institutions and agencies, structures, and many others. Here is a "must" tool for debates and social studies. Its rival is the comparatively recent *Information Please Almanac* (3–33), born of the famous radio program. It covers much of the ground of the *World Almanac,* and it has two notable features: special articles on timely events, and a good "who's who" section on people in the news.

A unique yearbook useful in the social studies is the *Statesman's Yearbook* (3–34). Although a British publication, it devotes one of its three major sections to the United States. The first section is reserved for the British Commonwealth and the third section for all other nations of the world, alphabetically arranged. Fundamentally, the *Statesman's Yearbook* is an annual guide to the governments of the world. For each country it gives area, population, constitution, government, religion, finance, defense, education, industry, commerce, agriculture, money, diplomatic representatives, and many other pertinent facts. There is also a section on the United Nations.

Another tool for the social studies is the *Statistical Abstract of the United States* (3–35), which each year summarizes all of the important statistics gathered from private sources and government agencies. One valuable feature is the comparative tables carrying statistics back for several years.

DICTIONARIES

No class of reference book is more vital to learning than the dictionary—a list of words of a language or terms of a subject, usually arranged alphabetically, with meanings and other data. The importance to language arts of this class of teaching tool is obvious, but its relation to learning is often not understood. Failure to appreciate the principal features of dictionaries and related language tools accounts for the inadequacy of present teaching use.

Dictionary Utilization

A high school teacher, some time ago, assigned an English class to look up a word in the "big dictionary." The next day about half of the class came back with one definition, and the rest with a different one. *All of the pupils had copied the first definition and stopped.* The reason for the divided result was obvious. Those pupils who had gone to *Webster's New International Dictionary,* one of the two American "big" dictionaries in an elephantine single volume, found a historical sequence of definitions, with the oldest meaning given first. However, those pupils who consulted the other "big" American dictionary, *Funk & Wagnalls New Standard,* found the most common meaning given first. Had the pupils been instructed to bring in all the definitions given for the word in the dictionary, every pupil would have had the definition the teacher wished to discuss.

Some dictionary information especially useful in teaching is the following:

1. *Meanings* of words, phrases, and expressions
2. *Spellings,* especially of troublesome words like "believe," "receive," "pneumonia," "Cincinnati"
3. *Pronunciations,* especially of controversial words (like "either"), regional variations (as of "house," "creek," "idea"), and British variations (as of "clerk" and "schedule")
4. *Usage* of such words as "awful," "complete," "reckon"
5. *Synonyms, antonyms, homonyms*
6. *Abbreviations, signs, symbols*
7. *Rhyming words*
8. *Slang and colloquial English*
9. *Illustrations*
10. *Foreign words and phrases* used in English writing

Dictionary Abridgment

English language dictionaries can be classified by vocabulary size and by age and grade level. Except for the unabridged dictionaries, all vocabularies are limited according to an abridgement principle. The earliest English dictionaries were limited to "hard" words; it was thought everyone knew the meaning of such "easy" words as "cat," "dog," "run." What is considered to be the earliest English dictionary, Robert Cawdrey's *A Table Alphabeticall* (published in 1604), was primarily an interlinear glossary of Latin and French texts and treated only difficult words. So also did the dictionary *New Worlds of English Words,* compiled in 1658 by John Milton's nephew, Edward Phillips. But by 1721 Nathan Bailey published the *Universal Etymological Dictionary,* which included easy as well as hard words, omitting only those not considered in good form.

Such word censorship was the vogue in the eighteenth century, not only in England, but on the Continent, and received its most dictatorial support from Dr. Samuel Johnson in his famous *Dictionary of the English Language.* Abridgement to Dr. Johnson meant prohibition of the uncouth words used by the uncultured, and this theory of dictionary-making persisted in England until the middle of the nineteenth century, when Dean Trench in a historic paper proposed that the dictionary should record all of the words used by the people. Out of that proposition the great *Oxford English Dictionary* was born. It took 70 years to prepare and engaged some 1300 scholars on both sides of the Atlantic. Although unabridged dictionaries had been undertaken before, the *O.E.D.* established the principle once and for all that unabridgement means all of the words of a language.

But if the principle of unabridgement was clearly established, the principle of abridgement for those who had no need for a full dictionary was not. The selection of words was based largely on the choices of subject experts, plus a general representation. Such choice was strengthened by the Thorndike-Lorge word count technique. In 1944 there was published *The Teacher's Word Book of 30,000 Words,* which was based on a tabulation of the frequency of occurrence of each different word in about 25 million words of running text in novels, essays, textbooks, monographs, pamphlets, magazines, and business and social letters. Most dictionaries are now abridged by suitable word counts supplemented by subject specialists' selections.

Types and Examples of Dictionaries

Today's English-language dictionaries can be classified by vocabulary size and age and grade level.

Classes of English-Language Dictionaries

Type	Vocabulary Size	Scope	Example
Primary Abridged	under 5000	For Kindergarten through Grade 3	Rainbow
Intermediate Abridged	30,000+	For Grades 4 through 8	Webster's Elementary
High School Abridged	60,000+	For Grades 9 through 12	Thorndike-Barnhart High School
College Abridged	125,000+	Selected from adult literature	American College
Adult Unabridged	400,000+	All words except obscene	Webster's New International

Selection of dictionaries for teaching use involves some knowledge of the scope and the features not only of all of the types shown in the table, but of the leading examples.

The Primary Abridged Dictionary. The picture dictionary for very young children evolved naturally from the child's ABC book ("A is for apple"). It is characterized by the omission of definitions and by the use of pictures and sentences to give meaning to words for children. Vocabularies range from a couple of hundred words for preschool use to several thousand for the early intermediate grades. Only a few representative titles will be mentioned here.

Rainbow's (3–36) 2300 words are selected by Wendell W. Wright, and its 1100 pictures are created by Joseph Low. One of the largest of the primaries, it lets pictures define wherever possible; otherwise sentences do the job. With somewhat fewer words (1030) but more pictures (1500) Ellen W. Walpole and Gertrude Elliott introduce the child to the dictionary habit in their *Golden Dictionary* (3–37). In *My First Dictionary* (3–38) there are only 600 entries selected by Laura Oftedahl and Nina Jacobs, but there are also exactly 600 Pelagie Doane illustrations. What distinguishes the *Picture Book Dictionary* (3–39) edited by Dilla MacBean, former Chicago school libraries supervisor, is its oblong format and the fact that each of its 325 words chosen from the primary list is illustrated by a picture and a sentence.

sew   We **sew** with a needle and thread. Mary will sew a dress for her doll.

sewed   She has **sewed** many dresses for her dolls.

sewing   Mary is **sewing** with black thread.

shade   John is sitting in the **shade** of the tree. Louise is sitting in the sunshine. A cloud covering the sun makes shade. An umbrella will give you shade from the sun.

shadow   When the light shines, almost everything has a **shadow**. You can see your shadow if you stand in the sun. Trees make lovely **shadows** in the moonlight.

> I have a little shadow that goes in and out with me,
> And what can be the use of him is more than I can see.
> He is very, very like me from the heels up to the head;
> And I see him jump before me, when I jump into my bed.

shake   Harriet will **shake** the dust from the rug. The wet puppy can shake himself to get dry.

shook   My mother **shook** the snow from her fur coat.

321

A page from the *Rainbow Dictionary. Courtesy World Publishing Company.*

The Intermediate Abridged Dictionary. When E. L. Thorndike produced in 1935 what the publisher called "the first dictionary ever made from scratch for use and understanding by children," he blazed a new trail in the intermediate grades. The dictionary was the *Thorndike-Century Junior,* which based its vocabulary selection on a word count and produced new simplified definitions rather than condensations from adult dictionaries.

Designed for grades three to eight, the intermediate abridged dictionary today tends to divide into upper and lower range subclasses. Examples of dictionaries in this class include three Thorndike-Barnhart (successor to Thorndike-Century) titles: the "Beginning," for grades four to five, with some 14,000 entries; the "Junior" (3–41) for grades five to eight with 43,000 entries; and the "Advanced Junior," for the upper intermediate grades. All of these feature sections on dictionary use and the Thorndike vocabulary selection technique.

Webster dictionaries for this age level are the "Elementary" (3–42) with 18,000 entries, and "A Dictionary for Boys and Girls" (3–43) with 38,500. *Funk & Wagnalls "Standard" Junior Dictionary of the English Language* (3–44) and *Winston Dictionary for Children* (3–45) also belong in the intermediate class.

The High School Abridged Dictionary. Aimed at grades nine through twelve, the high school abridged dictionary is also useful in the intermediate grades and sometimes in junior college. The same four firms which publish intermediate dictionaries also compete on the high school level. The *Thorndike-Barnhart High School Dictionary* (3–46) has over 80,000 entries and features a bound-in manual on dictionary use. *Webster's Students* (3–47), *Funk & Wagnalls Standard High School* (3–48), and *Winston Dictionary for Schools* (3–49), with somewhat fewer entries, are other titles in this class of dictionaries.

The Merriam-Webster and Thorndike-Barnhart publications on both the intermediate and high school level are distributed by textbook publishers—the former by the American Book Company and the latter by Scott, Foresman and Company.

gathering 408 gazellelike

gath·er·ing (gaᴛʜ'ər ing or gaᴛʜ'ring), n. 1. act of one that gathers. 2. that which is gathered. 3. meeting; assembly; party; crowd. 4. swelling that comes to a head and forms pus. —Syn. 3. See meeting.

Gat·ling gun (gat'ling), an early type of machine gun consisting of a revolving cluster of barrels around a central axis. [Am.E; named after R. J. Gatling (1818-1903), American inventor]

Ga·tun (gä tün'), n. 1. town in N Panama Canal Zone. 2. a large dam near there. 1½ mi. long. 3. an artificial lake formed by Gatun Dam. 164 sq. mi.

Gatling gun

gauche (gōsh), adj. awkward; clumsy; tactless. [< F gauche left] —gauche'ly, adv. —gauche'ness, n.

gau·che·rie (gō'shə rē' or gō'shə rē), n. 1. awkwardness; tactlessness. 2. an awkward or tactless movement, act, etc. [< F]

Gau·cho (gou'chō), n., pl. -chos. cowboy of mixed Spanish and Indian descent in the S plains of South America. [< Sp.]

gaud (gôd), n. a cheap, showy ornament; trinket: *Savages like beads, mirrors, and such gauds.* [apparently < AF *gaude* < *gaudir* rejoice < L *gaudēre*]

gaud·y (gôd'i), adj., gaud i er, gaud i est. too bright and gay to be in good taste; cheap and showy. —gaud'i ly, adv. —gaud'i ness, n.
Syn. Gaudy, flashy, showy mean done for display. Gaudy particularly suggests too bright colors, sometimes too much or too glittering decoration, and always suggests being in bad taste: *She would be attractive if she did not wear such gaudy jewelry.* Flashy emphasizes dazzling brightness and cheap and vulgar display: *He tries to impress people by wearing flashy socks and jackets.* Showy emphasizes making a great and striking display, often but not always in a flashy way: *Peacocks are showy birds.*

gauge (gāj), n., v., gauged, gaug ing. —n. 1. standard measure; scale of standard measurements; measure. There are gauges of the capacity of a barrel, the thickness of sheet iron, the diameter of a shotgun bore, wire, etc. 2. instrument for measuring. A **steam gauge** measures the pressure of steam. 3. means of estimating or judging. 4. size; capacity; extent. 5. distance between railroad rails or between the right and left wheels of a wagon, automobile, etc. Standard gauge between rails is 56¼ in. 6. position of one sailing ship with reference to another and to the wind. A ship having the weather gauge of another is to the windward of it. 7. length of the exposed part of shingles, tiles, etc., when laid in rows. —v. 1. measure accurately; find out the exact measurement of with a gauge. 2. estimate; judge: *It is difficult to gauge the character of a stranger.* Also, gage. [< OF]

Gauge for measuring wire

gauge·a·ble (gāj'ə bəl), adj. that may be gauged.

gaug·er (gāj'ər), n. 1. person or thing that gauges. 2. official who measures the contents of barrels of taxable liquor. 3. collector of excise taxes. Also, gager.

Gau·guin (gō gaN'), n. Paul, 1848-1903, French painter.

Gaul (gôl), n. 1. an ancient country in W Europe. It included France, Belgium, the Netherlands, and parts of Switzerland, Germany, and N Italy. 2. one of the Celtic inhabitants of ancient Gaul. 3. Frenchman. [(def. 1) < F *Gaule* < L *Gallia* < *Gallus* a Gaul; (def. 2) < L *Gallus*]

Gaul·list (gōl'ist), n. in France, a political follower of Charles A.J.M. de Gaulle.

gaunt (gônt or gänt), adj. 1. very thin and bony; with hollow eyes and a starved look: *Hunger and suffering make people gaunt.* 2. looking bare and gloomy; desolate; forbidding; grim. [origin uncertain] —gaunt'ly, adv. —gaunt'ness, n. —Syn. 1. lean, spare, lank. See thin.

Gaunt (gônt or gänt), n. John of. 1340-1399, Duke of Lancaster. English soldier and statesman. He was the fourth son of Edward III and founder of the royal house of Lancaster.

gaunt·let (gônt'lit or gänt'lit), n. 1. a stout, heavy glove, usually of leather covered with plates of iron or steel, that was part of a knight's armor. 2. a stout, heavy glove with a wide, flaring cuff. 3. the wide, flaring cuff. 4. take up the gauntlet, a. accept a challenge. b. take up the defense of a person, opinion, etc. 5. throw down the gauntlet, challenge. Also, gantlet. [< OF *gantelet*, dim. of *gant* glove < Gmc.]

Iron gauntlet

gaunt·let (gônt'lit or gänt'lit), n. gantlet[1]

Gau·ta·ma (gou'tə mə or gou'tä mə), n. 563?-483? B.C., Buddha. Also, Gotama.

Gau·tier (gō tyā'), n. Théophile, 1811-1872, French poet, novelist, and critic.

gauze (gôz), n. 1. a very thin, light cloth, easily seen through. 2. a thin haze. [< F *gaze*; named after *Gaza*, Palestine.] —gauze'like', adj.

gauz·y (gōz'i), adj., gauz i er, gauz i est. like gauze; thin and light as gauze. —gauz'i ness, n.

gave (gāv), v. pt. of give. *He gave me some candy.*

gav·el (gav'əl), n. a small mallet used by a presiding officer to signal for attention or order or by an auctioneer to announce that the bidding is over. [? var. of *kevel* hammer; origin uncertain]

Judge holding a gavel

ga·vi·al (gā'vi əl), n. a large crocodile of India that has a long, slender snout. [< F Hindu. *ghariyāl*]

ga·votte (gə vot'), n. 1. dance like a minuet but much more lively. 2. music for it. [< F < Provençal *gavoto* < *Gavots*, Alpine people]

Ga·wain (gä'win or gä'wān), n. knight of the Round Table and nephew of King Arthur.

gawk (gôk), n. an awkward person; clumsy fool. —v. *Informal.* stare rudely or stupidly. [? < dialectal *gaulick* (-handed) left (-handed)]

gawk·y (gôk'i), adj., gawk i er, gawk i est. awkward; clumsy. —gawk'i ly, adv. —gawk'i ness, n.

gay (gā), adj., gay er, gay est. 1. happy and full of fun; merry. 2. bright-colored; showy. 3. full of pleasures. 4. dissipated; immoral. [< F *gai*] —gay'ness, n.
Syn. 1. Gay, merry mean lively and light-hearted. Gay emphasizes being free from care and full of life, joy, and high spirits; merry emphasizes being full of laughter and lively pleasure and fun: *The gay young people were merry as they decorated the gym for the dance.*

Gay (gā), n. John, 1685-1732, English poet and dramatist.

gay·e·ty (gā'ə ti), n., pl. -ties. gaiety.

Gay-Lus·sac (gā ly säk'), n. Joseph Louis, 1778-1850, French chemist.

gay·ly (gā'li), adv. gaily.

gaz., 1. gazette. 2. gazetteer.

Ga·za (gä'zə), n. town in W Palestine, once an important city of the Philistines. 20,000.

gaze (gāz), v., gazed, gaz ing. —v. look long and steadily. —n. a long, steady look. [cf. Scand. (dialectal Norwegian) *gasa*] —gaz'er, n.
Syn. v. Gaze, stare mean to look long and steadily at someone or something. Gaze emphasizes looking steadily and intently, chiefly in wonder, delight, or interest: *For hours he sat gazing at the stars.* Stare emphasizes looking with wide-open eyes steadily and directly at someone or something or off into space, chiefly in curiosity, rudeness, surprise, or stupidity: *The little boy stared at the stranger for a few minutes before answering his question.*

ga·zelle (gə zel'), n. a small, graceful antelope of Africa and Asia that has soft, lustrous eyes. [< F < Arabic *ghazāl*] —ga zelle'like', adj.

Gazelle (about 2 ft. high at the shoulder)

< from, derived from, taken from; cf., compare; dial., dialect; dim., diminutive; lang., language; pp., past participle; ppr., present participle; pt., past tense; ult., ultimately; var., variant; ? = possibly.

A page from the *Thorndike-Barnhart High School Dictionary.* Courtesy Scott, Foresman & Co.

The College Abridged Dictionary. The teacher will choose one of the college abridged dictionaries for desk use. A dictionary of this class contains about 150,000 words, and there are four leading examples.

The *American College* (3–50) has 132,000 entries (including person and place entries), selected largely on the basis of the Thorndike-Lorge word count and compiled with the help of 355 authorities. The person and place entries are included within the main alphabetical listing and verbal descriptions of place names are augmented by some 300 maps.

A somewhat larger number of entries, 145,000, is included in Funk & Wagnalls *New College Standard* (3–51), which features *EM' · PHA · TYPE*, a device for indicating pronunciation.

The *Webster's New Collegiate* (3–52) dictionary has 125,000 entries. Included are some 5000 person and 10,000 place entries, which are placed at the back of the dictionary in keeping with the Merriam separate-alphabet policy. Featured, also, is a separate rhyming dictionary, which has long been a favorite of teachers.

Webster's New World (3–53) dictionary is not a Merriam Webster; it is published by the World Publishing Company. Its 142,000 entries include 4500 persons and 6000 places and there are some 1200 illustrations.

Finally, the *Winston* dictionary, with about 100,000 entries, is distinguished for its simple and sound definitions.

The Adult Unabridged Dictionary. Basically, the adult unabridged dictionary is a teacher's tool, but it has good possibilities for high school pupils and even the more verbally advanced children in grades above four. There are three outstanding examples—two American and one British.

Webster's New International (3–54), the oldest American "big" dictionary, has over 600,000 entries, with some 13,000 biographical and 35,000 geographical names in separate lists. About 29,000 quotations show word use by leading authors. A divided page, with three columns in the upper part of the page for the living language and six columns in the lower part of the page for obsolete words, is one feature that has distinguished the *Webster's New International* in the past. Definitions are given in historical order, the oldest meaning first. Pronunciation is indicated by diacritical marks, and although most of the simplified spellings recommended by the American Philological Association and the Simplified Spelling Board are given, they are not necessarily placed preferentially.

Webster's American rival, *Funk & Wagnalls New Standard* (3–55), has about 500,000 entries, including some 30,000 places and 16,000 persons. Its almost 10,000 pictures, both black-and-white and color, strengthen the verbal meanings. Definitions are given with the most common meaning first.

The *Oxford English Dictionary* (3–56), is distinguished most importantly by its nearly two million quotations used to trace the history of every word in the English language. Over 400,000 words are treated in the 12 volumes and supplement. There are no illustrations.

BIOGRAPHICAL AND GEOGRAPHICAL REFERENCES

Persons and places are the facts of most interest in learning. Many and various "R" books supplying this information are at the teacher's disposal in a good library.

Biographical Sources

Biographical reference must take into account time and place. Some "R" books are limited to people still alive; others are restricted to citizens of one nation. A few, known as universal biographies, include all times and places, insisting only that the people be notable enough to warrant world celebrity.

Such a universal reference tool is *Webster's Biographical Dictionary* (3–57), which includes the great names of world history. A pupil can quickly discover in this book who, when, and where about his hero or subject. The arrangement is alphabetical by last name.

Another universal biographical tool, unique in its arrangement is Miriam de Ford's *Who Was When?* (3–58). Groups of famous contemporaries from 500 B.C. to 1949 A.D. are revealed in large-sized chronological charts. Each year is assigned a horizontal division on a page vertically divided by eleven fields of human activity, such as government, military, science, literature, and music. It is thus possible to see what great names in one field were contemporary with famous people in other fields.

When it comes to famous people of our day, *Current Biography* (3–59), issued monthly but available also as an annual, provides both articles and pictures of people in the news. Birth date, occupation, and address for each individual are given in the heading, and in the case of death, a brief obituary and reference to *The New York Times* are included.

One out of every 33,000 Americans is listed in *Who's Who in America* (3–60), published every other year. This standard reference book, issued regularly for over half a century, selects biographies either because of notable success in a significant field of human endeavor or because of official position. A few persons who are not Americans but who have identified themselves with American life, such as Winston Churchill, are also included. Monthly supplements add names.

Several special biographical sources dealing with notables in one field can be used effectively. The *Kunitz Shelf of Authors* (3–61), including *American Authors* and *Junior Book of Authors*, may be put to excellent use in literature classes. Morgan's book of brief biographies, *Our Presidents* (3–62), is valuable in history and civics. Encyclopedias are full of information about people, and some dictionaries provide brief identifying biographies.

Geographical Sources

Gazetteers, guide books, and atlases, supplemented by separate maps and globes, are the teacher's stock-in-trade for places. These will be treated in detail in Chapter 6. Here it will be sufficient to mention Webster's *Geographical Dictionary,* a gazetteer which briefly describes most of the important places in the world, and the guide book *Guide to America,* issued by the American Automobile Association as an aid to travelers. On a stand in most school libraries will be found an atlas, or a collection of maps such as Goode's *World Atlas* or the older *School Atlas.*

A good reference collection will include a range of "R" books sufficient in quantity and adequate in quality to answer questions about all of the subjects represented by the curriculum.

In the Appendix is listed a representative collection of reference books such as you might expect to find on the shelves of a school library or Materials Center. Every teacher owes it to himself to recognize at least most of these titles and to call upon them appropriately as the learning situation suggests.

The big "R" books pack learning power. As fact-finders, as overviewers, as documenters, as reading guides, and as summarizers, reference books are among the most effective of all classes of Instructional Materials. Use them unsparingly every teaching day.

Readings

EAKIN, M. K., and BROOKS, A. R. "Picture Dictionaries," *Elementary School Journal,* XLIX (January, 1949), 260–61.

MOTT, CAROLYN, and BAISDEN, L. B. *The Children's Book on How to Use Books and Libraries.* New York: Charles Scribner's Sons, 1937. Pp. 123–47, 158–76.

SHORES, LOUIS. *Basic Reference Sources.* Chicago: American Library Association, 1954. Pp. 17–21, 56–69.

———. "Reference Books," in *Compton's Pictured Encyclopedia,* XII (1956), 88b–89.

THORNDIKE, E. L. "Improving Ability to Read," *Teachers College Record,* XXXVI (1934), 1–19, 123–44, 229–41.

WINCHELL, CONSTANCE. *Guide to Reference Books.* Chicago: American Library Association, 1951. Pp. xvi–xvii.

4

READING BOOKS

The world's books can be separated into "adult" and "juvenile" literature. The adult portion is by far the larger, and from it the teacher will make his own selection of recreational and informational reading. Only a segment of this adult portion will be mentioned in this chapter. Major attention will be given to the selection and use of reading books for classroom teaching.

The term "juvenile" as applied to books probably gained its first recognition when public library children's rooms began marking books with a "J" to separate them from the rest of the collection. But the term is really not very popular now, either in libraries or among young readers. It is being replaced by such terms as "children's" and "young people's literature."

As we look at literature for children and young people, several classifications by type suggest themselves. The first possibility is by age and grade level. In terms of school organization, we might group reading books as follows:

a. **Picture Books,** for preschool, prereading
b. **Easy Books,** for grades 1–3, including books to read out loud to the children
c. **Intermediate Books,** for grades 4–6
d. **Junior High Books,** for grades 7–9
e. **Senior High Books,** for grades 10–12
f. **Young Adult Books,** for grades 13–14

Among these grade and age levels, two major classes of books can be recognized: (1) the great books and (2) the subject books. In the former are the children's classics of the past and the potential classics of the present—primarily what we call imaginative literature, but including also a few subject books written with such creativity as to be worthy of inclusion among the greats. In the second group are the numerous books dealing with the subjects in the school curriculum and with the cocurricular activities and interests of children and young people.

In the school library or Materials Center, however, all of these books will appear on the shelves in approximately Dewey Decimal order, with the following exceptions: (1) easy and picture books, which are kept together, usually on large shelves with upright dividers about a foot apart, instead of the usual three feet; (2) fiction, which may be arranged alphabetically by author and by title; and (3) biography, arranged alphabetically by the biographee, and under biographee by author. The rest of the collection of so-called library books will be arranged in Dewey order from 000 to 999, with the numbers on reference books preceded by the "R."

The Reading Book Potential

Learning through reading is still a classroom staple. Economy in time, space, and money favor the book as a teaching format. The lack of visual, sound, or other sensory "props" inspires children to create their own mental images—sometimes incorrect of course, but often more vivid and colorful than any concrete experience that could be substituted. Above all, the mental effort to convert an abstract symbol to something real for the child is itself the very stuff of education, fostered by books in their own way.

What we must never forget is that there are still some children who learn better and more through reading than through almost any other kind of activity. Although it is true that most pupils will know more about the Roman Forum after taking hammer and saw and constructing a model of it, or will learn to appreciate dolls by working with scissors and paste, there is still the wonder-eyed youngster who reads and accomplishes all that the hammer and saw and scissors and paste could possibly do for him.

Let the child, therefore, read. Readiness will come much earlier than present educational research permits, if only we surround the child as much with books as we do with the pragmatic accoutrements of a very practical and realistic society. Let the child inspired by his reading of fairy tales and myths, fiction and verse, develop his own splendid colors for a happy and beautiful world.

Learning through reading is a classroom staple. *Courtesy Salt Lake County (Utah) Library.*

Within the subject books may be found everything practical the child needs to know. A rich, young people's library of how to live with other boys and girls, and grown-ups, too—running the gamut of government, civics, etiquette, economics, dating, correspondence, organization—is in this part of the reading book collection. Let there be no concern, therefore, that in books the child will find nothing practical and of this world. Together the "G" books and the "S" books contain within them the potential for learning both how to live and how to make a living.

But the real power in the reading book, from the teacher's viewpoint, relates to individual differences. Somewhere in that library is just the book to spark the child's special background. It may be a book in science which explains magnetism to him in terms of his experience. Or it may be a bit of inspiration that will show the way to a fruitful and creative life. In the hands of the skilled teacher the reading book is still a tool to conjure with.

Yesterday's Children's Books

The history of literature for children and young people appears to be a chronicle of conflict between those of the older generation who favored and those who spared the rod in the education of the young. Representative of early English books for children, intended to teach rather than to entertain, were catechism excerpts from the learned works of Aldhelm, Aelfric, and the Venerable Bede (all written before the Norman invasion) that set up a teacher-pupil question-answer design for the "three R's" and for manners-morals primers stimulated by the culture of the later age of chivalry. Of the latter, examples frequently cited are *The Babees Boke,* "a lytle reporte of how young people should behave" with the "whole duty of children" presented in 160 lines; William Caxton's *Book of Curtesye;* and *How the Good Wife Taught Her Daughter,* an early forerunner of the modern teen-age manual on etiquette and homemaking. What little entertainment literature the children got came from such adult classics as Sir Thomas Malory's *Morte D'Arthur,* Aesop's *Fables,* and the *History of Reynard the Fox,* which were not originally intended for children.

The conflict between the "Traditionalists" and the "Progressives" on the rearing of children found even stronger expression in the Renaissance and Puritan periods of the subsequent centuries. About 1550 the hornbook, already referred to in Chapter 2, made its contribution to the instruction side, with its alphabet, syllables, and prayer. So also did the *New England Primer* and its many imitations. But the morals-manner aspect of the literary effort for children took a more severe trend. Led by the adult classic, *Pilgrim's Progress,* which was adapted for children, several works expressly prepared for the younger generation created a new and more terrible tone. Their ominous titles alone were enough to convey the point: *Young People Warned* and *A Dying Father's Legacy to an Only Child.*

One of the much quoted English excerpts from this type of literature is this from James Janeway's *Token for Children,* "an exact account of the conversion, holy and exemplary lives and joyful deaths of several young children":

> When by spectators I am told
> What beauty doth adorn me
> Or in a glass when I behold
> How sweetly God did form me
> Hath God such comeliness bestowed
> And on me made to dwell
> What pity such a pretty maid
> As I should go to hell!

For the progressives, however, considerable hope appeared in this period. Such adult classics as *Robinson Crusoe* and *Gulliver's Travels* provided entertainment opportunities for the young along with some introductions to the eternal verities. And Comenius' *Orbis Pictus* presented the world of learning to children in newer and vivid dimensions by removing "scarecrows from wisdom's garden."

But the real stimulus to a great literature for children came from a French author and a British publisher of this period. In France, Charles Perrault, a lawyer, member of the French Academy and friend of La Fontaine, retold for his young son the delightful fairy tales he had heard at the court of King Louis XIV. Either the father or the son collected these into a book, published in 1697, called *Tales of My Mother Goose,* which included such subsequent English language favorites as *Bluebeard, Sleeping Beauty, Puss-in-Boots, Red Riding Hood.*

In England, John Newbery, a London bookseller and publisher, issued in 1744 his little *Pretty Pocketbook.* Because this is considered by many the first book expressly published for children's entertainment, the date is taken as the beginning and Newbery as the father of a real children's literature. At the sign of the "Bible and Sun" Newbery began a venture that produced the *Liliputian Magazine, Little Goody Two-Shoes, Mother Goose Melody,* and Perrault's *Tales* in English, among other titles for children. In recognition of his contribution, Frederick Melcher of *Publishers' Weekly* established in 1922 an annual award for the book considered by children's librarians to be the most distinguished contribution of the year to American literature for children. The Newbery medal book has since been honored every year at a banquet held during the annual convention of the American Library Association.

Origins of Today's Children's Literature

A knowledge of the historic groupings of the vast field of creative literature for children will enable the teacher to move among these books with a feeling of recognition.

The Didactics. The first of the groupings, the didactics, goes back to the *Instructional.* Though the didactics have a lesser place in contemporary children's reading, certain classics are still of interest to the teacher. Their origin can be traced back to John Locke, whose educational system called for teaching children the alphabet and other information through games, and to Jean Jacques Rousseau, who added the naturalistic and pragmatic tone to the child's education. Although neither Locke in his *Thoughts on Education* nor Rousseau in his *Emile* showed much consideration for the child's imagination, the impact of both these works on modern education has been, at least in the opinion of some, almost too heavy.

In the wake of this Locke-Rousseau influence came *Sandford and Merton* (1783) by Thomas Day (1748–1789), contrasting the character of bad boy Tommy and good boy Harry. More than one critic today considers this still a book with considerable humor and sympathy for childhood. Equal consideration for Mrs. Sara Kirby Trimmer's (1741–1810) *Fabulous Histories* (1793) is also given today by reviewers, who cite it as one of the first books to encourage children to be kind to animals. But highest recognition for all of the authors of this Rousseau-Locke instructional school goes usually to Maria Edgeworth (1767–1849), whose craftsmanship stands above her didacticism. Many of her stories from *Parent's Assistant* (1796) and *Moral Tales* (1801) have been incorporated in anthologies and readers. The little classic *Waste Not, Want Not* was read by the millions of children who were brought up on the McGuffey *Readers*.

Fairy and Folk Tales. A second grouping would include fairy tales and folk tales. After Perrault, a lady of the French court, Countess d'Aulnoy, produced a collection of fairy tales called *The White Cat and Other French Fairy Tales*, which were later illustrated in color by Elizabeth MacKinstry for an English selection.

The early nineteenth century produced the work of the Grimm Brothers. They were linguists and lexicographers first, but the by-product of their language study was the collection of wonderful folk tales that have fascinated children for over a century; Walt Disney drew their *Snow-Drop* in a new dimension as *Snow White and the Seven Dwarfs*. Jacob Ludwig (1785–1863) and Wilhelm Carl (1786–1859) produced *Popular Stories*, translated into English in 1823 and since reproduced many times; notably, Wanda Gag recreated for the very young child *Snowhite and the Seven Dwarfs* and, for children in the intermediate grades, *Three Gay Tales from Grimm*, including *The Three Fathers*, *The Clever Wife*, and *Goose Hans*.

After the Grimm Brothers came Hans Christian Andersen (1805–1875), the fabulous fairy and folk tale teller. To the Scandinavian folk story and to his own creations, Andersen brought that touch of wonder usually found only in the eyes of the young. The first book of "Wonder Stories," published in 1835, contained such perennial favorites as the *Tinder Box* and the *Constant Tin Soldier,* only recently produced as a 16-mm motion picture. Mary Howitt was Andersen's first translator into English, and Jean Hersholt his fullest.

Retold Classics. The third of the groupings are the rewritings of the classics for children—Homer and Shakespeare, Greek and Norse Mythology, and such epics as those of Robin Hood and King Arthur.

In 1807 Charles and Mary Lamb retold the story of 20 plays in *Tales from Shakespeare,* Charles presenting the tragedies and Mary the comedies. This collection had been preceded by individually published plays in sixpenny books, beautifully illustrated in color by William Blake.

The following year Charles Lamb alone produced *The Adventures of Ulysses,* with a distinguished frontispiece by the English painter and book illustrator Corbould. But the children's Homer remained to be retold over a century later by Padraic Colum as the *Adventures of Odysseus and The Tale of Troy,* with illustrations by the Hungarian painter Willy Pogány. Later, collaborating with the Russian artist Boris Artzybasheff, Colum performed similar wonders with Celtic and Norse folklore.

The retold classics form as distinguished a shelf in the children's library as any other single grouping. Look at the array of contributors. They include Nathaniel Hawthorne, Charles Kingsley, Andrew Lang, William Morris, Sidney Lanier, Walter de la Mare, and Sir Arthur Quiller-Couch. Of them all, Howard Pyle (1853–1911), the American artist, has had probably the greatest impact on the retold classic. Through his inimitable drawings for *Robin Hood* and *King Arthur* he influenced such illustrators as Jessie Wilcox Smith, Maxfield Parrish, and N. C. Wyeth, creating a new standard for this class of children's literature.

Poetry. The fourth grouping is poetry. Verse for children usually begins with the mysterious and mystical *Mother Goose.* Whether she was Charlemagne's mother, Queen Goosefoot, or Charles Perrault's Muse, or Thomas Fleet's mother-in-law, Elizabeth Vergoose, or whether she was any of these is less important than the fact that rhymes like *Jack and Jill, Simple Simon, Little Bo-Peep* and others are the stuff of which childhood poetry is made. Possibly the first collection of these rhymes was that published in Boston in 1719 by Thomas Fleet. Another early collection was that issued by John Newbery in 1765. *Mother Goose* has appeared since in a series of variegated and colorful editions. Some of the more famous include Marguerite de Angeli's *Book of Nursery and Mother Goose Rhymes;* Kate Greenaway's delicately illustrated collection; *The Little Mother Goose*, illustrated by Jessie Wilcox Smith, with 12 full pages of color and many black-and-white's; Tasha Tudor's soft-color and black-and-white illustrations; Blanche Fisher's *Real Mother Goose* in bright colors; *Ring o' Roses*, favored for little children because of its generous size, blue cover, and original pictures by L. Leslie Brooke; and the *Tall Book of Mother Goose*, illustrated by Feodor Rojankovsky. The odd size of the last (12 x 5 inches) is distinctive, and the pictures are most unusual.

Among the earliest poets who wrote for children were William Blake and William Wordsworth. Blake's *Songs of Innocence* contributed the *Little Black Boy* who shielded the little white boy from the extra hot rays the sun has in heaven. Wordsworth's *Alice Fell* and *Lucy Gray*, William Allingham's *The Fairies*, and Mary Howitt's fairies of *Caldon Low* belong with this earlier poetry for children. Christina Rosetti, Lewis Carroll, Robert Louis Stevenson, and Rudyard Kipling swelled the stream. Other early noteworthy contributors were Alice Meynell, Hilda Conkling, W. H. Hudson, Walter de la Mare, F. T. Palgrave, and Coventry Patmore.

Fiction. The fifth grouping is comprised of stories for entertainment rather than for instruction. *Robinson Crusoe* and *Gulliver's Travels* began the long line of children's novels. But these two were converted from adult purposes. Later novelists who wrote for adults turned their genius to writing especially for children, and without apology. Dickens wrote his *Christmas Carol* in 1843, Sir Walter Scott his *Tales of a Grandfather* somewhat before, and Thackeray his *Rose and the Ring* somewhat after.

But it is to Mary Mapes Dodge (1831–1905) that credit is generally given for beginning the line of children's novels. *Hans Brinker* was published in 1865. She wrote it for her two boys out of an impelling interest in Holland, in J. L. Motley's *Rise of the Dutch Republic*, and in her friends and visitors from The Netherlands. Eight years later Mrs. Dodge started the famous *St. Nicholas* magazines for children.

Around this periodical developed fiction writing for children. Louisa May Alcott (1832–1888), who gave the child's world *Little Women*, later contributed much of her talent to *St. Nicholas*. Kate Douglas Wiggin, who wrote *Rebecca of Sunnybrook Farm*, got her start with Mrs. Dodge's magazine. Kipling's "Jungle Books" began in *St. Nicholas*, and Mark Twain's *Prince and the Pauper* also appeared there first.

To these early fictional efforts for children must be added the novels and stories of many other nineteenth and early twentieth century authors such as Robert Louis Stevenson, Herman Melville, Jules Verne, Jack London, Joseph Altsheller, on whose precedents and foundations much of the current output is based.

Illustrators

In any children's literature course, recognition of the artists who augment the printed word for children is an essential. A few of the more famous illustrators will be mentioned here in historical order.

If one were selecting ten English artists, there would probably be considerable agreement on these: Thomas Bewick (1753–1828), the wood etcher and engraver used by John Newbery; George Cruikshank (1792–1878), who added his own universal touch to the immortal writings of Dickens and of the Grimm Brothers; Sir John Tenniel (1820–1914), identified with *Alice in Wonderland;* Walter Crane (1845–1915), whose decorative work for fairy tales, especially for Hawthorne's *Wonder Book*, distinguished him; Kate Greena-

way (1846–1901), who will always be known for her flowers
and landscapes and her fine *Mother Goose;* Randolph Caldecott (1846–1886), who achieved his fame largely through his
original use of color, and his reflection of the spirit of England, so evident in *John Gilpin* and in *The House That Jack
Built;* L. Leslie Brooke (1862–1940), whose style resembles
Caldecott's and who has been mentioned in connection with
Mother Goose and Edward Lear's *nonsense* books; Arthur
Rackham (1867–1939), another fairy tale designer with mysterious ivory tints who, in addition, distinguished himself
with a Dickens' *Christmas Carol,* a Swift's *Gulliver,* and a
Night Before Christmas, besides his own *Fairy Book;* and
Ernest Howard Shepard (1879–   ), whose black-and-
white drawings caught so perfectly the genius of A. A. Milne
in *When We Were Very Young.*

To match these ten Englishmen, there are several Americans. Inevitably, we begin with Howard Pyle (1853–1911)
of Robin Hood fame, and follow with three of his outstanding students: Maxfield Parrish (1870–   ), who did a wonderful *Arabian Nights* and who added to Eugene Field's
poems; Jessie Wilcox Smith, famous for her illustrations in
Little Women, Mother Goose, Heidi, and Stevenson's *Child's
Garden of Verses,* to mention only a few; and N. C. Wyeth,
whose work for *Treasure Island, King Arthur, The Last of
the Mohicans, Ramona, The Yearling,* and historical novels
generally, is not easily forgotten. Three husband-wife teams
deserve consideration: Berta and Elmer Hader, who have
been singularly successful for little children, with such joint
efforts as *Big City, Farmer in the Dell,* and *Cock-a-Doodle-
Doo;* Maud and Miska Petersham, who together have done
the Hungarian children's classic *Miki,* subject books on the
ABC's, stamps, and presidents of the United States, and a
beautiful book on the *Christ Child;* Edgar and Ingri D'Aula-
rie, whose history and Scandinavian background books and
biographies of Franklin, Buffalo Bill, Columbus, Lincoln,
Washington, and Pocohontas have justly won them acclaim.
Other illustrators to watch for are Boris Artzybasheff and
Willy Pogány, who represent naturalized-American talents

of the first rank, and Munro Leaf, Robert Lawson, Theodore
Geisel (better known as Dr. Seuss), Roger Duvoisin, and
William Pène du Bois.

LEVELS OF READING BOOKS

Against this sketch of origins, selection from the book
stock of a school library for specific learning needs is better
fortified. The following survey of reading books considers
five groups by level, in type and subject categories. These
groups are designated (1) preschool, (2) primary, (3) intermediate, (4) secondary (including junior and senior high
and young adult), and (5) professional for the teacher.
Within these groupings attention is given both to the "great"
books, which include didactics, fairy and folk tales, retold
classics, poetry, and fiction, and to the subject books classified by the Dewey Decimal system. The selection of titles in
the appendix can be supplemented by examining the selection aids described in the chapter on reference books.

Preschool Books

We have discovered much about child development and
we are sure to discover more; no matter how positive present
authorities sound, the best of them admit there is still much
to learn about why children behave as they do. Certainly
there is still much to learn about why children read, and how
and what. At present we believe children come to books first
through the spoken word and through pictures. Rhymes and
rhythms read by older folks arouse eager interest and that is
why *Mother Goose* is so fundamental. For little children
under three, such fundamental readings come in washable,
chewable, soft, and safe formats, with pictures that the child
can identify from association with things around him.

Since *Mother Goose* (4–1) is basic for this level, identification of several titles to look for in the Materials Center is
helpful. If DC classified, they bear the number 398, but more
than likely the books for children of this age will be in "E"
for "easy." *The Book of Nursery and Mother Goose Rhymes,*

illustrated by Marguerite de Angeli, is the aristocrat of them all. It includes 376 of the rhymes and 260 illustrations. But there are other, less expensive collections with advantages for the very young. For example, the Peggy Cloth Books include *Mother Goose*. The format will take rough handling without ill effects on book or baby, and attached to the volume is a foam-rubber stuffed animal which "speaks." There is also the *Tall Book of Mother Goose* with Rojankovsky's pictures, 50 of them in color. Wilma McFarland's collection of *Great Poems* (4–2) can supplement the *Mother Goose* readings for the upper reading age of this level.

Familiar objects in spoken word and picture have a primary allure and, of the many picture books that capture, those involving animals are irresistible. A favorite, about an inquisitive Scotch terrier, is Marjorie Flack's *Angus and the Ducks* (4–3), but no more so than Beatrix Potter's *Tale of Peter Rabbit* (4–4) and the other famous family members, Flopsy, Mopsy, and Cotton-tail. They are popular with the child because he identifies the animals at once as "my dog" or "my rabbit" and sees their relation to familiar objects around him—or at least we think so at this stage in our own knowledge of children. Because of his interest in the familiar, the young child appears to enjoy books like Maud and Miska Petersham's *The Rooster Crows* (4–5), which won the Caldecott award, and which augments its rhymes and jingles with pictures that fascinate; Margaret Wise Brown's *Good Night Moon* (4–6), a bedtime story in which the rabbit says good night to the many familiar objects that surround a child's bed; George A. Adams' *ABC Picture Book* (4–7) with full-color photos of easily recognized things, and Tash Tudor's *A Is For Annabelle* (4–8).

Additional titles for the older children of this level can be represented by Jean de Brunhoff's *Story of Babar*, about an elephant, and Wanda Gag's hilarious *Millions of Cats* (4–10).

It is impossible to mention here the many subjects which now, for the first time, can be presented to children. Pelagie Doane's *A Small Child's Bible* (4–11), which retells 70 Bible stories in word and picture and is offered in either a Catholic or Protestant edition, is outstanding among books on religion. Among books on etiquette, Munro Leaf's *Manners Can Be Fun* (4–12) can be cited as a far cry from the early manners-morals primers of the age of chivalry.

A full selection of titles, critically annotated, can be found in the "E-Easy Books" section of the *Children's Catalog*.

Primary Books

The grades represented here are usually up to the third, but because of reading ranges within grades, ages five to nine, approximately, are considered. There are rich opportunities on this level, both among the imaginative and informative books. Candidates for "classics" consideration are such titles as Dr. Seuss' *And To Think That I Saw It On Mulberry Street* (4–13), in which a small boy's imagination transforms a drab everyday street scene into a technicolor picture of circus elephant and giraffes. And there is Robert McCloskey's *Make Way for Ducklings* (4–14) with its spirited pictures of eight ducklings marching in line through the streets of Boston. Or there are the stories, already classics, of A. A. Milne (4–15): *When We Were Very Young, Now We Are Six, Winnie the Pooh*, and *The House At Pooh Corner*, and Kenneth Grahame's *The Wind in the Willows* (4–16), illustrated by Arthur Rackham.

Stories that cater to the young child's interest in things mechanical are *Little Toot* (4–17) by Hardie Gramatky, about a lighthearted tug boat, and Virginia Lee Burton's *Mike Mulligan and His Steam Shovel* (4–18), which really tells about the canals, highways, railroads, airports, and skyscrapers man and machine helped build. The animal bent is satisfied further with such a Newbery award winner as *Rabbit Hill* (4–19) by Robert Lawson, and *Frog Went A-Courtin* (4–20) retold by John Langstaff with the help of Rojankovsky's pictures. The folk tale can be represented by Marcia Brown's *Cinderella* (4–21), which won the 1955 Caldecott medal for its delicate illustrations.

Subject books begin to appear on this level in all of the school fields as supplementary reading. For instance, science is well represented by such titles as Lancelot Hogben's *First Great Inventions* (4–22), with cross-sectional pictures to support the text for camera, electric light, radio, and airplane; Herman and Nina Schneider's *Let's Find Out* (4–23), introducing elementary science with simple home experiments; John Lewellen's *True Book of Moon, Sun and Stars* (4–24); and the two biological science books *Let's Go Outdoors* (4–25) by Harriet E. Huntington and *Up Above and Down Below* (4–26) by Irma E. Webber. History is handsomely presented by Ingri and Edgar Parin d'Aulaire in *Abraham Lincoln* (4–27) and by Alice Dalgliesh in *Fourth of July Story* (4–28). There is no limit to the number of good subject books that might be cited, but one in religion deserves special mention. Florence Mary Fitch has in *One God* (4–29) beautifully described how Catholics, Protestants, and Jews worship God.

Teachers in the primary grades would do well to explore the basic selection aids described in Chapter 3 and select specific titles related to their grade and units for first-hand preview in the Materials Center.

Intermediate Books

The intermediate books are for the years of fantasy and realism. Available are Andrew Lang's varicolored fairy-tale books (4–30)—blue, red, green and yellow—packed with tales and legends from many lands. Open also is the way to the wonders of the fantasy masters—Hans Christian Andersen (4–31), the Grimm Brothers (4–32), and the treasure of the *Arabian Nights* (4–33). This is also a period to enjoy *King Arthur and His Knights of the Round Table* (4–34) and to dip into Aesop's *Fables* (4–35). The *Merry Adventures of Robin Hood* (4–36) will captivate boys and have some interest even for girls.

At this time, too, young readers will probably enjoy the stories that spellbound their parents when *they* were intermediates—*Pinocchio* (4–37), *Heidi* (4–38), *Black Beauty* (4–39), *Alice in Wonderland* (4–40), *Robinson Crusoe* (4–41), *Gulliver's Travels* (4–42). Stevenson's *Treasure*

Island (4–43) and *Kidnapped* will appeal especially to the boys, as will *The Three Musketeers* (4–44), *Tom Sawyer* (4–45) and *Huckleberry Finn*. Of the Louisa May Alcott trilogy (4–46), the girls would, of course, read *Little Women* first, and the boys *Little Men*, and both are likely to revel in *Jo's Boys*. *Hans Brinker* (4–47), *The Little Lame Prince*, and *Five Little Peppers* will inevitably find their way into the reading of many of the intermediates. A few will read *A Tale of Two Cities* now, as well as later in high school. Books that their parents did not have when they were very young are such fine Newbery hits as *Caddie Woodlawn, Hitty, Doctor Doolittle, Wheel on the School,* and *Miracle on Maple Hill.*

The titles mentioned in the preceding paragraphs are merely a small but popular fraction of the library of imaginative literature at the disposal of intermediates in a good Materials Center.

On the information side, subjects of absorbing interest like natural history, science and invention, and history and biography are abundantly treated in series and single titles. History and biography, for example, have the "Landmark Books" (4–48), which include titles dealing with prehistoric America, explorations, Indians, the American Revolution, and other highlights up through the exciting *Thirty Seconds Over Tokyo*. These books have the advantage, besides, of being correlated with other Instructional Materials, including recordings and filmstrips. "Land of the Free Books" presents history in some 20 novels, and there is a "Childhood of Famous Americans" series which includes biographies of Benjamin Franklin, Buffalo Bill, Sitting Bull, and Luther Burbank, among others.

Science and invention have comparable series. "Allabout" (4–49) books are surveys by top-notch authorities of subjects that range from dinosaurs to elephants, from atoms to jets, from weather to stars, and deal accurately and readably with the wonders of the basic sciences like geology and chemistry. There is also the "First Book" (4–50) series, beginners' introductions, in simple words and clear pictures, to bees and birds, to glass and cotton, to Indians of Asia and of America, to baseball and automobiles, to poetry and music, and to space travel and magic.

Secondary School Level Books

The secondary school level encompasses ages 12 and up. Because adolescent and adult interests begin to blend within this reading range, a library of major proportions is needed to satisfy the varied individual needs. Nevertheless, those books that are milestones along the way to becoming well read are worth mentioning.

The principal concern of both teachers and librarians is that young people of secondary age often do not devote a fair share of their time to reading. Concern is both for those who read much when they were intermediates and for those who never really got started at all. Frequently the hungry reader of childhood permits teen-age activity to eat up all reading time. Equally often, young people arrive in high school without ever having learned to read a book through or to enjoy the reading of it. In either case librarians and teachers begin with the boy's or girl's most compelling interest. Whether it is dancing or sports, homemaking or mechanics, animals or machines, reading on the subject of uppermost interest is offered first. Once the student is motivated, it is easier to cultivate other interests.

A high school football player who once boasted he had never read a book through was given the 15th volume of *Pageant of America*, devoted to the history of American sports, and asked to evaluate the section on football. The next week, by the boy's own blushing admission, he reported he had read the book through and wanted to read more. His interest took two directions—more sports, in the form of John Tunis's books, and Colonial America, an interest aroused by *Pageant's* treatment of sports in the colonies.

To arouse lagging interest and to convert new readers, the literature for young people offers many opportunities. The teen-age interests in vocation, etiquette, sports, homemaking, science, fashion, adventure, and travel are met both in imaginative and informational literature.

Fiction appeals are many. For boys who love adventure the Jules Verne books still appeal, as attested by the current revivals of *20,000 Leagues Under the Sea* and *Around the World in 80 Days.* Melville's *Moby Dick* and the Nordhoff-Hall "Bounty Trilogy" continue as perennial favorites. Science fiction has its most enthusiastic fans among young people. Robert Heinlein's *Space Cadet* and *Between Planets* are good examples of stories about outer space. Sports interests are met by such stories as Curtis Bishop's *Football Fever.*

For girls love stories abound. Two of the most popular are Maureen Daly's *Seventeenth Summer* and Rosamond Du Jardin's *Boy Trouble.* There are counterparts for boys, notably James L. Summer's *Girl Trouble* and Booth Tarkington's little classic, *Seventeen.*

Both boys and girls continue to enjoy the idyllic *Green Mansions* of W. H. Hudson, and there are common interests in the poetry of Browning and Burns, Kipling and Masefield, Stevenson and Whitman, and moderns like Edna St. Vincent Millay, Carl Sandburg, and Ogden Nash.

There is no brief way to list subject books for high-school-age readers. The best aids are *Standard Catalog for High School Libraries* and the two "Basic Book Lists" described in Chapter 3. Individual state lists will prove helpful also. As an example of the latter, *Recommended Library Books for Florida Schools* is suggested.

Professional Books

A small collection of professional books for teachers should be included in the school library or Materials Center, and a larger collection in the system Materials Center. Basic lists of recommended titles for a teachers' library have been published in various sources. A good example is the selected bibliography in *Collier's Encyclopedia* (v. 20, pp. 88-92). Current listings of new books in education are included in the *Education Index,* and such books are reviewed in many of the professional journals.

Among the professional areas which should be represented by titles are history of education; principles and philosophy; comparative education; educational sociology; preschool, kindergarten, elementary, secondary, higher, and
adult education; curriculum; teaching method; administration; and guidance. In addition, there should be books on the
teaching of individual subjects.

Areas of particular interest to teachers concerned with
Instructional Materials are libraries, audio-visual instruction,
reading and study, and reading guidance. No attempt will be
made here to describe all of the pertinent books in these related fields. Many references occur throughout this text and
in the chapter readings.

Teachers will find good introductions to library use in
the N.E.A. Department of Elementary School Principals 30th
yearbook, which is entirely devoted to elementary school
libraries. Mott and Baisden's *Children's Book on How to Use
Books and Libraries* (4–51) will suggest many teaching devices. Jennie Flexner's *Making Books Work* (4–52) is a
mature guide to library use.

Since World War II a number of audio-visual texts have
been published. Three of popular appeal are Wittich and
Schuller's *Audio-Visual Materials* (3–53), Edgar Dale's
Audio-Visual Methods in Teaching (3–54), and Lester Sands'
Audio-Visual Procedures in Teaching (3–55). All three ap-
proaches are stimulating.

Increased attention to improving students' study and reading habits has resulted in several good manuals. One of these,
Best Methods of Study, by Samuel Smith (3–56), is in the
Barnes and Noble "College Outline Series." Paul Witty has
prepared a helpful little book, *How To Become a Better
Reader* (3–57). Rudolph Flesch, through his controversial
best seller *Why Johnny Can't Read* (3–58), has stirred many
to re-evaluate our methods of teaching reading.

There is a fine library of books on reading guidance. Arbuthnot's *Children and Books* (3–59) offers solid help. Jean
Roos' *Patterns in Reading* (3–60) is equally helpful in coun-
selling young readers. The paperback best seller *Wonderful*

World of Books (3–61) has so many essays of reading encouragement that it should be regularly reread by all who work with Instructional Materials.

SELECTION OF READING BOOKS

The preceding catalog of reading books, level by level, has noted only a few titles. A more comprehensive selection of reading books for classroom use should be based on systematic checking of selection aids and the application of sound criteria in reviewing individual titles. Some assistance can also be obtained from the records of awards made by critical juries for distinguished writing for these groups.

Among the most famous awards are the annual Newbery and Caldecott medals. The Newbery Medal is given for the best writing, and the Caldecott Medal for the best illustrating. Both awards were established by Frederic G. Melcher of *Publishers' Weekly* and are announced at a banquet during the annual convention of the American Library Association.

Since 1922, the year of their establishment, the Newbery award titles have been:

1922   *Story of Mankind:* Hendrik Willem Van Loon
1923   *Voyages of Dr. Doolittle:* Hugh Lofting
1924   *Dark Frigate:* Charles Boardman Hawes
1925   *Tales from Silver Lands:* Charles J. Finger
1926   *Shen of the Sea:* Arthur Bowie Chrisman
1927   *Smoky, the Cowhorse:* Will James
1928   *Gay-Neck:* Dhan Gopal Mukerji
1929   *Trumpeter of Krakow:* Eric P. Kelly
1930   *Hitty, Her First Hundred Years:* Rachel Field
1931   *Cat Who Went to Heaven:* Elizabeth Coatsworth
1932   *Waterless Mountain:* Laura Adams Armer
1933   *Young Fu of the Upper Yangtze:* Elizabeth Foreman Lewis
1934   *Invincible Louisa:* Cornelia Meigs
1935   *Dobry:* Monica Shannon
1936   *Caddie Woodlawn:* Carol Ryrie Brink
1937   *Roller Skates:* Ruth Sawyer
1938   *White Stag:* Kate Seredy
1939   *Thimble Summer:* Elizabeth Enright

1940 *Daniel Boone:* James Daugherty
1941 *Call It Courage:* Armstrong Sperry
1942 *Matchlock Gun:* Walter D. Edmonds
1943 *Adam of the Road:* Elizabeth Janet Gray
1944 *Johnny Tremain:* Esther Forbes
1945 *Rabbit Hill:* Robert Lawson
1946 *Strawberry Girl:* Lois Lenski
1947 *Miss Hickory:* Carolyn Sherwin Barley
1948 *Twenty-one Balloons:* William Pène du Bois.
1949 *King of the Wind:* Marguerite Henry
1950 *Door in the Wall:* Marguerite de Angeli
1951 *Amos Fortune, Free Man:* Elizabeth Yates
1952 *Ginger Pye:* Eleanor Estes
1953 *Secret of the Andes:* Ann Nolan Clark
1954 *And Now Miguel:* Joseph Krumgold
1955 *Wheel on the School:* Meindert De Jong
1956 *Carry On, Mr. Bowditch:* Jean Lee Latham
1957 *Miracles on Maple Hill:* Virginia Sorensen
1958 *Rifles for Waitie:* Harold Keith

The Caldecott Medal has been awarded each year since 1938 to the illustrator of the most distinguished picture book for children published in America. The recipients have been:

1938 *Animals of the Bible:* Dorothy P. Lathrop
1939 *Mei Lei:* Thomas Handforth
1940 *Abraham Lincoln:* Ingri and Edgar d'Aulaire
1941 *They Were Strong and Good:* Robert Lawson
1942 *Make Way for Ducklings:* Robert McCloskey
1943 *The Little House:* Virginia Lee Burton
1944 *Many Moons:* Louis Slobodkin
1945 *Prayer for a Child:* Elizabeth Orton Jones
1946 *Rooster Crows:* Maud and Miska Petersham
1947 *The Little Island:* Leonard Weisgard
1948 *White Snow, Bright Snow:* Roger Duvoisin
1949 *The Big Show:* Berta and Elmer Hader
1950 *Song of the Swallows:* Leo Politi
1951 *The Egg Tree:* Katherine Milhous
1952 *Finders Keepers:* Nicholas Mordvinoff
1953 *The Biggest Bear:* Lynd Ward
1954 *Madeline's Rescue:* Ludwig Bemelmans
1955 *Cinderella:* Marcia Brown
1956 *Frog Went A-courtin:* Feodor Rojankovsky
1957 *A Tree Is Nice:* Marc Simont
1958 *Time of Wonder:* Robert McCloskey

Selection Aids

Selection has been simplified by the publication of standard lists, which teachers and librarians working together have selected. These lists are, of course, not limited to books. Included are not only the great books, but often pictures, pamphlets, recordings, films and filmstrips, maps and globes, and other types of materials.

There are both advantages and disadvantages to lists. In their favor is usually the competence of the selectors, the critical annotations, the classification, bibliographic information, and grading. The data provided in lists can save a tremendous amount of time for school librarians and teachers.

Perhaps the principal disadvantage is the hazard of being stereotyped. If individual differences mean anything at all in the multi-materials concept, they mean something in the materials themselves. It is conceivable that a best book for children in New York City is second best for children in Roadstop, and vice versa. Selection by and for the individual school has much to be said for it if checked against the standard list.

There are many good book-selection aids. The five described in Chapter 3 under bibliographies are of paramount importance. To these should be added current reviews of children's and young people's books. The *Booklist*, also described in Chapter 3, provides a continuous guide to the current output of trade books for children and young people. Other review sources are *The Horn Book Magazine*, published in Boston bimonthly since 1925, the *New York Herald-Tribune*, which inaugurated the annual spring festival of children's books in 1936, *The New York Times*, and the *Saturday Review*.

Virginia Kirkus' Service, New York, issues a Bulletin in loose-leaf sheets, multilithographed on both sides, which critically evaluates new books. On the blue cover sheet is a calendar of new books for the month, with the exact publication date for each title. There are yellow sheets which form a

"Juvenile Supplement," listing and evaluating children's and young peoples' books under six heads: (1) picture story books, (2) books to read aloud, (3) easy reading, (4) eight to eleven, (5) twelve to sixteen, and (6) young adults. Each of the last three classes are further subdivided into fiction and nonfiction. For each title a brief note is added to the bibliographic information.

There are many lists and reviews of children's books. The teacher cannot read them all, but it is a good professional habit to examine at least one of these sources regularly and to keep a notebook record on new books that sound promising. It is especially well to be alert for current titles that may contribute to a teaching unit or purpose. Such titles should be presented to the faculty selection committee or to the librarian for consideration when the school's book fund is to be allocated.

Evaluation of Reading Books

There are at least five basic criteria found in the various schemes for evaluating general reading books: (1) authorship, (2) scope, (3) treatment, (4) format, and (5) aids.

Two aspects of *authorship* are the author and the publisher. As a new book is examined the teacher must ask himself these questions: Is the book well written? Who is the author and what else has he written? Are his qualifications adequate? What about the publisher? Certain trade publishers have a consistently good record for producing children's books. What about the editor? There are now about 60 experienced editors of children's books in general publishing houses and in houses publishing only children's books. The presence of such an editor should contribute to the effectiveness of a book.

When it comes to scope, the purpose of the book must first be understood. Is its aim primarily to inform or to spark imagination and thought? Informational books must be authoritative and accurate; they must comprehend the subject. Inspirational books should show highly developed creativity, imagination, and perception on the author's part. They should be convincing, inspiring, contributing to the child's growth.

Treatment is largely a matter of style. Writing for children has evolved from a tone of condescension to one of equality. We now believe, with Anatole France, "When you are writing for children, do not assume a style for the occasion. Think your best and write your best." Good writing for children is clear, beautiful, challenging, inspiring. It never underestimates. If anything, it overestimates and flatters the child by appealing to him as an adult.

Much has been done with *format*. Bindings are not only durable but alluring. Make-up attracts the young reader from page to page by weaving text, legends, and illustrations into an inviting pattern. Illustrations, formerly isolated and drab, are now an integral part of reading. Bleeds have added a new dimension to pictures. There is a more brilliant tone to type and illustration, and occasionally a bit of three-dimensional novelty.

More attention is being given to *aids* in the subject books. Indexes are better in that the entries more nearly resemble curriculum units. Bibliographies are not afterthoughts, but, rather, carefully-planned steppingstones from the point where the book leaves off to the beginning of the path that leads to an advanced goal. Chapter and topic, readings, and even lead sentences in paragraphs are more carefully pointed toward the educational objective.

Evaluation Checklist for Reading Books

Authorship: Is the author qualified? Does the publisher have an established record? Is the editor experienced?

Scope: If informational, does the book cover the subject? If inspirational, does it contribute to the child's growth?

Treatment: Is the style clear, beautiful, challenging, inspiring?

Format: Are binding, paper, make-up, illustrations, attractive?

Aids: Do they include adequate index, bibliography, captions, legends?

Evaluation of Picture Books. Some supplementary criteria are needed in measuring the preschool and primary picture book. Several significant studies of the child and his picture book have resulted in the following conclusions.

According to dependable child authorities, children before two years of age are not interested in pictures. In the beginning of his book experience the child will show clearly that he does not distinguish between the picture and the object and will attempt to clutch the picture in the same manner as an object. Next he will identify pictures of objects he knows. If there is a cat in the home, he will readily recognize a cat in the picture, but he will also identify all animals as cats. From this point on the child will be curious about all unfamiliar objects that appear in pictures. It may be stated as a general principle that very young children prefer as subject matter simple and somewhat familiar objects, creatures, and actions with an obvious story.

Several significant studies indicate that for a book to be accepted in the nursery the first prerequisite is that the pictures tell the story. Reading matter should be brief and supplementary. Color is preferred over black and white, and the color should come not in pastels but in large masses, crude and elementary. Illustrations in which figures are strongly outlined and given simple treatment have the greatest allure. In general, a number of separate pictures, each a story in itself, with little or no text, appeals more than complex pictures with much reading matter. Medium to small pictures seem to be preferred over the very large.

UTILIZATION OF READING BOOKS

The reading book has a variety of teaching functions. Some of the most common can be identified by these professional terms: "supplementary," "extensive," "recreational," and "inspirational."

The supplementary reader in the primary grades begins a type of book use that culminates in the college reserve book system. The supplementary approach assumes that the textbook treatment can be amplified and individualized through additional readings. Part of the assumption is based on the pedagogical belief that repetition alone will strengthen learning. But part of the supplementary reading theory is also based on the idea of matching individual differences in pupils with individual differences in materials. Somewhere in the vast literature there is a treatment peculiarly fitted to the distinctive background of the reader. By the law of probability, many books are more likely than a single text to effect sound communication with the learner. So the supplementary reading assignment acts as a complement to textbook activity.

Extensive reading, introduced by the language arts teacher as an antidote to intensive reading, gains its strength from interest, rapidity, and volume. In earlier years it was not uncommon in high school and even in intermediate grade readings of the classics to spend a major school term on one book. Who among us of the older generation does not recall with impatience the slow reading that resulted from diagnosing *Ivanhoe* or *Silas Marner* or *Evangeline*? The process consisted of an exhausting search for dictionary meanings of polysyllabic words, concentrated sleuthing among complex and compound sentences for hidden and mysterious meanings that one sometimes suspected would surprise even the author, studying with great concentration a "famous" description of something in nature (the kind of description that Mark Twain once thought should be separated from the story and isolated in an appendix for the edification of those who sought recreation in such reading), and, finally, rolling these exercises into culminating themes which somehow related the whole subject to the countryside in winter. This was a certain way indeed to destroy young people's interest in the classics.

In reaction against that method, English teachers now encourage wide and rapid reading for the story. Instead of one classic intensively studied each term, pupils are encouraged to read a dozen or more books rapidly. The power of extensive reading is cumulative. The best way to learn how to read is to read a lot. Wide reading increases not only the vocabulary, but one's repertoire of allusions, the lack of which is often a major stumbling block to verbal facility.

Reading for *recreation* was not deemed important by those who wrote for children's instruction centuries ago. But within recreational reading are the preparation and potential for serious reading. The power of such reading lies in its beginning at the point of the reader's most intense interest. This is a sure way to start the nonreader on the reading road.

The secret is to discover what interests the child or young person most at any given time. Whether it is football, drawing, television, a crooning singer, airplanes, or distant planets, reading matter exists on the subject. Impelled by the earnestness of his current interest and surprised by the discovery that well-informed people with comparable absorption have written on the subject, the young person will overcome vocabulary obstacles with surprising ease. Reading for entertainment can therefore become a steppingstone to serious reading.

Great men and women attest that certain books have proved to be turning points at critical stages in their lives. Many recall certain books which affected their outlook on life and major decisions. Although such reading experiences are probably not too frequent in a single lifetime, they are worth hoping and trying for. It is part of our teaching responsibility to place as many opportunities to read great books in our pupils' paths as the school day will permit.

Readings

ARBUTHNOT, MAY H. *Children and Books.* Chicago: Scott, Foresman Co., 1947. 626 pp.

DUFF, ANNIS. *Bequest of Wings: A Family's Pleasures with Books.* New York: The Viking Press, 1944. 204 pp.

HAZARD, PAUL. *Books, Children and Men,* Translated by MARGUERITE MITCHELL. Boston: Horn Book, Inc., 1944. 176 pp.

MILLER, BERTHA MAHONY, and FIELD, ELINOR W. *Newbery Medal Books: 1922–55.* Boston: Horn Book, Inc., 1955. 455 pp.

SMITH, LILLIAN H. *Unreluctant Years; A Critical Approach to Children's Literature.* Chicago: American Library Association, 1953. 193 pp.

5

SERIALS

Serials are printed publications issued in parts or in series at more or less regular intervals. Included in this class of Instructional Materials are (1) periodicals and newspapers, (2) government publications, and (3) pamphlets and miscellaneous printed materials such as broadsides.

Serials are not usually included in the main Dewey Decimal arrangement on the shelves but are housed separately. There are exceptions: Some government publications, like the *Statistical Abstract* and the *Congressional Directory*, are good reference books and are shelved with the "R" collection. An occasional pamphlet may prove to be less ephemeral than this class of materials implies and be classified, cataloged, and shelved as a reading book. But, in general, serials receive separate housing and treatment from the rest of the book collection.

One difference in treatment is found in the Library records. Though a serial title entry may be found in the card catalog, the serial records are kept in a separate file. Here the librarian checks in each part as it is received. The expected frequency of receipt—weekly, monthly, quarterly—is noted, so that, if the serial does not arrive as expected, the librarian can check with the dealer or publisher.

Another difference is in housing. Current issues of serials are usually displayed on slanting or sloping shelves. Back numbers may be kept on standard shelving just below or nearby. If issues of the serial are retained for over a year, they are usually bound into a volume or tied together.

Serial literature is vast and rich. It provides a current and vital support to the "T," "R," and other books. Selectively approached, serials can furnish the missing link between pupil and book. Certainly there is an element of "today" in the magazine and newspaper—and often in the government publication and pamphlet—that may stir the child who is allergic to the book's "yesterday."

In order for the teacher to move freely among these serials as teaching tools, certain guideposts must be reviewed.

PERIODICALS AND NEWSPAPERS

Potentials and Trends

The definitions of periodical, magazine, and newspaper are not too convincingly differentiated even in the best dictionaries. A periodical can be approximately defined as a publication issued at intervals of more than one day. From the meaning "a storehouse of information," a magazine can be defined as a periodical publication, paperbacked, containing stories and articles by various writers and an assortment of advertisements. A newspaper can be described as a publication issued regularly, usually daily or weekly, and containing news, opinions, feature stories, background and interpretive articles, and cartoons and advertisements. Dis regarding these definitions, most readers assume they can tell the difference between a magazine and a newspaper even when the Sunday paper comes with a magazine section.

For the teacher, the newspaper and magazine carry an extra meaning. These may be the media through which a youngster apathetic toward books may be aroused. Both newspapers and magazines have been in the vanguard of format innovation. Eye appeal through page make-up and picture has long been the stock in trade of these mass media, each in its way. The newspaper has created an idiom with an impact that John Doe and his family have absorbed without resistance. For example, baseball teams never "win" or "lose" on the sports page; rather, "Cubs Trump Cards." Nor is a treaty signed; instead one reads "Pact Inked After Parley." Around the copydesk of one metropolitan newspaper there is considerable banter about "not using simple words, because they may confuse the public." The magazine's very existence has depended on discovering or creating interests in the daily requirements of food, clothing, and shelter, and the desire to get along. Into the large-circulation periodicals, therefore, has gone the best communication talent that money from advertising revenue can buy. If good teaching is fundamentally clear communication, then the teacher can and should exploit the work of America's leading communicators.

Headlines that arouse interest, provide eye appeal. *Courtesy Civil Education Service, Inc.*

There can be no question that American adults learn much, if not well, from the newspapers and magazines published in this country. What about their children? The older ones read many of the same publications as their parents. For the younger children there is much that comes to them from the press and periodical by way of grown-up discussions. But there is also a magazine and newspaper literature addressed specifically to the next generation. Among the children's magazines and newspapers there is considerable range both in content and level. In some instances the format approaches the lure found in the adult mass media. Indeed, in a few instances, the juvenile publications are the products of adult magazines. *Jack and Jill*, for instance, is a child of the *Saturday Evening Post*, and there is the group of publications fathered and mothered by the *Parents' Magazine*.

The children's magazines today are having their troubles no less than their adult counterparts. The collapse of such multimillion-reader media as the Crowell-Collier publications and the consolidation or decease of many daily newspapers long regarded as American institutions have been duplicated on a smaller scale among the junior publications. In fact, the precariousness of nearly all children's serials has made the mention of specific titles here an extreme hazard.

Many ask, is the children's magazine a declining medium? Must it give way inevitably to the comics, the Saturday movie, and television? Can it ever recapture an audience as faithful as its grandparents were to *St. Nicholas* and *Youth's Companion*? Authorities offer conflicting answers to such questions. On the pessimists' side are the recent records of one short life after another for children's periodicals. On the optimists' side is the fact that several good magazines are flourishing.

The high mortality among children's magazines is not difficult to understand. Certain casualties may be attributed to the short subscription life. Children outgrow magazines in a way adults do not. The average subscription period for a children's magazine is not more than three or four years. Limited advertising, especially for the publications that cater to the very young, makes economic survival extremely precarious. Increasing subscription prices, on the other hand, threaten circulation. Yet despite these handicaps, certain juvenile magazines continue to flourish and to contribute as significantly to the education of the young as do their big brothers and sisters to the learning of the old. Representative publications from both the senior and junior magazines and newspapers have a tremendous potential for classroom learning. The teacher who draws on their power adds another approach to individual differences among his pupils.

Materials Center Handling

The school library, old or new, has always considered periodicals and newspapers an integral and significant part of the collection. But they have always been handled differently from books. From selection to dissemination, libraries have established a procedure with certain features that should be known to teachers.

Current periodicals—sloping shelves for the latest issues, straight shelves for back issues. *Courtesy State College of Washington.*

To begin with, periodicals are selected for subscription on the basis of standard lists and teachers' choices. Where a school faculty does not indicate strong preferences, the librarian relies on the professional training in selection he has received in his library school, and the qualified appraisals of the juries that select basic lists for school libraries. The fact that a periodical is or is not indexed in one of the periodical indexes also may influence the librarian's decision.

After the list has been made up, it is submitted for bid to a periodical agency. Fortunate is the school that does not have to take the lowest price. Service factors are also important; supplying of back numbers, follow-up on missing or delayed issues, and prompt delivery of index at the end of the volume must be considered. It is, of course, not impossible to get lowest price and highest service from the same agency, and that is what the library seeks.

As periodicals come into the library, they are checked in the special serial file previously mentioned. Then they are placed on the sloping shelf in place of the previously current issue. It has been the custom in the past for all periodicals to be used in the library and not to circulate them for home use. When all of the issues of a volume have been received and if the title is one previously agreed upon as worthy of binding, they are collated and prepared for the bindery.

Modifications in the above standard operating procedures have been developing in school libraries steadily, especially since World War II. In the matter of selection, the trend has been to relate more closely than ever to school subject interests. A much more generous circulation policy now prevails. Classrooms may have the use of periodicals for as long as a week at a time, always observing of course the unselfish principle of sharing if other demands arise during that time. Individual teachers and pupils are given the privilege of loan overnight and in some instances for even longer periods. Always to be remembered in this consideration of circulation is the fact that a single issue of a general periodical might contribute to several classes and various assignments, and commitment to one class for a long period of time inevitably may handicap the others.

There is also a tendency to bind and retain a smaller portion of back issues than formerly. Though the reference value of bound volumes is very high, especially for some magazines, the nature of periodical material favors current use. Consequently libraries in schools are tending to consider most periodicals expendable. In keeping with this newer philosophy, libraries are saving some of their periodical subscription money to buy single issues of value of a wide variety of titles. Also, libraries are binding only a few periodicals—such as *National Geographic,* largely because of its colored pictures of customs and costumes of many lands and peoples and of its valuable maps.

Certainly libraries and Materials Centers now more than ever seem particularly anxious to increase teacher and pupil use of periodical literature.

Lists and Indexes

One aid to increased use of periodicals and newspapers is a knowledge of lists and indexes. The lists can be broadly divided into two classes: inclusive and selective. Among the inclusive lists, which serve primarily to provide the facts of publication, are those obtainable free of cost from the library magazine agencies. Examples are the *Librarian's Guide to Periodicals* issued annually by the F. W. Faxon Co., Boston; and the *Periodical Handbook,* also yearly, offered by the Mayfair Agency, New York City.

The most inclusive list of American newspapers and periodicals containing the greatest amount of information about them, currently revised, is Ayer's *Directory of Newspapers and Periodicals* (5–1). Some school libraries include this title in their reference collection. It is always available in a public or college library. Arranged by state and locality, the directory gives for each title information about circulation, publisher, editor, format, price, political affiliation, and features. There are also classified lists of periodicals and magazines arranged by subject interests. Ulrich's *Periodicals Directory* (5–2) is a world, classified bibliography of periodicals. Its value to teachers is for its lists of professional and subject journals in nearly all school subject fields.

Among the selective lists, those specifically compiled with school libraries in mind are most useful, although some help can be found also in the lists prepared for public and college libraries. Laura K. Martin's thoughtful and intelligent volume, *Magazines for School Libraries* (5–3), the latest revised edition of which appeared in 1950, is worthy of a careful reading by all teachers. Although the lists include some titles now defunct, the information is still useful. Certainly the background discussion, the overviews of subject areas and interests in relation to magazines, the individual annotations, and the tabular groupings of titles are nowhere as well done in the professional literatures of either education or librarianship.

Perhaps the most up-to-date selections of periodicals for the school library can be found in the "Basic Book Collections" (1–6, 7, 8) compiled by special committees of the American Association of School Librarians in co-operation with various educational groups. The elementary and junior high school lists were reissued in 1956; the senior high school list somewhat earlier. Classified into broad subject groupings, each entry is bibliographically full, and the annotations are critical, spirited, and revealing. Omissions and inclusions will inevitably be applauded by some and regretted by others. A case in point is the preference for *Newsweek* over *Time* in the elementary list. It is such differences of opinion, however, which serve at school faculty meetings as a prelude to intelligent selection.

It is true that one of the bases for periodical selection is indexing in one of the major periodical indexes. The value of a magazine is enhanced, especially for reference, by such indexing. In the school field three periodical indexes are especially useful. For the elementary grades the *Subject Index to Children's Magazines* (5–4) provides not only a helpful reference tool but a check on subscription lists. Published monthly (except during June and July) since 1948, it indexes 38 children's magazines, cumulates twice yearly (in February and August), and lists bibliographic information about the magazines indexed.

The other two indexes important to periodical selection and use in schools are the *Readers' Guide to Periodical Literature* and the *Abridged Readers' Guide* (3–9). The former is an index to over 100 popular American and Canadian periodicals of a "general nature received in libraries of all sizes." It appears semimonthly in September through June and monthly during July and August, cumulating frequently during the year and into annual and biennial bound volumes. Its arrangement is alphabetic by author and subject for articles, and by author and title for stories and other imaginative writings. Poems, motion pictures, and plays also appear as such. Full bibliographic references are given and it is needless to say *RG* can be a big help to the high school teacher and student in locating magazine articles on almost any subject.

The *Abridged Readers' Guide* (3–9) indexes only 35 magazines but is adequate for most school use. It appears monthly September through May, with June, July, and August publications listed in the September issue. The list of periodicals indexed is indicated in front of each issue of *ARG* and provides a selection guide for teachers and librarians. Both *RG* and *ARG* are described in the two pamphlets issued to teachers free by the H. W. Wilson Company: *How To Use the Readers' Guide* and *Cataloging and Indexing Service*.

Evaluation Criteria for Magazines

Published critical appraisals of our press and periodicals suggest many principles for evaluation. Perhaps an eclectic guide for the teacher can be constructed around four criteria: (1) format, (2) content, (3) treatment, and (4) authority.

The elements of *format* are about the same as for books except for binding. They include paper, type, make-up and illustration. Newsprint, used by some magazines, cannot support as fine a picture as calendered paper. Paper opaque enough to prevent print from showing through to the other side of the page, however, should be a requisite in evaluating format. Similarly, legibility of type, usually aided by adequate leading (spacing between lines), if not by size, is essential for children's reading.

Content will vary with age level and subject, but one or two general criteria can always be applied. The cover should appeal to the oldest reader. Age interests should be clearly differentiated so that younger and older children can find their features. There is a consensus that "how-to-do" departments should aim at the top age in the range unless there are different sections for each level. Pictures should be aesthetic, challenging, dramatic, and related to the text.

PERIODICAL LITERATURE March 1957—February 1958

ATOMIC power plants—Continued
First atom power plant gets nuclear furnace;
   Shippingport, Pa. il Pop Mech 109:126 F '58
Getting it straight. Newsweek 50:82-3 Ag 19
   '57
Girding for atomic power. M. J. Fitzgerald.
   America 97:253-6 My 25 '57
Good news on atom power. Bsns W p 138 Ja
   11 '58
Lagoona controversy. R. Moley. Newsweek
   50:128 N 11 '57
Municipal nuclear power planned for Piqua,
   Ohio. J. P. Gallagher. Am City 72:128 S
   '57
Nuclear operating procedure. Sci Am 197:68
   D '57
Nuclear plant turns on power; Shipping-
   port plant. il Bsns W p32-4 D 7 '57
Nuclear power for Italy soon. G. Valerio.
   Am City 72:204 Je '57
Nuclear power in Britain. J. Cockcroft. Vital
   Speeches 24:107-10 D 1 '57
Piqua, Ohio, to build nuclear power plant.
   Am City 72:209 Ap '57
Power from atoms of peace; Shippingport
   plant; photographs. diag N Y Times Mag
   p 14-15 O 27 '57
Power from the atom. New Repub 136:6 Je
   24 '57
Private a-power at Vallecitos. Newsweek 50:
   80+ N 4 '57
Shippingport reactor starts. Science 126.1280
   D 20 '57
   See also
Strikes—United States Atomic power plants

   Accidents and injuries
Atom industry safe place to work. Sci Digest
   41:24 Ja '57

Europe, Western
   See also
Euratom (European atomic energy com-
   munity)

   Great Britain
Control h-bomb reaction. il(p65) Sci N L
   72:67 F 1 '58
Monster tamed? Newsweek 50:62 O 28 '57
Toward h-power. il diag Time 71:51 F 8 '58

   Iran
Atoms-for-peace agreement with Iran. U S
   Dept State Bul 36:629 Ap 15 '57

   Russia
Has Russia pushed ahead in the atom race?
   interview, J. E. Van Zandt. U S News 43:
   50 J N 1 '57
Reds try taming h-power. Sci N L 73:71
   F 1 '58
USSR a-power hits snags. Sci N L 72:66 Ag
   3 '57

   Scandinavia
   See also
Nordic institute for theoretical atomic
   physics

   United States
   See Atomic research
ATOMIC research laboratories
   See also
Brookhaven national laboratory
ATOMIC theory
   Picture history of the atom. H Kondo. il
   diags Sci Digest 43:69-71 F '58
ATOMIC warfare
   About disarmament. E. Rabinowitch. bibliog f

Thorium's in the race for sure. Bsns W p 153
   Je 1 '57
Three times at bat for U.S, three hits: a-
   bomb, h-bomb, clean bomb. il U S News
   43:86-8 Jl 12 '57
What the atom will do for you. Changing T
   11:43-8 Ag '57
   See also
American nuclear society

Mr 22 '57
Much more than the h-bomb is needed. H. W.
   Baldwin. il N Y Times Mag p7+ Ag 18 '57
Nature of nuclear warfare. E. Teller. Bul
   Atomic Sci 13:162-5 My '57; Reply. L.
   Fermi. 13:232 Je '57
No place to hide. Time 69:23 Ap 1 '57
NATO and nuclear weapons. D. Acheson.
   New Repub 137:14-16 D 30 '57

A page from *Readers' Guide to Periodical Literature*. *Courtesy H. W. Wilson Company.*

Treatment involves style and ethics. Much has been written on writing style for children. There is now almost a universal objection to "writing down." Young people want to be grown folks and treated as such. They celebrate arriving of age and what they expect from a teacher is to be talked with as adults. That very feeling is being recognized increasingly in writings for children—tempered, however, by the realization that adult selections of best children's books do not always correlate with the children's own preferences.

Consideration of ethics should not be overlooked in evaluating literature for young people. Although the didactic extremes of the Puritan period are anathema both to children and to those who publish for them, an awareness of man's relation to man and to God is a debt owed by the older generation to the generation which will continue our human destiny. In consequence, the good juvenile magazine must strive to reflect as much of the truth and beauty the adult world has achieved as it is possible to convey within the more limited scope of literature for children.

Authority in children's magazines takes publisher, editor, and contributors into account. Publications sponsored by well-known firms, or by agencies such as the Girl Scouts and Boy Scouts, carry with them from the start a weight that must be earned by new enterprises. The experienced editor of a trade publisher's children's department or a junior encyclopedia, or the successful children's librarian or school leader, frequently introduces a rich experience from a related field into the direction of a juvenile periodical. Name contributors are as important in young people's magazines as in their adult counterparts, but no more. There is certainly opportunity in the literature for children for the discovery and encouragement of new talent.

Evaluation Chart for Magazines

Format: Is type legible, paper opaque, make-up inviting? Are illustration and text related?

Content: Does cover appeal? Is age range correct? Are activities graded? Do pictures complement the words?

Treatment: Is writing "up" or "down"? Does ethics permeate without preaching?

Authority: Who are the publishers or sponsors? What is the background of the editors? How adequate are the contributors?

Evaluation Criteria for Newspapers

Although the newspaper is, like the magazine, a serial, it has certain publication problems of its own. For one thing, the average frequency for the output of the press is generally greater. For another, deadlines permit much less deliberation on make-up in the editorial rooms of a daily newspaper than those of a monthly or even weekly magazine.

Relative to *format*, a conventional eight-column newspaper page must be compared with a tabloid. School newspapers tend toward the smaller page. Page make-up in general and of the front page in particular, headline style, and the strategic use of illustrations, as well as a legible and pleasing type, contribute to the physical appearance of a newspaper.

Relative to *content*, *The New York Times* slogan, "all the news that's fit to print," is open to interpretation. The *Christian Science Monitor*, for example, would consider much of the news in *The Times* unfit. There are also differences on advertising. Some newspapers will not accept liquor or tobacco ads.

In *treatment*, there are all the ramifications of political affiliation. One newspaper will present the case for the "honorable opposition" no matter how sharp the disagreement; another will hardly deign to notice a difference. The attitudes of a newspaper toward labor, government, education, defense, foreign relations, social security, and other key issues of the day enable one to analyze the character of the paper and predict the treatment which will be accorded a subject not only editorially but in the handling of the news itself. If the paper is one in a chain, its policy will be largely predetermined. Even if the newspaper is locally owned, its perspective may be shaped entirely by the owners. A striking difference between owners and staff was illustrated by the poll that established the fact that although 80 per cent of the newspaper publishers of the United States opposed President Roosevelt and the New Deal in their editorial columns, and often in their handling of the news, nearly 90 per cent of those who wrote and edited the news favored Roosevelt policies.

In evaluating *authority*, the news services and syndicated features should be considered. Of the two major news services, the Associated Press is considered more conservative and reliable; the United Press, somewhat more liberal, and the International News Service, inclined to favor the sensational aspects of the news, are now combined as United Press International. There are many syndicated services, including feature articles by authorities, picture services, comics, serial fiction, crossword puzzles, and articles of household interest. Choices of columnists and local editorial talent also contribute to authority. A predominance of feature writers who espouse either political extreme—liberal or conservative—or the employment of reporters and editors with an eye for the sensational, weakens the authority of a newspaper.

Evaluation Checklist for Newspapers

Format: Conventional eight-column or tabloid size? Page makeup, typography, illustration suitable?

Content: All the news—or limitations? All kinds of advertising—or restrictions?

Treatment: Political affiliations and attitudes on key issues?

Authority: Chain or local ownership? Kinds of news services?

Selection of Magazines and Newspapers

Every teacher has his favorite magazines and newspapers, but no library can afford to subscribe to them all. Selection is usually affected by funds available and the relative needs of the school program. A more effective selection will come about if teachers and librarians will continually review the subscription list, taking into account curriculum, standard lists, indexes, personal preferences, nature of proposed use, and teachers' and pupils' personal subscriptions.

The publications mentioned in the following sections do not represent an actual selection for any school. They are merely some titles teachers should know and consider both in selection and utilization. They have been arbitrarily grouped. In the average library or Materials Center they will probably be arranged on the sloping current shelves, in alphabetical order.

Here they are considered in three groups: (1) "chain publications; (2) general and story magazines; (3) special-area periodicals, such as those which stress book reviews, scouting, girls' interests, boys' interests, science, health, geography, or news. All of these groups overlap to some extent. Under each group the titles are considered in grade order, from preschool to grade twelve or above.

Chain Publications. Here the term "chain" is not used in the same sense as a "chain" of daily newspapers. Rather, it refers to a group of newspapers and magazines published for classroom use by a single publisher. Four such chain publishers will be mentioned here. Three distribute their publications primarily as classroom subscriptions. At least one copy of any title subscribed to by a classroom should be in the library.

American Education Publications (5–5), Middlebury, Connecticut, is the oldest of the chain publishers. Founded by Charles Palmer Davis, a school board member of Agawam, Mass., who was appalled by boys' and girls' ignorance of current events, AEP issued its first children's newspaper *Current Events* on May 20, 1902. As the success of this idea grew, more papers were established, one to fit each of the grade levels. At present AEP issues:

My Weekly Reader, for grades 1 to 6
Current Events, grades 6 to 8
Every Week, grades 8 to 10
Our Times, grades 10 to 12
Read, for junior high school English and social studies
Current Science and Aviation

Children's newspapers undertake to fill the gap between the textbook and today. Distinguished editorial advisory boards add authority to the content and to the treatment given the material. The formats are pleasing and suggestive of things to come in the adult newspaper. The papers are sold in groups to classes—at reasonable cost, so that each child may have his individual copy.

The Civic Education Service (5–6), Washington, D.C., was founded on the campus of Kansas State Teachers Col-

Children's newspapers. *Courtesy Civic Education Service, Inc.*

lege, Emporia, by Walter E. Myer, chairman of the department of sociology and economics. In response to a request from the college's president for a more systematic study of current history, Professor Myer undertook a weekly mimeographed summary and analysis of the news which soon was distributed to the high schools of Kansas and other states as the *Weekly News Review*. At present, Civic Education Service publishes the following newspapers:

Young Citizen, for grades 5 and 6
Junior Review, for grades 7 to 9
Weekly News Review, grades 9 to 11
American Observer, grades 10 to 12
Civic Leader, for social studies teachers.

All of these newspapers draw upon wire services and other Washington resources to bring to pupils a reasonable facsimile of adult newspapers. An advisory board of distinguished educators lends authority to the content, and the quality of paper, make-up, and illustration contributes to an effective format.

The Scholastic Corporation Publications (5–7) are more like magazines in format and organization than newspapers, although they include news. Founded by M. R. Robinson, a Pennsylvanian, in 1920, the magazines now have editorial offices in New York. The list of publications and services offered by Scholastic includes:

Newstime, grades 4 and 5, language arts, social studies, science
Junior Scholastic, grades 6 through 8, English and social studies
World Week, grades 8 through 10, social studies
Senior Scholastic, grades 10 through 12, social studies
Practical English, grades 9 through 12, English
Literary Cavalcade, grades 9 through 12, English
Co-ed, grades 7 to 12, homemaking

To accompany these children's magazines, there are teacher publications: *Scholastic Teacher*, issued weekly, includes professional news about teachers and teaching, conventions, timely articles, audio-visual techniques, and teaching guides; *Practical Home Economics* is the teacher edition of *Co-ed;*

and *Scholastic Coach* is a professional magazine for athletic directors.

Nor are these all of the services which Scholastic offers. To encourage reading, *Summertime,* a magazine of recrea-

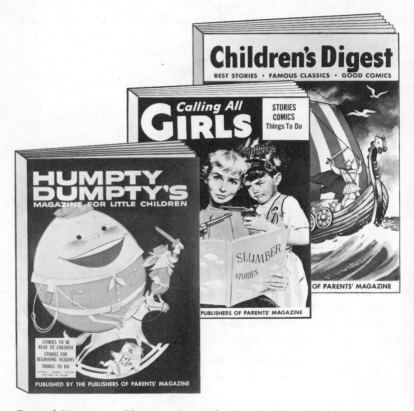

Parents' Magazine publications for children. *Courtesy Parents' Institute, Inc.*

tional reading, is issued biweekly from June 15 to August 15. TAB, the Teen-Age Book Club, enables students to obtain at a cost of 25 to 35 cents a selected list of good books. Also offered is a budget service for low-cost pocket-size books known as "Readers' Choice." Other services include an Institute of Student Opinion which conducts national polls on questions to which the answers of youth are significant. Scholastic also sponsors national competitions in writing, painting, sculpture, graphic arts, and photography, all open to students in grades seven through twelve in both public and private schools of the United States and possessions.

A distinguished national advisory council and staff of editors give authority to all of the Scholastic undertakings. Format ranges from newsprint to good magazine make-up, with generous illustration supplementing carefully edited text.

The Parents' Institute, Inc., publishers of *Parents' Magazine* (5–8), entered the children's field some time ago with *True Comics* presenting heroic subjects in comic-book format in an effort to neutralize the sordid content of the usual comics. Librarians differed as to the success of this effort. But *Parents' Magazine* has since ventured with additional periodical titles. *Humpty Dumpty's Magazine for Little Children* is a 128-page paperbound volume of read-aloud stories, games, puzzles, and things to do. *Piggity* is an animal story magazine printed on so-called eye-ease tinted paper. Parents, however, seem enthusiastic about *Children's Digest*, intended for children of all ages, with retold stories and classics that continue the "true comic" effort. *Calling All Girls*, for ages 7 to 14 is also enjoying a measure of success. The value of the *Parents' Magazine* venture continues to find both its supporters and critics among librarians and teachers.

General and Story Magazines. From preschool through high school, the general and story magazine is a staple. Three titles can be cited as examples for the very young. *Child Life*, issued monthly in October through May and bimonthly during June through September, is intended for preschool and primary children. It includes poems, stories and a play, book and record reviews, recipes, puzzles, and photos and prints. Very thin paper weakens its format. *Highlights for Children* covers a broad age span but is preferred by primary children. Stories, features and things to do, as well as some verse, are popular. The tone, however, seems somewhat didactic. The best of the three is *Saturday Evening Post's* little magazine

Jack and Jill. Its stories, articles, puzzles, songs, photos, drawings, and such features as the "Girl's Page" and the "Boy's Page," seem to have child appeal through the fifth grade.

For ages 6 through 10 and 6 through 12, respectively, are *Children's Playmate* and *Children's Activities.* The former, a monthly, is the product of the A. R. Mueller Printing & Lithograph Co., Cleveland, and has been issued since 1929. Because it stresses handicraft coloring and cutout, it is of less value for the library than for individual subscription. The latter, monthly September through June, is planned to encourage reading and wholesome activity. A typical issue is comprised of stories; verse; brief, well-illustrated articles in geography, history, and nature; and how-to-make-and-do features. Somewhat more mature, despite the suggestion that it is useful from the fourth grade up, is the British *Young Elizabethan*, "the magazine for boys and girls." It is gracious and elegant in its presentation of story and article through text and picture.

There are other children's and young people's magazines that can be classified as "general and story," but it might be well to look at some of the adult counterparts found in school libraries, elementary as well as junior and senior high. *Life, Readers' Digest*, and *Saturday Evening Post* are almost universals. Other adult magazines may have more to offer youngsters, and many will be found in school libraries. There is, however, enough in the fine pictorial and cultural features of *Life* to overcome any aimlessness some contend this magazine encourages.

The *Saturday Evening Post* is attractive to the younger generation. Its stories and articles are of a consistently high calibre. There is enough in any issue to support classroom learning on a variety of units, from the intermediate grades through high school.

Greater difference of opinion on the value of the *Readers' Digest* has always existed. Some English teachers' testimonials have exaltingly praised the coming of the magazine to their classrooms. But others have contended the digests represented a further weakening of the educational fiber and that its ethics were Pollyannish, paternalistic, and downright reactionary. Libraries, however, universally subscribe to *Readers' Digest* for its brief, readable, and timely articles, many of which are now originals rather than condensations. The humor and book briefs apparently appeal to pupils, also.

Special-Area Periodicals. There are so many special-area periodicals that only a few areas and some representative titles can be indicated. The standard lists and indexes will suggest many more. First of all, the review periodicals for children's and young people's literature include at least two "musts" for all teachers. One of these is the American Library Association's *Booklist* (to which is now attached the *Subscription Books Bulletin*), dedicated to a critical appraisal of the junior book output. The other is the *Horn Book*, exclusively devoted to careful evaluation of current children's books, their authors and illustrators.

Scouting is an area of interest to both boys and girls. For the latter, the *American Girl* is the official monthly aimed at the 11 through 15 age level. Stories and articles relate to adolescents—dates, grooming, fashions, etiquette, sports, cooking, movies, art, and books. A typical recent issue includes articles about flowers, shoes, horses, and double-daters, and regular features include "Headline News in Girl Scouting" and photos of events of interest to girls.

Boys' Life does a comparable job as the official monthly of Boy Scouts of America. Sports, outdoor life, adventure, careers, and hobbies find outlets in such regular features as stories, articles, photos, "color section," "Duffel Bag," "Hobby Hows," "Gifts and Gimmicks," and "Think and Grin." With circulation well over the million mark, *Boys' Life* takes on the attributes of a junior mass medium.

Aside from these two, girls and boys have other separate media of note. Emphasizing fashion, homemaking, etiquette, grooming, and entertainment is the teen-age monthly *Seventeen*. Its attractions are such as to appeal from the seventh grade up. To complement it, there are a host of woman's magazines, including *American Home, Better Homes and Gardens,* and *Good Housekeeping.*

The boys, too, are supported in their special interests by such magazines as *Young Men,* formerly *Air Trails,* which concentrates on model planes, boats, cars, with detailed drawings and directions, and on careers for the mechanically minded that lead also into radio, photography, and guncraft; *Sport,* which can be read enthusiastically by fifth graders as well as high school boys because of the good balance between "how-to" directions and "Who's Who" biographies of the major sport stars; *Popular Mechanics* and *Popular Science,* the difference between the two indicated by their title emphases, and their similarity by the abundance of "opportunity" advertisements and "do-it-yourself" articles.

Girls as well as boys have caught the spirit of the scientific age. *Science News Letter,* usable at least from the seventh grade up, is compact in its brief reports of progress on all fronts, including medicine and technology. For the biological sciences *Junior Natural History* and *Nature Magazine* present material on complementary age levels. The former, with its animal, bird, and plant lore in text and picture, plus puzzle and quiz sections, lures children of the fourth to eighth grades, wide-eyed, into love of nature, and on to the advanced content on conservation, species, stars, botany, and zoology found in *Nature Magazine.*

In the area of health, the American Medical Association and the American National Red Cross sponsor periodicals of inestimable value to young and old lay readers. AMA's monthly, *Today's Health,* formerly called *Hygeia,* writes about the prevention and cure of diseases in articles and fictionized features, in advice departments, and even in cartoons and pictures. For somewhat younger readers, ANRC's two publications approach health subjects through nursing. *American Junior Red Cross Journal* aims at about seventh and eighth grade level with a galaxy of inspiring articles idolizing nurses, and includes news of the Red Cross. *American Junior Red Cross News* does about the same job for younger children.

Perhaps attention should also be called to the news magazines and newspapers for which the children's chains prepare the young reader. Between *Newsweek* and *Time*, teacher preferences will undoubtedly influence pupils. The coverage of a national newpaper like *The New York Times* is broader than that of a local paper or of a regional or state metropolitan daily, and for that reason, if for no other, every school library will want to include two or more such national dailies in its subscription list.

PAMPHLETS AND GOVERNMENT PUBLICATIONS

Pamphlets

A thin, paperbound booklet is the format most usually associated with the pamphlet. From a content standpoint the pamphlet has frequently been related to crusading, proselytizing, and propagandizing. But today this is in no way true of all pamphlet literature. For among the paperbounds the whole gamut of human activities and interests can be found. Every curriculum subject, every cocurricular interest, indeed, every aspect of life is encompassed in the vast pamphlet literature.

Pamphlets are usually found in one of two places in Materials Centers. Most often they are housed in a steel vertical file, arranged alphabetically by subject, but they may also be found in pamphlet boxes on book shelves, arranged separately by subject, or classified as a pamphlet box in the regular Dewey Decimal listing.

When housed in a vertical file, pamphlets are stamped v.f. or PAM or INF FILE. They are usually arranged alphabetically by subject headings taken from a list such as is found in the *Readers' Guide* or in Sears' *List of Subject Headings for a Small Library*. Because of the great number of pamphlets available and received, a process known as "weeding" is carried on by the librarian. This consists of reviewing from time to time the amount of use made of individual pamphlets by teachers and pupils and discarding those not used. The librarian also does the opposite at times: removes

Pamphlets in vertical files (left) and pamphlet boxes (right). *Courtesy Appalachian State Teachers College.*

pamphlets from the vertical file that have given evidence of sufficient value to be made a permanent member of the book collection.

Circulation of pamphlets is usually simplified. Groups of them may be taken out at one time and charged, not by individual title, but by subject and number. Entries in the card catalog are also usually made by subject rather than by author and title. The card may read "For further materials on this subject consult the Vertical File under the following headings: . . . ."

The greatest problem that confronts both teachers and librarians on pamphlets is selection. Norma Ireland in her definitive volume on pamphlets (5–10) lists about 660 organizations that issue pamphlets. This is a highly selected list that omits travel agencies, educational institutions and book publishers. Since each of these 660 organizations is publishing pamphlets almost continually, the threat of inundation in the library is constant, but that threat can be met and converted into a powerful teaching force by united teacher-librarian selection and weeding.

Fortunately there are several aids. As in the case of magazines, lists and indexes are wonderful allies. To begin with it is well to recall that *Publishers' Weekly* also lists in its "Weekly Record," pamphlets issued during the week. Because this is a fairly inclusive list, it will be less helpful than some of the more selective ones. But the teacher will find it a good idea to scan the "Weekly Record" for pamphlets as well as books.

Most of the standard booklists mentioned so far include some pamphlets. *Children's Catalog*, which does not include pamphlets in the basic volume because of their ephemeral nature, does list them in the annual supplements. Pamphlets are also included in the periodical indexes, in many periodicals, in the *Booklist*, and in separate bibliographies of pamphlets.

The basic pamphlet list is Wilson's *Vertical File Index* (3–6). It is "a subject and title index to selected pamphlet material." Formerly it was known as the *Vertical File Catalog*.

It is now issued monthly, except in August, and cumulated into an annual January through December volume. Pamphlets included in this by no means complete list are considered to be of interest to libraries; and inclusion of a pamphlet is not intended to be an endorsement.

Another important list is the *Elementary Teachers' Guide to Free Curriculum Materials* (5–11) published by the Educators Progress Service, of Randolph, Wisc. The 13th annual list included 1222 pamphlets, bulletins, maps, charts, exhibits, and books available free to elementary schools and junior high schools. The materials are listed under 15 major areas, such as agriculture, business education, home economics, etc. Title, annotation, and source are given for each item, and directions for requesting these materials. There is a section devoted to teachers' materials. There are three indexes—by title, subject, and source, the last giving complete addresses. Selection has been made from twice the number of candidates. This is a tremendously useful teachers' tool with inestimable aid for pamphlet selection. The arrangement of the list is for the most part very sensible. To assist in utilization, several special units on free materials in such areas as conservation, atomic energy, transportation, etc., have been prepared by specialists.

Since pamphlet materials are overwhelmingly what are called "sponsored" materials—that is, materials issued by a firm or association to advocate its product or cause—teachers must be on guard against mere propaganda. No rule of selection can be written that will cover all individual titles. Judgments of librarians and teachers will have to reinforce each other in final selections.

Government Publications

Reference to any publication issued by a government as a "government document" is not strictly accurate, since the document is the original and the publication is a duplication in print or by some other process. Nevertheless the terms "government documents" and "government publications" have persisted as synonymous.

Local, state, federal, foreign and international governments issue publications. In all, the volume is beyond any but the very largest of libraries to handle. What the school library must do is select from the vast output those items that will support the school program. As in the case of other classes of Instructional Materials, selection aids exist.

The largest single source of government publications is the United States Government. The most comprehensive current list is the *United States Government Publications Monthly Catalog* (5–12), always referred to as the *Monthly Catalog*. This is a tool worth looking at. It lists all of the publications issued by the office of the Superintendent of Documents, which is the official distributing agency. It omits, however, some "processed" publications; that is, those duplicated on office equipment, such as mimeograph, by the various agencies. In the *Monthly Catalog*, publications are arranged first by agency author and then by publication, with each entry being assigned a number. There is a title and subject index each month, and the monthly indexes are cumulated into a January through December annual. Some of the special features of the *Monthly Catalog* include "Previews" of forthcoming publications and information on how to obtain publications.

In general, federal government publications may be obtained free or by purchase. Certain designated libraries are "depositories" and by law are entitled to the publications they request. Other libraries obtain free copies of publications from their congressmen or by writing to the agencies concerned. The Department of Agriculture is particularly generous in considering such requests. Otherwise, government publications may be purchased from the Superintendent of Documents by paying for them in advance with cash or money order, or with coupons issued by the Superintendent of Documents in sheets of twenty for one dollar.

If subscription to the *Monthly Catalog* is not within the Materials Center budget, then the free semimonthly *Selected United States Government Publications* (5–13) can be consulted. This is an annotated list of particular value to the teacher in search of government publications related to her teaching unit. Also free are the *Price Lists* (5–14), issued from time to time, which are lists of government publications on specific subjects such as American History.

Other listings of government publications are in the U.S. Office of Education periodical *School Life*, and in the *N.E.A. Journal*. In addition, there are the standard booklists and periodical and pamphlet lists previously mentioned. Retrospective subject lists of government publications can be found in Leidy's *Guide to Government Publications* (5–15).

The basic list of state publications is the Library of Congress monthly *Checklist of State Publications* (5–16), which is arranged by state and, under state, by subject. There is no comparable tool for local publications, but the Bureau of the Census issued in 1948 a *Checklist of Basic Municipal Documents* which contained about 2000 items from 92 American cities with populations over 100,000. There is now an extensive listing and indexing system for United Nations documents, but the best of these for school purposes can be found in the standard booklists.

Readings

BOYD, ANNE M. *United States Government Publications*. New York: H. W. Wilson Co., 1949. 627 pp.

BROWN, E. S. *Manual of Government Publications, United States and Foreign.* New York: Appleton-Century-Crofts, Inc., 1950. 121 pp.

CUMMINGS, H. H., and BARD, HARRY. *How to Use Daily Newspapers* ("How To Do It Series," no. 5). Washington, D.C.: National Council for the Social Studies, 1952. 6 pp.

IRELAND, NORMA O. *The Pamphlet File*. Boston: F. W. Faxon & Co., Inc., 1954. 220 pp.

MARTIN, LAURA K. *Magazines for School Libraries*. New York: H. W. Wilson Co., 1950. 196 pp.

PETERSON, THEODORE. *Magazines in the Twentieth Century*. Urbana: University of Illinois Press, 1956. 457 pp.
   (Chap. I for overview and Chap. XIV for evaluation, especially)

WILSON, MARY C. *How To Use Multiple Books* ("How To Do It Series," no. 16). Washington, D.C.: National Council for the Social Studies, 1953, 7 pp.

WRONSKI, S. P. *How to Locate Government Publications* ("How To Do It Series," no. 11). Washington, D.C.: National Council for the Social Studies, 1952. 8 pp.

Part II

The World of Graphics

6

PLACE MEDIA

We are everywhere at once in this day of air travel, global cruises, and instant communication. At even the beginning grade levels children want to identify places near and far. This desire on the part of boys and girls has been given added impetus since World War II by some 12 million GI fathers and mothers who will sometimes mention the name of some exotic place they have visited. Since these places are not in the old geography books, new teaching media are needed to tie them to older landmarks.

Such regions as the Pacific Islands, the Persian Gulf, and the top of the world have now taken on a new dramatic significance in even the child's mind. No longer is it acceptable to keep one finger on the map of Europe while looking at the map of Asia in order to put together the two parts of Russia. The reality of the new continent of Antarctica cannot be verbalized simply by the concept of the South Pole. These and other one-world dramas spur geography interests as never before.

Nor are these interests limited to geography and history. The environments of plants and animals need to be located. Place tools alone can provide such support for nature study. Stories from many lands cry for map locations to augment language arts study. Customs and games, clothing and foods, famous people and events, all are part of some locale. Without forcing, it can be proved that place media will enrich nearly all school study. Place media may be defined as teaching tools that help describe our entire world and locate places on it.

SELECTION OF PLACE MEDIA

There are five types of place media: (1) gazetteers, (2) guidebooks, (3) atlases, (4) maps, and (5) globes. The first two are basically verbal, the others heavily visual. All five have their place in grades from at least three up.

Gazetteers

Gazetteers are essentially dictionaries of place names. Arranged alphabetically, gazetteers give, under the name of each place, a brief identification which includes type (city, island, lake, mountain, etc.), location (latitude-longitude or distance from a well-known point), statistics (size, population, etc.), history, and pertinent facts.

Although lists of place names with descriptions were compiled probably as early as the sixth century by Stephen of Byzantium, the earliest gazetteer in the modern sense was Lawrence Echard's *Gazetteer's or Newsman's Interpreter* (1703). As geographical knowledge and interest increased, attempts were made to compile complete gazetteers. Some of the more famous ones include two produced in Scotland in 1850—Johnston's and Blackie's; Bouillet's in France, 1857; Ritter's in Germany, 1874; Longman's in England, 1895; and Garollo's in Italy, 1898. The United States produced Lippincott's Gazetteer in 1865, a basic reference tool that continues today through the recent *Columbia-Lippincott Gazetteer*, now America's largest geographical dictionary.

Lists of places, with identifications, can also be found in dictionaries, encyclopedias, and almanacs. In some of these general reference tools, place names are in a separate alphabetical list, as in *Webster's New International Dictionary*; in others, such as *Funk and Wagnalls New Standard Dictionary*, the place names are incorporated in the same alphabet with all other words and terms.

Among separate gazetteers *Webster's Geographical Dictionary* (6–1) is basic. It lists about 40,000 places in every part of the world, with pronunciation, location, identification, and description briefly indicated. For example, all incorpo-

Learning more about their world. *Courtesy Monroe County (Florida) Schools Materials Center.*

rated communities in the U.S. and Canada with a population of 1500 or more are included. For other parts of the world, localities are included when the population equals at least:

3000 in South Africa
5000 in the British Isles, Australia, and New Zealand
5000–10,000 in Western and Central Europe
10,000 in the USSR
20,000–25,000 in all other places

Islands, mountains, rivers, lakes, counties and other places and features are also included. Among the facts cited are area, population, geographical features, economic data, historical records, and such miscellany as state mottoes, flowers, capitals, chief cities, and date of admission to the Union.

Although gazetteers are usually entirely verbal, *Webster's* supports its words with 177 maps, 24 of which are in color. There is a full-page map for each U.S. state, and there are color maps of such subjects as Bible lands, U.S. territorial growth, and European folk migrations.

The *Columbia-Lippincott Gazetteer of the World* (6–2) is the big one, with over 130,000 articles—more than three times the number of places found in *Webster's*. It is descended from the historically famous *Lippincott Gazetteer*. Nations, continents, regions and major cities of the world are treated in long, comprehensive articles. Shorter entries identify towns and villages. Detailed and thorough descriptions of countries, provinces, and districts, and of such features of the world as islands, deserts, canals, lakes, seas, dams, mountains, rivers, peninsulas, ocean currents, and volcanoes, provide aid to teachers and to pupils in upper grades. *Columbia-Lippincott* is especially strong on such elements as variant pronunciations and spellings, climate, cultural institutions, industry, agriculture, natural resources, and monuments.

Besides *Webster* and *Columbia-Lippincott*, there is a shelf of gazetteers and near-gazetteers with popular appeal for adults, children, and young people. For example, the Rand McNally *World Guide* (6–3), based on *Columbia-Lippincott*, is selective, illustrated, and very much less expensive. Jane Werner's *Golden Geography* (6–4), "a child's introduction to the world . . ." with pictures by Cornelius DeWitt, intended for grades four through six has more than 300 color paintings which present the world in all of its regions, climates, and environments as they relate to human life.

For the early grades (two through five) there is Munro Leaf's *Geography Can Be Fun* (6–5). Here, through delightful, pointed, and frequently amusing drawings, the earth's external relations to the sun and moon and the internal composition of its regions and peoples are fitted together in a unity of understanding.

These then are some gazetteers—tools to identify places and to locate them so that children, young people, and adults may have verbal comprehension. Most of these should be available in a good school library or Materials Center.

Guidebooks

Another type of verbal place tool, the guidebook, intended primarily for the traveler, has possibilities for classroom use. A guidebook may be defined as an aid to travel. Its purpose is well stated in that most famous series of guidebooks, Baedeker: "to enable people to travel with the greatest economy of time and money and to widen their experience by acquainting themselves with the scenery, the manners and customs, and the artistic treasures of foreign countries." The guidebook literature available is overwhelming; part of it is free or inexpensive.

The vast travel literature issued by railroads, steamship lines, bus companies, airlines, travel agencies, and oil companies constitutes an important, though free or inexpensive, class of place media. The school Materials Center should be on the free mailing list of many travel agencies and should seek other items as they are announced in library, audiovisual, and general professional journals. Librarians and teachers working together can maintain a fresh supply for classroom use by continual vigilance that compares output with curriculum.

In addition to the free material, there is inexpensive locational material in magazines, government publications, and the publications of geographical societies. Such periodicals as *Holiday, Travel,* and *National Geographic,* as well as the more general magazines, feature travel articles.

From the U.S. Government, as well as from individual states, attractive folders, posters, and booklets describe national and state parks, monuments, resorts, highways, industry, and agriculture, usually in striking formats that feature color illustrations. Such travel and geographic organizations as the American Automobile Association, the National Geographic Society, and the American Geographical Society publish maps and texts about places.

There are a number of commercially published guidebooks that are found in most libraries. The Baedeker series covers many countries and has been periodically revised ever since its first volume appeared in the English language in 1861. The *Blue Guides*, issued in the U.S. by Rand McNally, in Great Britain by Benn, and in France by Hachette, concentrate mainly on Europe.

For the United States the *American Guide Series*, produced by the Federal Writers' Project, includes separate volumes for each state, some cities and regions, and points of interest along the federal highway U.S. 1. *Guide to America* (6–6) prepared by the travel director of the American Automobile Association, condenses information about points of interest in all of the States. There is travel help in the *Official Hotel Red Book and Directory*, which is issued annually, in the *Official Guide of the Railways*, issued monthly, and in the *United States Official Postal Guide*.

Atlases

An atlas is a collection of maps bound together in a volume. One of the earliest of these bound map collections was that by the famous Flemish cartographer, Gerhardus Mercator (1512–1594). (Because it had a picture on the cover of the giant Atlas holding up the world, such collections have borne the mythological character's name ever since.) It could be said, however, that atlases were issued as early as the second century A.D., when Claudius Ptolemaeus included a collection of maps in one of the eight volumes of his work on map-making, *Geographia*. It is this work which is supposed to have been revived in time for Columbus' trip to the New World.

Essentially an atlas is a cross between a verbal and a graphic medium. Its gazetteer and guidebook parts are dominated by words, and its maps by representations of the earth's surface. From cover to cover, an atlas begins with a sort of gazetteer table of contents, which locates by map and page the principal major divisions of the world; then follow all the maps, in a sequence that generally starts with the universe and the world as a whole and then proceeds from country of publication to points farthest away; the final part may consist of a gazetteer-index and guidebook.

Atlas Evaluation. First, there is the matter of *format.* In size, atlases vary from the folio 16 x 22 inches of the *School and Library Atlas,* for example, to the standard book size 6 x 9 inches and even smaller. Other format considerations for atlases are legibility and color and the adequacy of the legends and symbols. These will be considered in detail in connection with maps.

A most important atlas criterion is *scope*: how much of the universe and of the world is represented. Some atlases begin with the solar system; others omit such extra-earth representations. In one atlas the world and all of its regions may be represented in proportion to size and significance; in another, the country of origin may receive disproportionate attention.

Another criterion involves type of map. There are physical, political, economic, historical, and other types, and maps showing population density, climatic conditions, or agricultural and mineral resources.

Since an atlas includes a gazetteer, the value of that part must be measured by the standards for gazetteers. In some works the gazetteer feature is confined to the back of each map, but in other atlases a real gazetteer index is provided in the back of the volume.

One must also consider whether the atlas has a *guidebook.* Many atlases feature attractive sections of this kind, with photographs, often in color, of places of interest.

A final and important check on an atlas is its *authority.* What is the standing of the publisher? Of the cartographer?

Basic Atlases. There are many good atlases available, ranging widely in size and in price.

Evaluation Checklist for Atlases

Scope: Regions covered—universe, world, hemispheres, continents, countries, localities?

Type of map: Political, physical, economical, historical?

Gazetteer: Back of each map or back of volume?

Guidebook: Word and picture description of places of interest?

Authority: Qualifications of publisher and cartographer.

Format: Color, legibility, symbols, legends, map size.

Goode's World Atlas (6–7), issued from 1922–1949 under the title *Goode's School Atlas*, is a standard in most school libraries and Materials Centers. The maps are excellent, and the information about surface, climate, vegetation, soils, economic resources, trade, communication, race, language, religion, and a host of other geographical subjects is basic. There is a superior discussion of the difficult subject of map projection.

A more ambitious tool is the *School and Library Atlas of the World* (6–8). It is 16 x 22 inches in size and comes with its own metal stand (at an extra charge). The 133 pages of maps cover the United States and foreign countries. Additional pages provide outline and insert maps, and there are about 115 pages of reference material, including a gazetteer index and guidebook. Ten outstanding geographers have assisted the editors, and the publisher has been issuing geographical materials since 1903.

Other basic atlases are produced by the great cartographic publishers of the United States, including such names as Cram, Denoyer, Hammond, Rand McNally, and others.

The Rand McNally *Cosmopolitan World Atlas* (6–9) includes in its 114 pages of colored maps a number of important features. For example, foreign areas are mapped on the so-called regional basis in such a way that areas surrounding show up in exactly the same detail. A marginal outline locating the area covered is also provided. Maps for the parts of each continent are represented on the same scale as the continental map or on multiples of that scale. Each map indicates scale in four different ways—in miles, kilometers, ratio, and miles to the inch. Topography is revealed on all maps by hachuring, and by the land form method. The *Cosmopolitan*, created shortly after the close of World War II and developed in connection with *Collier's Encyclopedia*, pays particular attention to the new geography created by the air age.

From Hammond comes a whole library of atlases. The 6 x 9-inch *Complete World Atlas*, for example, will fit an ordinary bookshelf. It has virtually the same information that some of the larger atlases have, but its maps are smaller. Perhaps the most comprehensive of the Hammond atlases is the *Ambassador World Atlas* with its 151 large pages of full-color maps, its extensive gazetteer, its statistical data, its street maps of important U.S. cities, and its vast guidebook collection of photographs. Because the *Ambassador* and Rand's *Cosmopolitan* are probably the two most frequently found atlases in libraries, teachers would do well especially to acquaint themselves with their features.

Cram's Unrivalled Atlas of the World features 120 color maps, 56 of the United States, its states, and possessions and the rest of foreign countries and ocean groups. Among notable features are the gazetteer and index to domestic and foreign places, the 74-page history section supported also by maps, and the special unit devoted to the United Nations.

There are other good atlases, and a selected list is included in the appendix. Also, the collection of maps in a good encyclopedia constitutes an atlas of considerable teaching value. In some of the encyclopedias—*Britannica*, for example—all the maps are together in one volume. In others, like *Collier's*, *Compton's*, *World Book*, the maps are scattered throughout the text so as to be proximate to the discussion of the area concerned.

Maps

A flat-surface representation of the earth or of the sky or of a heavenly body or of any part or aspect of them is called a map.

Man has been making maps for a long time. About 200 B.C., Crates of Mallus created his famous "Orb of Dominion," a map of the world which divided our earth into four equal parts. The known part he labeled "the human race"; of the three unknown parts he labeled one "Antipodes." Leonardo da Vinci (1452–1519) devised the "Mappemonde" from a Portuguese globe, dividing his map into eight parts in a way that approaches the modern gore or butterfly projection. But it was Mercator who introduced the famous cylindrical projection that bears his name and that persists in even our modern maps and atlases. Since it is based on parallel meridians, a Mercator map distorts polar areas. This exemplifies the difficulties that confront the cartographer in his quest for a perfect flat-surface representation of the round earth.

As surveying methods improved, so did cartography, and the eighteenth century produced the two names that ushered in many of the modern mapmaking techniques—Guillaume Delisle and J. B. B. d'Anville. In that century some of the European governments began systematic mapping of their own countries. C. F. Cassini headed the first important national project in France, and in 1801 Great Britain began its Ordnance Survey. The United States established the Geological Survey in 1879, which undertook to create topographic sheets at a scale of 1:62,500. Although about one half of the country has now been so mapped, nearly half of these map sheets have become obsolete.

In addition to these national projects, the nineteenth century produced quality maps in some significant atlases by famous cartographers. These included Adolf Stieler, Heinrich Berghaus, K. T. Andree, and John Bartholomew, whose famous *Times Atlas of the World* remains a British classic.

The present century saw the launching of the great world map planned for and presented to the International Geographical Congress by Albrecht Penck. Under this plan the world is being mapped in about 1500 sheets, each sheet of which covers four degrees of latitude and six degrees of longitude, on a scale of 1:1,000,000.

Meanwhile, a considerable contribution to world mapping has been going on in the United States both by government agencies and learned societies, on the one hand, and by commercial publishers, on the other. For example, the American Geographical Society (as a part of the 1:1,000,000 world

A photograph used in aerial mapping. *Courtesy Fairchild Aerial Surveys, Inc.*

map) has issued a 107-sheet *Map of Hispanic America*, and the National Geographic Society, through its magazine and in separates, serves the map needs of a great segment of the people. Among government agencies, the Army Map Service, established during World War II, has provided coverage for many neglected world areas, and aerial mapping by the Air Force and other agencies has contributed significantly to cartographic technique.

Rand McNally, which celebrated its centennial in 1956, has produced some 250 million maps and globes in its history.

In observance of the centennial, the firm has innovated a "merged-relief" map which achieves a three-dimensional effect through the "skillful and dramatic use of oblique shading," showing gradual changes in elevation which previous flat tints could not. Such other American firms as Hammond,

A representative wall map. *Courtesy A. J. Nystrom & Co.*

Denoyer-Geppert, Nystrom, and Weber-Costello have also made important contributions to school map and globe use, and today offer the teacher a variety of effective place media for classroom use.

Map Evaluation. Maps exist for a variety of purposes. Some concentrate on the location of land and water areas. Others identify political units. Still others pinpoint specific places, trace movements and migrations of peoples, describe climatic conditions, or reveal topographic heights and levels. This great variety of map purposes is reflected in the tremendous quantity of maps now available to teachers. Intelligent map selection from the current output should be based both on the quality of the map and on the purpose for which it is to be used. There are about a dozen points to be considered in an intelligent evaluation of maps.

To begin with, *size* is an important element. For individual pupil work, desk maps that range from 6 x 9 inches to large atlas dimensions of 16 x 22, and even larger, are desirable. These come in different formats. They include the maps that occur in text relationships within textbooks, reference books, trade books, and periodicals. But they also include separate maps—maps in loose-leaf notebooks, in atlases, in folders, and on individual sheets. Some of these are outline maps to be written on and developed by pupils. Others are erasable, with slate or cellophane surfaces on which chalk or colored pencils, respectively, can be used.

For class work, there is the wall map. It must be large enough to serve the pupils in the back of the room. For a class of 30 pupils, Arthur Robinson ("Size of Lettering for Maps and Charts," *Surveying and Mapping*, 1950, p. 37–44) has recommended a 6-foot width, and for a world map preferably a 7-foot width. However, most of the good wall maps are closer to a 5-foot width and some of them are produced at 3- and 4-foot widths.

Comparable to the wall map is the projected map. Any desk map can be projected on an opaque projector, even those larger than 8 x 11 inches, simply by projecting particular segments one at a time. Transparencies of maps can also be made for projection on a 10 x 10-inch overhead projector, and 2 x 2-inch and 3 x 4-inch slides can also be made for a class.

Closely related to size is the *area* covered by a map. There are maps of the universe, world, hemispheres, continents, regions, nations, states, and particular localities. All of these areas have a place somewhere in the school program. It is safe to say that the classroom needs a wall or projected map for each of the following: (1) the world, (2) the Western Hemisphere, (3) the United States, (4) the school's state, (5) the school's locality—city or county, or both—and (6) any areas related to a classroom's particular subject field. It is probable that the school's library or Materials Center will include several maps for each of these areas, plus additional maps for both hemispheres, all continents, regions, countries, states, and major localities.

The *type* of map is also an important criterion. The simplest maps for the lower grades are confined to land-mass and water-mass identifications, with a minimum of political boundaries and physical features. More advanced and specialized maps introduce other elements. For example, a full political map will present many units, even down to county, township, and in some cases ward and precinct boundaries. Likewise, a detailed physical map will include, in addition to mountains, plateaus, plains, rivers, lakes, and coastlines, such details as deserts, harbors, and water depths. In this connection, the relief map, employing shades, hachures, contours, and three-dimensional effects, produced through photomapping, is most effective. Stereographic effects, such as "trimet" photography, produced through stereo-pairs selected from a series of continuous photographs, enhance the physical representations.

Other types of maps stress special elements. Statistical maps are combinations of graphs and maps. A population map, for example, may indicate density by a series of symbols on a surface representation. Historical, literary, art, religious, and other subject maps portray information in relation to their locale by pertinent picture symbols. There is, indeed, hardly a school subject that cannot be effectively reinforced by a map.

Other criteria for map evaluation involve cartographic problems and solutions: color, legend, projection, scale, and locater.

Color must be varied enough to accomplish distinctions among physical features and political units. Most good wall maps use about eight colors. Most of them also follow the international scheme for elevations. This is:

Water (sea level)	Blue
Lowlands (less than 1000 ft. above sea level)	Green
1000–2000 ft. above sea level	Yellow
2000–5000 ft.	Tan
5000–10,000 ft.	Orange
10,000 ft. and above	Brown

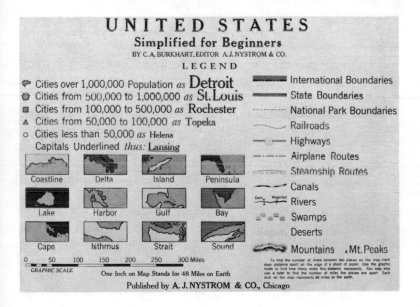

Basic map language. *Courtesy A. J. Nystrom & Co.*

But when it comes to color for political units, a variety of pastels and glosses may be enlisted to separate lands between the borders. To differentiate among several units crowding around a place like Cairo, Illinois, the publisher sometimes uses garish, dark colors that all but make invisible the legends identifying places.

The *legends* themselves must be clear not only typographically but orthographically. Employment of Anglicized forms for foreign names is important, especially for the lower-grade levels. "Wien" (Vienna) and "Moskva" (Moscow), while more accurate, can disturb learning by creating confusion over the names.

The problem of *projection* is more difficult, since it is still subject to limited solutions. A simple criterion is adequacy for the area under consideration. Various "equal-area" projections have advantages, since they are based rather closely on careful study of the particular region. A "grid-comparison" method for evaluating projection in relationship to classroom needs has been devised by Professor A. H. Robinson ("An Analytical Approach to Map Projections," Association of American Geographers *Annals*, December 1949, pp. 283–89).

Scale is stated in a ratio of map to area, such as "1:30,000,-000"—a "Representative Fraction" (RF)—or "75 miles equals 1 inch," which is a ratio of about 1:4,788,000. Kilometers as well as miles are usually indicated on scale bars.

Various *locater devices* are employed by mapmakers to assist users in locating specific places. The most common type is latitude-longitude. Almost as usual is the letter-figure method. Another locater device is the grid graph, a transparent sheet of numbered squares placed over the map. Hearne maps are equipped with a tape location finder keyed to an alphabetical index.

A final set of map criteria is bibliographic and includes such elements as have already been met in connection with book evaluation—*recency, authority,* and *special features.* Some publishers date their maps and all of subsequent revisions in an obvious manner; others hide the dates in keys and symbols. As in books, the standing of the publisher and the qualifications of the cartographers and editors are clues to the quality of the map. Special features are indexes, gazetteers, and accompanying handbooks.

Evaluation Checklist for Maps

Size: Wall or desk proportions?

Area: Universe, world, hemisphere, continent, country, locality?

Type: Political, physical, economic?

Color: Varied, pleasing, standard? Relation to lettering.

Legends: Legible? Vernacular or Anglicized?

Projection: Adequate for purpose?

Scale: Adequate for area?

Locater device: Adequate?

Recency: What is the last revision date?

Authority: Publisher's reputation. Cartographer's and editor's qualifications.

Special features: Gazetteer? Index? Handbook?

Map Sources. Maps are available from a variety of sources. For convenience the sources can be grouped in two classes: (1) Government, societies, and other nonprofit organizations; (2) Commercial firms. The following are representative map producers:

A. *Government, Societies, and Other Nonprofit Organizations*

American Automobile Association, Washington, D.C.—Road Maps, Guidebooks, and Accommodations Directories.

American Geographical Society, New York—Wall Maps, Geographical Aids, Bibliographies, Color Filmstrips.

British Information Services, New York—Wall Maps on the Commonwealth Nations.

National Geographic Society, Washington, D.C.—*National Geographic Magazine* and Wall Maps.

National Council of Geography Teachers, Chicago—*Journal of Geography,* published nine times a year.

Newsweek Educational Bureau, New York—Newsmaps sent monthly to teachers who use *Newsweek.*

U.S. Coast and Geodetic Survey, Dept. of Commerce, Washington, D.C.—Nautical and Aeronautical Charts, Topographic and Planimetric Maps of Coastline and Adjacent Land Areas.

U.S. Geological Survey, Dept. of Interior, Washington, D.C.—Maps for Schools and Colleges.

U.S. National Park Service, Dept. of Interior, Washington, D.C.

B. *Commercial*

George F. Cram Co., Indianapolis, Ind.—Globes, Maps, Atlases.

Denoyer-Geppert Co., Chicago, Ill.—Globes, Maps, Atlases, Models, Charts.

Farquar Transparent Globes, Philadelphia, Pa.
C. S. Hammond Co., Maplewood, N.J.—Maps and Atlases.
Hearne Bros., Detroit, Mich. Specialize in Student Participation Maps on which students can write and erase each day's work.
Historical Publishing Co., Monroe, Mich.—Outline Maps for History and Geography and Special Ones made to order.
Keystone View Co., Meadville, Pa.—Map Slides.
McKinley Publishing Co., Philadelphia, Pa.—Outline Maps.
A. J. Nystrom & Co., Chicago, Ill.—Globes, Maps, Blackboard Outlines.
Rand McNally Co., Chicago, Ill.—Globes, Maps, Atlases, Gazetteers, Guidebooks.
Replogle Globes, Inc., Chicago, Ill.—Globes.
Weber Costello Co., Chicago Heights, Ill.—Globes and Maps.

Representative Maps. All of the producers listed in the foregoing section have maps of value for some learning situations. In keeping with the over-all suggestion of having certain basic wall maps for each classroom, a table of representative map series issued by eight leading publishers is here presented. In each of these series there is a world, continent, U.S., and state map of note:

Publisher	Title	Features	Size in inches	Series
Cram	Simplified	"Markable-Kleenable"	51 x 44	CSP
Denoyer	Physical-political	Graphic-pictorial legend	64 x 44 to 72 x 44 to 64 x 84	SRP
Hammond	International (World) Superior (Continent)	Accompanying handbook	50 x 32 to 44 x 32	International-superior
Hearne	Student Participation	Cellophane surface	44 x 65	SP
McKinley	Wall Outline	No lettering	32 x 44 to 32 x 48	Wall Outline
Nystrom	Barton Simplified	Relief outstanding	64 x 57 (average)	LS
Rand	Simplified Ranally	Globe correlation	65 x 45	SR
Weber	Reality	Related globe-map scale	58 x 44 to 58 x 65	R

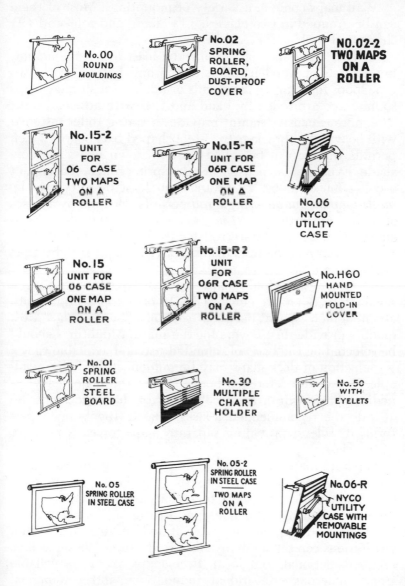

One map company's line of wall map mountings. *Courtesy A. J. Nystrom & Co.*

Wall maps come in a variety of mountings. Most of them can be grouped in two classes: (1) "hang and roll" and (2) "hang and fold."

Of the "hang and roll" group, the least expensive mounting consists of wooden rollers at top and bottom, with two tape loops for hanging from nails or hooks. For storage, maps so mounted are rolled by hand and tied with attached tape. The more expensive mount provides a spring roller fastened with heavy-duty brackets to a steel shaped backboard, which permits the map to be rolled up and down like a window shade. Even more expensive are the spring rollers that mount a collection of maps. These are of at least three types: the *multi-map mount on a single roll* permits selection by a series of index tabs; the *multi-map mount on multiple rolls* is equipped with a separate roll for each map; and the *twin-display map rack* permits display of two maps, side by side, at the same time.

The "hang and fold" maps are less expensive and quite satisfactory. They are cut into 8 x 10 or 9 x 11 sections with about ¼-inch space between sections for folding. Most mounts provide dust covers for the maps. Mountings should be selected on the basis of intended use and available space.

Selection of desk maps may be influenced by those available in text and reference books. All of the major encyclopedia sets provide a good collection of desk-size maps. So also do the recommended atlases. The textbook again performs its role of providing separate maps for each member of the class.

Separate maps are available in a variety of formats ranging in sizes of from 5½ x 7½ to 15 x 20. These are purchasable in quantities of a score to a thousand. The average cost for purchase of 50 to 100 maps is as little as one-half cent each.

Many good maps are available at no cost. Road maps from gas stations can satisfy many state study situations as well as regional, national, and local. Free maps are also available from numerous educational foundations and commercial firms and from the various federal, state, and even local government agencies.

Globes

The most satisfactory map from the standpoint of surface representation is, of course, the globe. A globe may be defined as a reduced replica or model of the sky or of the earth, with the astronomy of the former or the geography of the latter represented on the convex surface. A globe of the sky is known as a "celestial globe." A globe of the earth is called a "terrestrial globe."

The year Columbus began his epochal voyage, Martain Behaim (1450–1506) constructed a globe for the town of Nuremburg that would show the world's news. But this was by no means the first globe. The Greek grammarian Crates, whose "Orb of Dominion" map had been among the first two-dimensional representations of the world, also created a globe. The ancients did know that the world was round, even though many people in the Middle Ages apparently forgot or stubbornly preferred to believe that the earth was a flat circle with Jerusalem in the center. Assisted by Eratosthenes, of the famous Alexandrian library, Crates was able to establish measurements of the earth that were 99 per cent correct. In this way he filled the proper spaces with the Mediterranean countries he knew and then for the rest of the world guessed at three large island continents that almost coincided with North and South America and Australia.

The Behaim globe, 17 centuries after Crates, had the advantage of knowledge gained from the voyages of Marco Polo. But it lacked modern globe-construction techniques. In Behaim's day, the production of a globe involved (1) a ball-shaped mold, (2) a hollow ball made by pasting layer upon layer of paper over the mold, (3) an iron rod on which the globe could turn, (4) a coating of plaster and parchment, and (5) painting (for 15 weeks) of maps and pictures. This slow process was used for many years; for example, Tycho Brahe (1546–1601), the famous Danish astronomer, took 25 years to make his globe.

During the following century, the great popular interest in globes led to national competition. The race to produce the largest globe probably was stimulated by the famous Gottorp model ordered by Duke Frederick of Holstein-Gottorp in 1664. It is 11 feet in diameter, big enough to serve as a comfortable living room inside. As many as 12 people could be accommodated at one time, and when they entered through the door in the side they were met with the sight of a small planetarium consisting of stars painted on the wall in silver, and a crystal moon and sun which rose and set by machinery. In 1713 the Gottorp globe was given to Peter the Great of Russia, but in 1942 the Germans brought it back to Lübeck, where it may be seen today.

Not to be outdone, Louis XIV of France ordered in 1683 not only a larger globe, but a pair of them. The Venetian monk Coronelli made them each 15 feet in diameter and large enough to admit 30 people. Machinery was devised to spin the globes with a flip of the finger.

By 1750 globes were so popular that Englishmen were carrying tiny 3-inch diameter pocket globes designed by a Scotsman named James Ferguson. The Ferguson globe came in a black leather case with a map of the stars pasted inside.

America's first globemaker was a Vermont farmer-blacksmith, James Wilson, who sold his farmstock for $130 in order to follow through his hobby of studying maps and making globes. In 1810 he converted his Bradford blacksmith shop and enlisted all of his skill with hot metals to forge globe balls. The demand for his globes became so great that he had to establish another plant in Albany, N. Y.

Improvements in various printing techniques sped up the globemaking process. Today globes are produced by all of the major map publishers. Replogle devotes itself exclusively to globes and has become the greatest producer in the world.

Globe Evaluation. Since the globe is the only map capable of truly representing the earth's surface, its *accuracy* is of utmost importance. It is generally accepted that handmade globes, because the gores are hand-stretched and wetted, are more accurate than machine-made globes; but they are also more expensive. In purchasing a globe, it is important to determine whether the land areas are proportionate in size, true in shape, and correct in direction and distance from each other.

Globes differ in *scope*. Like maps, some are limited to physical differentiations while others are both physical and political, and still others incorporate a number of additional items of information. Relief is usually indicated through the international color scheme, but some globes provide raised surfaces to show various elevations.

The *legibility* of a globe is important. Although map details on even the largest globes are not discernible in the back of a classroom, it is frustrating when important information is not visible even close up. Consequently legibility of the principal boundaries and land and ocean marks is a requisite.

Globes vary in *size* from 3 inches in diameter, like the Ferguson globe of the eighteenth century or the modern dime-store variety, to the huge 15-foot diameter of Coronelli's historic globe. But the most common sizes found in the nation's schools are the 6- and 8-inch diameter globe for individual study, the 12- and 16-inch for classrooms and libraries, and the 20- and 22-inch slated or project globes used both in classroom and Materials Center. The following table shows the relation between diameter and surface area:

Diameter	Surface Area
6 inches	113 sq. inches
8 inches	201 sq. inches
10 inches	315 sq. inches
12 inches	452 sq. inches
16 inches	804 sq. inches
32 inches	3200 sq. inches

Several kinds of *mounts* are used for globes. The cradle type is most flexible because it permits the ball to be removed, carried about, and measured most easily. A horizon ring is sometimes provided for measuring distance and dividing the hemispheres. The pedestal or floor-stand mount includes an axis on which the globe can rotate. A meridian ring, either split or full, measures distance and helps locate points on the map. The table or plain-stand mount is least expensive

and has the advantage of obscuring no part of the surface. However, because of the inclination of the axis, it is difficult to see the extreme southern areas from the horizontal. Finally, the pendant or hanging mount, counterbalanced by a pulley and cord arrangement, is convenient in rooms where floor space is at a premium, since the globe can be raised when not in use.

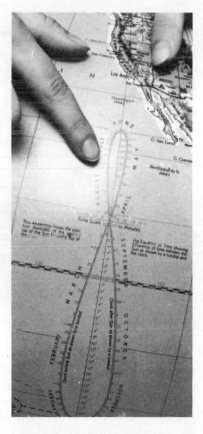

(*Left*) Examples of globe mounts. Top: Cradle mount (*Nystrom*). Right: Stand mount (*Nystrom*). Bottom: Variation of the pendant mount (*Denoyer-Geppert*).

(*Right*) The Analemma. *Courtesy Denoyer-Geppert Company.*

Two *measures* found on some globes have already been mentioned. One is the horizon ring found on cradle globes, and the other is the meridian ring on some stand and hanging globes. A time dial is also provided on some globes along with the meridian ring. This is a sort of world clock which makes it possible to compare time in different parts of the world. It is usually a metal disk, loosely capped over the north pole, and divided into 24 equal parts, one for each hour of the day; one half of the ring is painted black for night hours, and the other half light for day. To operate the time

A slated outline globe. The children are chalking bird flights on the globe.
Courtesy A. J. Nystrom & Co.

dial, the globe is rotated until the meridian ring indicates one's present location. The time dial is set there for the hour of that place at that time. Then by rotating the globe until the meridian is over any place of your choice you can tell the time at that moment in that place. The Analemma, found on some globes, is a figure-eight scale across the torrid zone showing the latitude of the sun's vertical rays every day of the year.

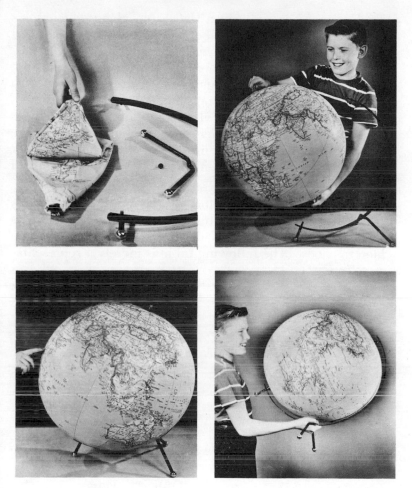

Deflatable globe. *Courtesy C. S. Hammond & Co., Inc.*

Special features found in connection with some globes are worth noting. The slated outline globe, relatively inexpensive because it does not require the meticulous application of gores, is useful at all grade levels in providing opportunity for pupil activity and experience in mapping on a sphere. In

1955 Hammond introduced a deflatable globe which folds into a small package and can be inflated with any pump and deflated by a twist of the valve. It is made of three-ply plastic, printed in bright colors and sharp type. Protected by a laminated sheet of heavy gauge Krene, it can be marked with a grease pencil, and the markings can then readily be erased. A wire stand is provided on which the globe spins freely, as well as a time dial and half-meridian. If punctured, the globe leaks slowly and can be repaired with the furnished kit, or with Scotch tape. It is an 18-inch globe, with an assembled height of 21 inches and a weight of 2½ pounds.

Representative Globes. Most of the producers of maps already listed also manufacture or distribute globes. The teacher can find many globes in the producers' catalogs from which to choose. The following table is merely a representative selection.

In order for each globe are given (1) catalog no.; (2) size (in parentheses); (3) mount; i.e., c-cradle, s-stand, h-hanging.

Producer	6 to 8-inch	10-inch	12-inch	16-inch	Special
Cram	78(7)s	102(10½)s	151(12)s	1603 E (16)s	
Denoyer			G10 Bxo (12)c	G173a (16)s	G203(20) Slated s
Hammond			PP 135 (13½)s		1821(18)s Deflatable
McKinley			(12)s (12)c		
Nystrom	GMP 82(8)s		GM 121 (12)s	GG162 (16)s	GG222 (22)s
Rand			4544ES (12)c 4531E (12)s	1644E (16)c	
Replogle	LM65 (6)s LM85 (8)s	P102 (10)s	P212 (12)s	R1602 (16)s	R3205 (32)c
Weber	604(6)s 808S(8)s		1212S (12)s	430S (16)s 2695 (16)c	

Evaluation Checklist for Globes

Scope: Physical or physical-political?
Accuracy: Accurate area sizes, shapes, directions, distances?
Size: Diameter of 6, 8, 12, 16, or more inches?
Relief: Indicated by color or raised surfaces?
Legibility: Legible boundaries, physical features, and legends?
Mount: Pedestal stand, table stand, cradle, or pendant?
Measures: Horizon, meridian, time dial?
Special features: Slated outline? Deflatable? Other?

UTILIZATION OF PLACE MEDIA

Place media have a language of their own. They present the earth in words, symbols, color, shapes, distances, and direction. Since they tend to be highly abstract, whether verbal or graphic, they may fail to communicate unless time is taken to teach them. The best way to teach them is to relate them to something familiar to the children.

The obvious start is with the elementary classroom. Map it. Convert actual sizes of tables, chairs, and other room furniture to proportionate symbols that will fit on an 8 x 11-inch sheet of notebook paper. This will be the beginning of an understanding of scale and distance.

Then go outdoors at noon on a sunny day. Have the children stand so that their shadows are directly in front of them. Say "You are facing north"; tell them that if they will remember to face the same way tonight they may see the North Star straight ahead of them. Continue with, "To your right is east, where the sun rises in the morning." If you wish, later on, you may add, "We call the morning A.M. because it is antemeridian—before the meridian—because the sun hasn't reached it yet. To your left is west, where the sun sets in the P.M., postmeridian." This will be the start of understanding direction. Now point in the direction of various landmarks— a pupil's home, the public library, the grocery store, the movie, and the river, lake, or mountain—and then determine whether each is north, south, east, or west.

At the next class session, undertake to map the town or the neighborhood. In addition to direction, it will be necessary to use some symbol for each feature. This will introduce map symbols and demonstrate the necessity for them.

Here is an experiential approach to map language. It can be carried through successive steps until the major map concepts are at least meaningful. What these concepts are and at what grade levels they belong have now engaged many teachers, and their findings are available in a vast and rich professional literature. Some of these writings are included in the Readings.

Major Map Concepts

Three of the major map concepts have already been mentioned—scale, direction, and legend. Three more—color, relief, and projection—are also fundamental to map reading. They may be introduced in part at each of several grade levels.

With regard to *scale* and *distance*, the implication of a definite proportion between map and ground must be developed. The classroom and neighborhood first-hand experience can be extended to state, country, and world. As the area grows larger and the map page stays the same, it is necessary to make the same space on the paper cover more ground in the world. To do this the proportion, which is called the RF (Representative Fraction) is changed.

For example, an RF of 1:63,360 means 1 inch to 63,360 inches, or 1 inch to 1 mile. But even such an RF is an inadequate proportion to show Florida on a 9½- x 12½-inch map, which requires a scale of 1:2,425,000 or 1 inch to 38 statute miles. The International World Map is scaled 1:1,000,000, or 1 inch to 15¾ miles, showing how much more detail will be possible on the 1500 map sheets which will eventually cover the globe.

Scale is usually indicated on a map by two lines or bars —one in statute miles and the other in kilometers. (Since the term "statute mile" has come up, it might be well to point out it equals 5,280 feet, while the nautical mile equals 6,080 feet.) On both bars the numbers run outward from zero in both directions.

Direction involves two major aspects besides the points of the compass. One of these is latitude—which provides an opportunity to explain climate relationships, including definition of the low, middle, and high latitudes, the reasons for the seasons, the revolution of the earth around the sun, and the calendar. The other is longitude—which provides an opportunity to explain time, including the reason for the time zones, the rotation of the earth, the Greenwich meridian, and the international date line.

Drill in locating places on a map or globe can become fascinating exploration. Latitude-longitude location of home town or various places of interest can be an enjoyable and competitive contest. In this connection the two Replogle booklets, *World-o-Fun* for children and *See the World on a Globe* for young people, are full of suggestions and information.

With the globe the time concept can be illustrated. Since every degree of longitude equals four minutes, and 15 degrees one hour, the reason for the 24 time zones in the world and the four time zones in the United States becomes apparent. The international date line in the Pacific should stimulate endless discussion. And the calendar with its leap year every fourth year—decreed by Julius Caesar, more accurately modified by Pope Gregory, and revised by the Russians to allow for the extra five hours, 48 minutes and 46 seconds above 365 days required for the earth to travel around the sun—should arouse curiosities that will send pupils to reference books, reading books, and textbooks, and to magazine and newspaper articles. Thus is born classroom research.

The *legends* on maps are now legion. Signs and symbols for cities, capitals, rivers, roads, railroads, mountains, valleys must be recognized. Further, such terms as "peninsula," "archipelago," "bay," "harbor," "island," "isthmus," and "canal" must be translated through pictures. Finally some explanation must be given for differences in spelling—for example,

Vienna (Wien) and Moscow (Moskva). Identification of signs and symbols, definition of geographical terms, and differentiation between vernacular and anglicized spelling of geographical names are all part of the concept of map legends.

Nor can *color* be taken for granted. When Tom Sawyer and Huck Finn were kidnaped in the mad professor's balloon, it was perfectly natural for the boys to doubt that they had left Missouri and were now flying over Indiana. "Why," said Tom, "it is still green down there, and in my geography book map, Indiana is red!"

There are at least two phases to color in maps. The first involves Tom Sawyer's natural doubt. It must be emphasized that there is no standard color scheme for political units, such as states, but that different colors are used to differentiate neighboring political units. The second concerns color language for elevation. For this the international scheme should be introduced.

In this connection the idea of *relief* can be discussed. A collection of maps for this purpose can be displayed which will indicate in succession relief shown by shading, color layering, hachure, contour, three-dimensional photography or drawing, and finally by raised surfaces. The effect of heights on climate should be considered here and latitude relations recalled.

The final concept, *projection*, is a difficult one. It can best be explained by one of several good motion pictures on the subject, such as United World's *Introduction to Map Projection.* But there are also effective readings in encyclopedias, in the introduction to Goode's *World Atlas,* and in several of the trade geography books. Demonstration of the problem of representing a round surface on a flat piece of paper can be accomplished by peeling an orange and flattening the skin, or by constructing a globe and map together. Reasons for the distortion in the size of Greenland should be illustrated through the Mercator projection.

Examples of other projections can be found in motion pictures and in reference books. The end papers of *Webster's Geographical Dictionary,* for example, illustrate six types of map projection. The filmstrip, *Flat Maps of a Round World* is helpful.

Readings

"Geographic Approaches to Social Education," in *19th Yearbook, National Council for the Social Studies*. Washington, D.C.: 1945, 282 pp.

GUYETTE, MERCEDES. "Famous Globes of Long Ago," in *See the World on a Globe*. Chicago: Replogle Co., 1951. Pp. 8–16.

"Interpreting Maps and Globes," in *24th Yearbook, Skills in Social Studies, National Council for Social Studies*. Washington, D.C.: 1953. Pp. 146–77.

JERVIS, W. W. *World of Maps*. New York: Oxford University Press, 1937. P. 208.

ROBINSON, A. H. "An Analytical Approach to Map Projection." *Association of American Geographers Annals* (December, 1949), 283–89.

SHORES, LOUIS. *Basic Reference Sources*. Chicago: American Library Association, 1954. Pp. 111–25.

Subscription Books Bulletin. Chicago: American Library Association, XIII (1942), 1–4; and XVI (1945), 45–62.

Teaching and Learning Geography with Maps, Globes, and Pictures. Chicago: A. J. Nystrom & Co., (n.d.). 14 pp. Reprints of five helpful articles.

Toward Better Understanding and Use of Maps, Globes, Charts. Chicago: Denoyer-Geppert Co., 1953. 23 pp.

Webster's Geographical Dictionary. Springfield, Mass.: G. & C. Merriam Co., 1955. Pp. xxvi–xxvii.

WHIPPLE, GERTRUDE. *How to Introduce Maps and Globes*. ("How To Do It Series," no. 15). Washington, D.C.: National Council for the Social Studies, 1953. 8 pp.

Catalogs of the major map and globe producers contain teaching suggestions.

Viewings

"Airplane Changes Our World Map." EBF. (Film, 22 min., sd., b & w)

"By Map and Compass." International Film Bureau. (Film, 28 min., sd., b & w)

"Flat Maps of a Round World." Popular Science. (Filmstrip, 56 frames, si., b & w)

"Introduction to Map Projection." United World. (Film, 20 min., sd., b & w)

"Maps and Men." Popular Science. (Filmstrip, 44 frames, si., b & w)

"Maps and Their Meaning." Popular Science. (Filmstrip, 53 frames, si., b & w)

"Maps Are Fun." Coronet. (Film, 10 min., sd., b & w)

"We Live on a Huge Ball." Popular Science. (Filmstrip, 52 frames, si., b & w)

7

PICTURES

The ancients valued one picture as 10,000 words, and today, regardless of the word count, the picture remains a potent medium of communication. Its power sells countless products to the adult consumer, and its lure can stir learning in the classroom.

A picture may be defined as a likeness of a person, place, thing, or idea on a flat surface produced by means of drawing, painting, or photography.

This definition can apply to all kinds of pictorial representation—photographs, drawings, paintings, posters, murals, post cards, cartoons, comics, and such graphics as charts, diagrams, and graphs. This chapter deals with their potential, selection, production, organization, and use.

Definitions of pictures and graphic materials are many and the terminology is varied. For example, in audio-visual literature the term "flat picture" is used to indicate a two-dimensional likeness. The terms "three-dimensional" or "stereographic" are used to describe pictures that create an illusion of depth.

Audio-visual literature also contains references to the "still picture." This is a less definite term. Although a picture usually shows motionless scenes, figures, or objects, it is equally true that many "still" pictures convey motion. A race track scene certainly leaves the impression of moving vehicles. Stroboscopic photos of athletic events give an impelling effect of movement.

Finally, audio-visual literature differentiates between "projected" and "nonprojected" pictures. Almost any picture can be either. Whether opaque or transparent, pictures of all types can now be projected, in part or as a whole.

What these definitions really do for the teacher is to herald the teaching potential of pictorial and graphic teaching materials. All around us we see the picture selling consumer goods. The verbal-visual gimmicks created by advertising agencies first catch the consumer's eye and then infiltrate until his sales resistance has been reduced to impotency and replaced by enthusiastic advocacy. Purchase should inevitably follow.

Perhaps a parallel can be created in the classroom. Learning resistance can be capitulated by an eye-catching picture and be replaced by a desire to know. There can be no question that good pictures motivate. They can stimulate expression, develop understanding, add spice and variety to a verbal lesson, and provide opportunities for individual or group study. Pictures are, besides, plentiful, inexpensive, and often timely and carefully documented. They present tremendous potentials for extending verbal experience, reducing misinterpretations that result from vagueness, assisting in the organization of learning, showing processes step by step, revealing comparisons and contrasts, and visualizing quantitative concepts.

Various researches in New York City and Cleveland public schools and by the U.S. Office of Education have shown that even now pictures rank high as teaching tools among all of the classes of Instructional Materials. In general, the larger schools have used more pictures than the smaller schools, and the lower grades seem to rely more heavily on pictures than do the upper grades. A study of 1037 school systems by the N.E.A. showed that 95 per cent used pictorial materials. Other studies seem to indicate that pictures are more effective with children than are verbal descriptions but that the combination of words and pictures is more effective than either alone.

If somehow this picture power can be allied with verbal efforts, a new teaching strength can be gained.

CLASSES OF PICTURES

One way to begin a classification of pictures is to divide them into two broad groups: (1) those produced by hand and (2) those produced by camera.

Within the second group, subdivisions of photographs as black-and-white and color, two-dimensional and three-dimensional, suggest themselves. In books photographs may be conventional, that is, framed, or *bleed*, running off into the margins or edges of pages. Furthermore, photographs may be grouped by size, subject, photographer, and a dozen other ways.

Handmade pictures present even more types and classes than do camera-made. First of all, drawings can be distinguished from paintings and each in turn subdivided by the nature of the materials used, surfaces and instruments (crayons, brushes, pens, pencils, etc.).

To simplify all this the following groups of pictures are considered: (1) photographs and stereographs; (2) drawings and paintings; (3) posters, murals, and postal cards; (4) cartoons and comics; (5) charts, diagrams and graphs.

Photographs and Stereographs

The two-dimensional photograph is by far the most plentiful and useful of all pictures. It abounds everywhere. Because of the unlimited supply, it is both an easy and a difficult material to come by: easy to procure in general, but hard to locate in particular. Yet even this problem is being solved by improved indexing and organizing and the studied relating of visual aids to the curriculum. Pictures for every purpose are now accessible.

Much teaching value can be found in the actual taking of original photographs. Powers of observation, appreciation, and creation are developed by the very process of selecting a camera subject. Pupils who become camera addicts gain not only a critical sense in selecting their subject, but an esthetic appreciation from the effort to develop a good composition. Furthermore, knowledge of the community and its resources results from the search for suitable material for photographing.

Besides the original photographs of amateurs there are the many excellent printed photographs of professionals. Textbooks today abound in superior teaching photos. Encyclopedias and other reference books often arrange for the taking of a special photograph in order to extend the word meanings of an idea, person, place, or object. One of the criteria for a children's picture book is that the picture must convey the message to the very young child without the use of words. Magazines, pamphlets, documents, and other printed material give evidence of the increased reliance on the photograph.

Sometimes depth is produced effectively even in a two-dimensional picture, but there are also three-dimensional photos. They are known as stereographs and are viewed through a stereoscope or the old-fashioned stereopticon. A stereograph consists of a pair of pictures taken of the same subject by a camera with two lenses set in the same relationship as the human eyes. Through the stereograph the two pictures are seen simultaneously, producing a very realistic three-dimensional effect. The modern stereograph employs color to good advantage.

Drawings and Paintings

A drawing is a representation by lines made on a surface with pencil, pen, or stylus primarily, whereas a painting is a picture made on a surface with brush and paint, oil, or water color. The range of drawings and paintings extends from the masterpieces of the great artists to the beginnings attempted by kindergarten children. Reproductions have made available to the classroom the works of the great artists. These have many teaching possibilities. From the files of Materials Centers and libraries can be borrowed good reproductions suitable for framing in the classroom. Some libraries circulate these to the home, already framed, for hanging. Who can measure the effect of a reproduction of a famous work of art hung on the wall of a classroom or in the child's own bedroom?

As in the case of amateur photography, drawings and paintings by teachers and pupils have their added values. There is learning in the very process of creating them. Besides, picture subjects may thus be selected for special classroom purposes.

Posters, Murals, and Post Cards

Posters are large pictures printed on cards or sheets of paper for the purpose of advertising, announcing, or publicizing an idea, event, place, person, or thing. They are sometimes called placards.

Posters are issued by many agencies, and most of them are available free. Travel posters are exceedingly effective in connection with history, geography, language, literature, and other studies related to places. Many commercial firms issue posters specifically for school use. Toothpaste manufacturers have done much for dental education; auto manufacturers for safe driving; meat packers and cereal distributors for dietetics. Many Materials Centers collect posters and make them available for classroom use.

There is much learning value in teacher-pupil production of posters. The best of these deserve inclusion in the Materials Center. Poster prize contests in connection with an event or campaign often produce posters of value as well as desirable learning situations.

Murals, school-made, are usually posters on a grand scale. But murals can also be much more. Dictionaries usually define them as large pictures painted directly on a wall or, by extension of the definition, on a ceiling. But school murals can be made on a roll of paper stretched out on the wall, or on the chalkboard, or on several cards put together on the side of the room.

Special advantages lie in the making of a mural. The cooperative effort which it usually involves is in itself a lesson in teamwork. The esthetic effect of converting a bare-looking room into one that feels lived-in is a lesson in beauty not soon forgotten.

Almost everything is reproduced on post cards—unfortunately, the bad as well as the good. Post cards are available in color as well as in black and white, and they contain pictures of places, persons, objects, as well as reproductions of art masterpieces. Although even the so-called jumbo-size is too small for class viewing, cards can be projected with the opaque projector and, in any case, can be examined by small groups as well as by individuals.

Some teachers keep their Christmas cards for the following year and put them on display immediately after the Thanksgiving holiday. Materials Centers are also beginning to collect Christmas and Easter cards of distinction for loan to classrooms.

Cartoons and Comics

Controversy over the teaching value of cartoons and comics continues unabated. Those who favor the use of cartoon and comic contend they help the child to learn; those who oppose insist they are driving reading out of the child's life. As the terms are defined, cartoons and comics are not necessarily alike. A cartoon is a drawing that symbolizes or caricatures, often satirically, some person, place, object, or event of current interest. In distinction, a comic is a series or strip of cartoon drawings that tells a story.

Editorials on subjects of serious concern frequently find their most effective expression in the cartoon. All of us have found humor in a cartoon that has driven home more effectively a current problem than any number of words possibly could. Cartoons have educational value if they provoke thought and discussion. Their sheer exaggeration often arouses the child's interest in a way almost no other medium can. Cartooning by children may have real learning value and sometimes develops latent talent. Libraries that collect and index cartoons are engaged in activities that may be of real assistance to classroom learning.

Comics present a somewhat different problem. It is estimated that 20 million copies are sold weekly at newsstands. Many parents and teachers are alarmed by this phenomenon. Some contend the comic is a threat to real learning, to character, to community morals. Recent years have witnessed efforts by parent-teacher groups, churches, aroused citizens, and the publishers themselves to regulate and to "purify" the comics. These efforts have taken several directions. One trend has been to stamp with a seal of approval those comics that conform with good taste and are considered "safe" for children. Another movement has undertaken to convert the classics to comic form. A third attempt to make comics palatable has attempted to teach lessons of tolerance. M. C. Gaines, who claims to be the originator of comics and whose All Star Comics sell in the neighborhood of 650,000 copies a week, employs children's reading specialists as advisers, as well as psychiatrists, athletes, authors, and movie stars. Special effort is made to inculcate high moral and ethical principles in his comics.

Nevertheless the older generation continues to ask questions. Do comics lure good readers away from book reading and to lazier media of communication? Are the comics providing the poor reader with the only medium he can understand? Does the comic rob the child of the opportunity to develop those subtler appreciations of life that can never be pictorialized?

The answers to these questions are not yet documented. Some believe that Superman will go the way of Nick Carter and Horatio Alger. Others maintain that the comics will continue to flourish because their allusions to rockets, atomic power, electric eyes, and guided missiles are more meaningful for the children of this age than are the classical references to dragons, chariots, and the Holy Grail.

Graphics

The term "graphics" has long had a dictionary meaning of making drawings. Audio-visual literature, however, developed a whole subject field around this word, concerned with

Cartoons provoke thought and discussion. *Courtesy S. J. Ray, The Kansas City Star.*

the production of all kinds of Instructional Materials. Out of this has developed the professional term "graphics," which describes a class of Instructional Materials that communicates information through a forceful combination of symbols and pictures. Most representative of graphic materials are probably diagrams, graphs, and charts.

By definition these terms are not mutually exclusive. Diagrams are most usually identified as sketches that explain by outlining. A graph is defined as a line (usually a curve) or series of bars showing variable quantities. The whole subject of graphical representation has been developed in a professional field called "statistography." A chart is defined as a sheet that informs by means of symbols and pictures. Dictionaries usually add that a chart may employ diagrams and graphs as well as tables and illustrations. Charts, therefore, appear to be the inclusive media.

Although there are numerous types of charts, the principal forms they may take are tabular, flow, and tree. Comparisons of national armaments, industrial production, or pupil achievements can effectively be shown in tables. Lines of work or direction of processes and procedures in jobs and production setup are represented by so-called flow charts. Genealogy is best indicated in what is known as the tree chart, which shows several roots leading into a single family trunk and offshoot branches that relate descendants. These three forms may be found in nearly all the various types of charts. Possibly the most popular types of charts can be limited to the following:

The *diagrammatic chart or diagram* is usually a sketch that explains by outlining. Shop instructions for equipment operation are aided immeasurably by diagrams. So also are mathematics and science. The language arts have long employed diagramming to clarify grammar, including syntax, construction, conjugations, and declensions. The social studies literature is replete with diagrams of social progress, institutional organization, and government functions.

Graphic charts, or graphs, present numerical data in several ways. Line graphs plot trends or relationships between two sets of data and are usually considered the most accurate graph form. Bar graphs are generally considered easiest to read. Data can be represented by either vertical or horizontal bars, but effectiveness declines when the number of values to be compared exceeds eight. The circle, or pie, graph indicates the portion of a whole devoted to different parts. The federal government's budget expenditures, for example, can be pictorially conveyed by representing the total as a pie or circle and the portions spent for defense, education, highways, etc., as proportionate segments. Pictographs, said to have been introduced by Otto Neurath, Vienna sociologist, have been used effectively in school encyclopedias such as *Compton's* and *World Book*. The figure-symbols Neurath constructed and which he called "isotypes" soon gave promise of becoming an international language.

Data charts present information usually in tabular form and may often make use of drawings and symbols in tables to clarify relationships. An example would be a data chart on sizes of pipe fittings with sketches in scale to show comparisons.

Pictorial charts make use of enlarged photographs or drawings and label the various parts of the item shown for clearer understanding.

Closely related to the pictorial chart is the *phantom-view chart*, an outline view of an object showing the inner workings of a system within it. For example, a phantom-view chart of a house might show the duct-work system for a central heating unit.

The *schematic chart* is similar to the diagrammatic chart in that it uses outlines to show relationships.

SELECTION

Picture Evaluation

A prelude to selection is evaluation. Five criteria for selection are: (1) pertinence, (2) organization, (3) accuracy, (4) artistry, and (5) detail.

The *pertinence* of a picture must be determined by the teacher in relation to what he wants to teach. Only he can judge finally whether the picture is suitable for his purpose.

Several elements enter into the criterion of *organization*. A good picture for teaching purposes has a clear cut center of interest. There must be a key idea and it must be in the foreground, not the background. The visual message must be simple and convincing.

Accuracy can only be estimated against the background of subject knowledge the teacher brings to his teaching. The picture should be technically correct, and there should be proper scale, that is, proper size relationships among the parts as related to the whole.

Artistry is a highly qualitative criterion. There are certain standards of composition, color and shading that are part of any esthetic evaluation of pictures. A good photograph, for example, should provide texture contrasts between metal and rock, between foliage and sky, and among people. There should be a solid base, vertical lines that tie top and bottom together, and a center of interest. In some pictures, of course, specifics of this kind are violated and yet the pictures are nevertheless suitable in terms of the teacher's needs.

Detail is of great importance for learning. Elements must be true as far as possible. The correct impression must be left in the child's mind.

Evaluation Checklist for Pictures

Pertinence: Does the picture show what you want to teach?
Organization: Is the key idea dominant?
Accuracy: Is the picture technically correct?
Artistry: Is the esthetic quality high?
Detail: Does it leave the correct impression?

General Sources for Pictures

Pictures are everywhere. We may begin with *textbooks,* as we did in the second chapter, since pictures abound there. If the modern textbook is distinguished from its predecessors by any one physical aspect, it is the attention given to illustration. It is worth-while, therefore, for the teacher to begin that quest for the right picture in his own textbook and in all of the related textbooks shelved in the Materials Center. To help him, there are such guides as the Rue indexes mentioned in Chapter 3, and picture references in the books' own indexes. But chiefly, discovery of the right picture will come from browsing in the books themselves.

Next there are the *general reference books*. No publisher devotes more of his resources to illustration than does the producer of the school encyclopedia. Few book publishers can afford to invest as much money in the selection, procurement, and reproduction of illustrations. Color pictures in sets like *Compton's* and *World Book*, overlays like those found in *American Peoples'* and *Collier's*, and black and whites in all of the major encyclopedias aid learning effectively and, what is more, are accessible because of superior indexing.

But there are general reference books other than encyclopedias that are good sources for pictures. Consider the dictionaries and their use of illustrations to support their definitions. The teacher should consider particularly the picture dictionaries for little children; these count on pictures to carry the full load of definition in most instances. Annuals like the *Britannica Book of the Year* feature dramatic shots taken of the previous year's major events.

Then there are certain *special reference books*. In the area of art the *American Art Annual*, Reinach's *Apollo*, Gardner's *Art Through the Ages*, and Hourtiq's *Encyclopedia of Art* are only a few suggestions. Literature offers Gayley's *Classic Myths*, Harper's *Dictionary of Classical Literature and Antiquities*, and Garnett and Gosse's *English Literature*, the last especially noteworthy for its facsimiles of the handwritings of famous authors. History presents such pictorial records of the past as the *Pageant of America*, with its full-of-wonders 15th volume containing pictures of the great in American sports; the *Album of American History*, a story of our nation in pictures; and innumerable single volumes that have tried to re-create the past for us in famous photos and drawings.

This is by no means an exhaustive list. It is rather an incentive to search among the "R" books for pictures.

Reading books from preschool through high school are increasing their reliance on illustration. The easy books are, of course, all pictures, one of the criteria being that the child must be able to understand the story from the pictures without dependence on a single printed word. Many publishers' series, such as the Beckley-Cardy "Americans in Action," Doubleday's "Young Moderns Series," Grossett's "Children's Library," Random House's "Landmark Books," Row Peterson's "Basic Science Education Series," Simon & Schuster's "Golden Books" and Whitman's "Pictured Geography," just to mention a few, are strong in illustrations. Book jackets, too, should be saved for their pictures.

A rich source is *serial literature*. Magazines like *National Geographic* and *Holiday* specialize in pictures. *Life's* "Speaking of Pictures," always thought-provoking, is sent to schools free. But most magazines have some illustrations, and the desired picture may be among the least suspected location. Advertisements often are helpful. Teachers will frequently find the best pictures of trains or ships or planes in transportation and vacation ads. Often the advertiser offers these pictures—at low or no cost—printed on a heavier stock and in larger sizes. Periodical indexes are a timesaver for locating magazine illustrations. If a public library is accessible, the *Education Index* and the *Art Index* will prove especially helpful in locating illustrations in periodicals.

Newspapers offer almost an unlimited number of timely pictures. The magazine sections should be especially canvassed for pertinent illustrations. For historical pictures scan the anniversary issues.

Alert libraries and Materials Centers cut out pictures of value from all books, magazines, and newspapers that are about to be discarded. These cutouts are frequently mounted and filed for ready reference under curriculum units or standard subject headings. In addition, librarians index pictures found in various books and serials in their collection. Cooperative indexing by libraries has resulted in a number of worth-while lists of sources for pictures. Indexes to indexes, such as the A. L. A. *Local Indexes in American Libraries,* can establish the existence of various picture lists.

Special Sources for Pictures. Special sources for pictures are legion. So that the teacher may not feel overwhelmed,

there should be co-operation among all of the teachers in a
school with the librarian or co-ordinator. Systematic selection will pay dividends in a tremendous amount of free and
inexpensive teaching materials. There are now aids to picture
selection that offer short-cut suggestions for picture choice
and organization. Two worthy of special mention are Norma
Olin Ireland's *The Picture File* (7–1) and Bruce Miller's
booklet *So You Want to Start a Picture File* (7–2). Mrs. Ireland's *Index to Indexes* and her *Index to Monologs and Dia-
logs*, as well as her book on the *Pamphlet File* already mentioned, are examples of her professional sensitivity to school
and library needs. Mr. Miller is a superintendent of schools
who early in his career discovered the power of the picture
as a teaching tool and devoted himself to the problems of
selection and utilization. His contagious enthusiasm perme-
ates his well-organized booklet.

There are a few specific source lists to remember. Two of
the H. W. Wilson Co. "standard catalogs," one for high
school libraries (1–4) and the other for public libraries
(7–3), are especially helpful. The *Art Index* (7–4) is not
only an index to art periodicals but to museum catalogs as
well. There are also several older indexes. The oldest one,
A. L. A. Portrait Index (7–5), is good for locating portraits
of famous people. The newest is Monro's *Index to Reproductions of American Paintings* (7–6). Ellis' indexes to nature
and travel illustrations and Shepard's *Index to Illustrations*
(7–7) help find pictures on many subjects. The *Costume
Index* (7–8) does a special job on locating illustrations of
clothing, shoes, hats, and other apparel worn at various times
and in various places. A selected list of "Picture Finders" is
included in the appendix.

A few direct sources for pictures include promotional literature of all kinds, especially the type produced by cham-
bers of commerce (to "sell" their community to prospective
visitors and industries), by boards of trade, and by business
and industrial firms. The American Iron and Steel Institute,
for example, will supply pictures and pamphlets on making
steel. The major airlines have aviation education pictures

available. Pictorial maps are available from railroads, oil companies, and food producers. Examples are the Great Northern Railroad of St. Paul, Minn., which issues an attractive free pictorial map of Glacier National Park; Armour & Co., Chicago, who provide a food sources map of the United States; and Conoco of Denver, long famous for its map services to motorists. Calendars, too, are rich in pictorial opportunities. Travelers' Insurance Co., for example, features Currier and Ives prints. A selected list of picture sources is included in the Appendix (7–11).

A simple grouping of picture procurement opportunities around the classes of pictures defined at the beginning of this chapter may prove helpful.

Drawings and Paintings. The *Art Index* is one of the key sources for pictures of drawings and paintings; so also are the reference books previously mentioned, especially Reinach's *Apollo* and Gardner's *Art Through the Ages*, which are virtually dictionaries of the art masterpieces of the past. Most of the museums of the nation issue catalogs (many of them with photographs of the works on display), original lithographic prints, reproductions of paintings and drawings, and also post cards bearing reproductions. Teachers who travel in Europe can collect prints and reproductions at comparatively little cost.

In addition, there are publishers who produce art reproductions for sale (7–12), including Artext Prints, Inc., Westport, Conn., and Art Research Associates, New York. Bruce Miller has a considerable list of these agencies in his booklet *So You Want to Start A Picture File*, already mentioned.

Posters, Murals, and Post Cards. The number of good posters available for school use is countless. General criteria for picture selection should be applied severely. A few posters of high value can be mentioned here. First of all, those issued by the National Safety Council are worthy of inclusion in every school collection. These can be supplemented by many safety posters that appear in large factories as part of their employee education program.

Then there are the many posters relating to citizenship, some issued by governments—local, state, and federal—and some by such organizations as various voters' and taxpayers' leagues. The 17 x 22-inch posters produced by the National Association of Manufacturers are deserving of special mention. Two of these, *Vote Now—Vote Later*, and *One Nation Indivisible* have proved popular.

Travel posters are always effective in geography, history, language, and literature classes. They are produced by airlines, steamship companies, railroads, bus lines, and travel agencies.

Sources for post cards have already been mentioned. Purchase of them in stores is not always necessary. Many libraries have induced teachers and pupils to send picture post cards from wherever they go, which has resulted in some fine teaching collections.

It is generally agreed that the value of murals is in making them. Consequently, most of these should be produced in school. Once produced and used, however, they should not be discarded, but preserved and later shared. They can become an important part of the picture collection in the Materials Center.

Cartoons and Comics. Cartoons and comics belong. A well-selected collection of them in the library is an asset to learning. Careful choice and clipping for the vertical file, organized by curriculum-related subject headings, can make cartoons and comics a useful medium of communication between teacher and pupil. Clippings from magazines and newspapers, cartoon and comic books are obvious sources and can be posted and selected. Good ones may be filed to complete a collection of dramatic value. Pupils and teachers can be encouraged to be on the lookout for examples of lasting value by posting the best on the bulletin board.

Charts, Diagrams, Graphs. Pertinent charts, diagrams, and graphs are found in books, magazines, newspapers, pamphlets and documents; *U. S. News and World Report* features many examples of all three. Because the subjects are timely, the library might do well to index some of them, and eventually, if the magazine is not bound, clip them for the vertical file.

Professional Prints and Sets. This heading is used to distinguish the pictures produced and distributed by educational producers of pictures specifically for the classroom. It is recognized that many of the pictures obtained free or inexpensively are professional in quality. But there are now educational publishers who are creating useful teaching pictures, individual and in series (7–13).

Picture maps should be distinguished from pictorial maps; the former provide activity opportunities for children to color and cut out. The Friendship Press, New York, offers 38 x 50-inch maps in black and white wrapped in cellophane. They include maps of the world, the United States, Africa, Alaska, Mexico, China, Japan, Southeast Asia, and India, and the "Bible in Many Lands."

From the R. R. Bowker Co., publishers of *Publishers' Weekly*, teachers can obtain wall maps, 20½ x 27 inches, that dramatize books.

Informative Classroom Picture Publishers, Grand Rapids, produces a series of *Life in America* classroom pictures. These come in six portfolios, one each on New England, Northeast, Midwest, South, Great Plains, and West. A rather good list of other picture agencies is included in Mrs. Ireland's *Picture File*. This includes museums, societies, publishers, and such government agencies as the British Information Service, which is an unusually good source for pictures.

Creative Educational Society, Mankato, Minn., produces three major series of pictures for classroom use. The first of these is the *Visualized Curriculum Series* in the area of the social studies, with the general theme "Living Together in the Modern World." It is a sequence of 8½ x 11-inch photographs lithographed on heavy card stock, each card also containing text on the back. In all there are some 914 documentary photographs organized into 55 teaching units under such broad subjects as food, shelter, clothing, transportation, communications, and conservation of human and natural resources. Under food, for example, there are 10 units with 177 pictures. A good review of the set can be found in *Subscription Books Bulletin* for April, 1956.

Pictures that tell stories. *Courtesy Informative Classroom Picture Publishers.*

This picture sequence is worthy of consideration by librarian and teacher. It represents a conscientious and careful effort to harness the teaching power of the picture in some systematic sequence and has several features of particular professional interest. The pictures are graded from one through nine for elementary and junior high school. Librarians experimenting with aspects of their indexing techniques have come up with some workable devices. One of these is the picture-finding guide which contains miniatures of all of the pictures. The filing and cross-indexing are other features. And the bibliographic aspect, which includes a list of sources for free pictures to supplement the files, will aid the teacher in selection. This is a teaching tool with unlimited possibilities. For projection purposes, so that a picture may be seen by an entire class at one time, the card format is definitely superior to the bound volume, although opaque projectors are increasingly being adapted for book projection.

Two other sequences are now available or in process. The "Community of Living Things" sponsored by the Audubon Society, contains over 600 full-page pictures with text on the back. The photos were taken by nature photographers of note. A "Creative Science Series," described as a "visual approach to the physical sciences in co-operation with the American Museum of Natural History," is also available. Both of these series are issued in book form. With these three series, the Creative Educational Society has established itself as a creator of teaching picture sequences for three of the major curriculum areas—social, physical, and biological sciences.

PRODUCTION AND ORGANIZATION

Production of Pictures

Most pictures will be selected, but some need to be produced. Even the selected ones will need occasional treatment for preservation and enhancement, such as good mounting and manipulation. Production of pictures and other graphics in the school is desirable for several reasons. Aside from the skill developed in whatever graphic technique is employed, children acquire a content mastery from constructing or re-constructing the facts. The mural is a case in point. A panorama of colonial life drawn on the wall involves checking and rechecking of the facts for the production of accurate pictures. This learning-by-doing device inherent in picture production and the morale-building that results from creation of something tangible are stressed by all audio-visualists. But one additional factor not adequately recognized is the application of the selection procedure to all school-made pictures. The best of them, chosen by teachers and pupils for their inherent qualities and their promise of future use, not only in one class but in other classes in the school, should be selected by teachers, pupils, and librarians together for accession in the Materials Center or library. The selection should be critical and based upon criteria agreed upon in advance. Periodic exhibits in the Materials Center can be used as a basis of judging and voting by a jury of teachers, pupils, and librarians.

The Equipment for Production

Children naturally take to making pictures. Expression with pencil, crayon, brush, or finger seems almost first nature. But as children grow older they seem to become more self-conscious and critical of their efforts. By adulthood most of them are convinced they have no talent and refuse to expose their efforts to possible ridicule.

Many of these same adults are teachers and, like other adults, have no confidence in their ability to perform graphically, even on the chalkboard. Yet I have seen the instructor in graphics in my own Library School perform miracles within days with both college students and teachers-in-service. Indeed, our graphics laboratory, dedicated to helping librarians and teachers gain confidence in their own ability to express themselves graphically, has become entirely too small to accommodate the number of students who seek instruction there. Every teacher could profit from a summer course in graphics. But if that is not possible, considerable help can be obtained on the job with the assistance of the art or drawing teacher, or the audio-visually trained librarian, or even a good manual on drawing.

There are, besides, many equipment aids. These range from devices for lettering and drawing to photoelectronic equipment for photographing and reproducing. There are also materials and gadgets for mounting and manipulating.

Lettering. Free-hand lettering is not as popular as it once was. Before Melvil Dewey introduced the typewriter into the library, a good Spencerian hand was a professional requisite for librarianship. Now librarians must be able to type, and teachers find themselves handicapped without some typing skill. Special typewriters help with specific graphics requirements. There are now bulletin board typewriters useful for display lettering, and script typewriters that emulate the old Spencerian, and a primary typewriter for little children.

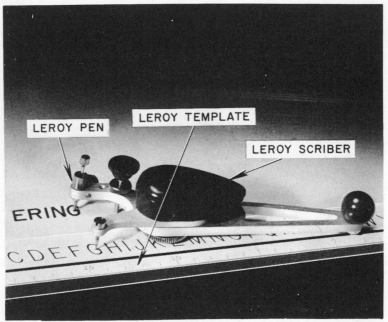

Leroy lettering equipment. *Courtesy Keuffel & Esser Co.*

Still some hand-lettering is necessary in connection with graphic production and reproduction. If for no other reason, pictures must be labeled, and they frequently will not take typewriter treatment. The teacher can use a "Speedball" pen, which comes in six widths and is available in four styles in most art stores. If the school can afford it, he can learn to use a letter scriber. Several types are on the market. The *Leroy* System, produced by Keuffel & Esser Co., Chicago, consists of a scriber, a pen and pin, and templates of the various fonts of lettering. Either vertical or 15-degree slant lettering can be produced by Leroy. *Letterguide,* manufactured in Lincoln, Neb., provides a scriber that offers various sizes and slants of letters, from 40 degrees left to 60 degrees right. Adhesive letters are also available. An example is *Paratype,* sold by Paratone, Chicago, each sheet of which includes one complete font.

One of the newer developments is the electronic and photolettering device developed by the Davidson Corp., Brooklyn, N. Y., called *Protype.* It consists of an incandescent light, lettering film, and a developer. Each film includes capital and lower-case letters, symbols and figures. The process requires only a half minute for development, and the result is lettering by photography. The *Protype* can be used for almost any lettering assignment. It produces certificates and diplomas, for example, perfectly. Sources for lettering equipment are given in the Appendix (7–14).

Drawing. Drawings and paintings; posters, murals, post cards, charts, diagrams, and graphs are always available ready-made. But they can also be made in the school by teachers, pupils, and librarians. Only a minimum list of supplies is needed to produce fairly usable and artistic graphics. From the basic supply given to graphic students in college classes at the beginning of the term, the following are selected:

drawing board	detail paper
ruler, transparent	corrugated display cardboard
T-square	scissors
triangles	paste
drawing pencils	gummed or cardboard letters
soft pencil or charcoal	cellophane tape
colored pencils or crayons	dry mounting tissue
inks and poster colors	masking tape
lettering and ruling pens	tracing paper, glazed and non-
lettering brushes	glazed, for India inks
oil paint	art gum erasers
construction paper	pantograph
	glass, plain and etched

Many working suggestions are contained in manuals. Some of the general principles of importance are: (1) make a miniature working sketch first; (2) choose a size that will enable the entire class to see it, and if possible decide on one size as more or less standard; (3) present one central idea; (4) the filled-in space should not exceed the open space; (5) either contrast dark on light or vice versa, or choose harmonious colors; and (6) make your captions brief and incisive. The day is coming when drawing kits will be made available to all teachers.

Photographing. In photography, the able novice of today can surpass the expert of yesterday in short order. This is so because of new, powerful flash bulbs, sensitive film, efficient cameras and ready-made charts and scales. The variety of cameras available to the amateur range from inexpensive box cameras to expensive and versatile reflex cameras of the press type. All types of cameras have their place in the production of school photos.

No attempt will be made here to discuss technical phases of photography. What will be considered is the kind of photographing that can be used to supplement for teaching purposes the many photos available.

There are several kinds of photos that students and teachers can make which are not obtainable commercially. Pictures of their own activities in class can have much value. Snapshots of group planning, of projects in successive stages of completion, of exhibits, of demonstrations and play-acting can be of use in evaluation, for subsequent undertakings, and for other classes.

Similarly, snapshots taken of school journeys can be used as a basis for class review, documentation of discussions, and future reference. Recreational activities, too, lend themselves to home photography. School camera clubs can be enlisted here.

In all of this photography, the principles of composition should be kept in mind. Center of interest, balance, some attention to detail, and texture contrasts are desirable in photographs.

The production unit of the Materials Center should include a well-equipped photographic laboratory.

Duplication and Reproduction. Mimeograph and other duplicating devices also contribute to picture production.

A compact Materials Center photo laboratory. *Courtesy Alameda County (California) Schools Materials Center.*

Remarkably good drawings have been reproduced by spirit duplicators, as well as by mimeographs and multilithographs. Rubber stamps, stencils, gelatin-pad hectographs, and silk screens are other duplicating devices. Libraries have for a long time used the photostat to reproduce pages from a book, including pages with pictures.

Within recent years a number of photoelectronic rapid duplicators have appeared on the market. The competition among them has been so great that each has sought to reduce the cost and time element below that claimed by the competitors. For example, *Transcopy*, the Remington Rand model, advertises a black-and-white facsimile in less than a minute per copy. *Thermo-Fax*, product of Minnesota Mining & Manufacturing Co., claims to copy in four seconds flat at a

Verifax copier, Viscount model. *Courtesy Eastman Kodak Company.*

cost of four and one-half cents a copy. *Photorapid*, manufactured by Photorapid of America, Inc., promises "unlimited" prints at a cost of two cents each. And the Kodak *Verifax* copiers, offered in four models, provide several copies in one minute at a cost of two and one-half cents each. The important point for this chapter is the fact that now any picture in print can be copied quickly and inexpensively and more libraries are equipped to do this than ever before. Through their contacts with other libraries, school libraries and Materials Centers can obtain that missing picture for the teacher even if it is available only at a great distance.

Organizing the Picture Collection

Selection and procurement are important aspects of picture use, but once selected and procured, pictures must be organized for use. Nothing is more discouraging than mountains of unassorted graphic materials. Such a situation will destroy whatever incentive teachers and pupils may have to communicate graphically. Good organization involves as a minimum adequate storage and filing. Artistic mounting and manipulating can add much to the utility of pictures.

Storage

Materials Centers and libraries favor vertical files for pictures and other graphics that do not exceed the dimensions of an 8- x 11-inch letter, or the larger 11 x 14 legal size. For posters, map-size cabinets are often used; and for murals, map or window-shade rollers. Horizontal filing is also found on occasion, but it is cumbersome and requires digging for the desired item. Since classrooms also need to file pictures and other graphic materials, it would be desirable for every classroom to be equipped with at least one vertical file and with a cabinet for larger materials.

Within the vertical file, manila folders or envelopes can be used as containers. The folders or envelopes should either be numbered and keyed to a separate index or carry subject headings. If numbered, the folders should, of course, be arranged numerically; if subject-headed, alphabetically.

Filing

The vertical file with subject headings is most satisfactory. Headings should be based on a standard list either constructed from the school curriculum or borrowed from a printed standard list. Among possible standard lists of headings are those found in the *Readers' Guide*, the *Vertical File*

Index, the Sears *Subject Heading List for Small Libraries,* or the list in Mrs. Ireland's *Picture File.*

Mounting

Mounted pictures are usually more effective than unmounted and are more lasting. However, if the picture is ex-

Picture mounting. Locally-produced materials are being mounted on heavyweight pebbleboard by means of a dry-mount press. *Courtesy Alameda County (California) Schools Materials Center.*

pendable, of poor quality, and not likely to be used more than once, mounting is unnecessary.

There are several types of mounts. The best all-around mount appears to be the dry mount. This requires equipment: a dry-mount press, a tacking iron, dry-mounting tissue, and a paper cutter. But the process is simple, fast, neat and lasting. Equipment and a booklet with simple directions can be obtained from Seal, Inc., Shelton, Conn.

Mounting can be accomplished by other means. (1) Rubber cement is unsatisfactory if picture is to be shown through an opaque projector as the heat will loosen the cement. (2) Tape, especially of the double-surface masking type, is satisfactory. (3) Wet mounting is best for oversize material like large charts or maps. A cloth, sizing removed, or unbleached muslin and wheat paste and vegetable glue are used in this process. (4) Lamination, in which the picture is imbedded between two pieces of plastic, may also be used.

Manipulation

Often when the exact picture wanted is not available, it can be created from several pictures by fitting together the related parts. Artistic pictures showing the furnishing of a room have been made by cutting out pieces of furniture from other pictures and fitting them into place. Photos of individuals around a conference table have been similarly manipulated. Again this process of manipulation offers a learning opportunity as well as a finished product for class use.

UTILIZATION

There are many ways to use pictures in teaching. A particularly striking one can start a unit off with flying colors. Strategic introduction of others may keep sagging interest up. In the end, pictures may provide review stimulation. Regardless of where in the unit plan they are used, certain general principles are worth considering.

First of all, each picture should be selected because it teaches what the teacher has in mind. It must make its point clearly and forcefully. There must be no question about its relation to the subject. Few rather than many pictures should be used.

Pictures may be displayed on the bulletin board or projected through an opaque projector. One device used successfully in projection is to mount them in sequence on lightweight boards like that used for manila folders and fasten them together with masking tape. Then they can be drawn through the projector almost in filmstrip fashion. Afterward they can be accordion-folded for storage.

Let the pupils help select the pictures for the unit. A period of browsing in the library or Materials Center picture collection, with the opportunity to show, compare, and defend their selections before the entire class, is in itself a learning experience.

Picture discussion should avoid question-answer forcing of points. Rather, comparisons of picture features with details found in readings, films, objects, or on field trips will accomplish more effectively the teaching objective. Even where a picture partially fails to communicate the point, pupil criticisms of deficiencies may serve to emphasize the very elements that need greatest stress. There is even the possibility that the picture may challenge pupils' graphic interests sufficiently to result in the creation of drawings, posters, and photographs by individuals and murals by groups or the whole class. In that case, the old saying may again prove true—one picture will be the equal of 10,000 essay words.

Readings

Audio-Visual Way. Tallahassee: Florida State Department of Education (Bulletin 22B), 1948. Pp. 16–24.

BROWN, J. W. and LEWIS, R. B. *AV Instructional Materials Manual.* San Jose, Calif.: Spartan Book Store, 1957. Pp. 17–97. Compact description of graphics materials and methods.

DALE, EDGAR, et al. *How to Teach With Pictures.* Grand Rapids, Mich.: Informative Classroom Picture Publishers, 1947. 45 pp.

DEKIEFFER, ROBERT, and COCHRAN, L. W. *Manual of Audio-Visual Techniques.* Englewood Cliffs, N. J.: Prentice-Hall, Inc., 1955. Pp. 14–79. Compact treatment of nonprojected materials.

RESS, ETTA S. *Use of Pictures to Enrich School Resources.* Mankato, Minn.: Creative Education Society, Inc., 1953. 32 pp.

SANDS, L. B. *Audio-Visual Procedures in Teaching.* New York: The Ronald Press Co., 1956. Pp. 234–69.

WITTICH, W. A., and SCHULLER, C. F. *Audio-Visual Materials: Their Nature and Use.* New York: Harper & Bros., 1957. Pp. 71–105.

Viewings

"The Language of Graphs." Coronet. (Film, 15 min., sd., b & w)

"Wet Mounting Pictorial Materials." Indiana University. (Film, 11 min., sd., b & w)

8

OBJECTS AND
COMMUNITY RESOURCES

"The more senses we involve the more we learn." That is one of the professional tenets behind our belief in sensory learning. We need only watch elementary school children reach for things as they appear and be convinced that touch, taste, and smell supplement visual and auditory education. The modern school library or Materials Center therefore stocks much more than books, maps, and pictures; it selects, procures, and organizes things and offers them for classroom display. These "things," for want of a better term, have sometimes been called "realia."

Realia, or objects, are tangible *things* used in learning. They constitute a whole format class of Instructional Materials. Included are (1) objects in general, specimens, and relics; (2) replicas, models, mock-ups; (3) dioramas, panoramas, and cycloramas; and (4) displays and exhibits; (5) boards of all kinds—chalk, bulletin, flannel, magnetic, peg.

Instructional Materials of these types have a three-dimensional characteristic predominantly and a five-sensory approach potentially. They should satisfy the most pragmatic educator and assure him of as direct learning as the classroom can afford. They will delight teachers who like to work with the concrete. Those teachers with a flair for doing and making will revel in the opportunities for display and demonstration. And the fact is that they will have most of the children with them.

But what about the rest of our profession? It is easy to condemn them as disinclined temperamentally toward gadgets, or backward in the face of pedagogical progress, or procrastinating with one excuse after another, such as the bulk or inaccessibility of such activities, time-consumption, menace to health or fire hazard. Such condemnation, however, applies to only a small minority of a profession that has always dedicated itself to the next generation. The majority of those who object to what appears to them to be an overemphasis on learning by doing and learning through direct sensory experiences do so on professional philosophical grounds. It is their contention that American education neglects the extrasensory approach to learning, underestimates the mystery of intuition and instinct, almost ignores the intangibles that the child apparently inherits. Consequently, they say, the danger is that as more emphasis is placed on things of this world, the pupil will create less with intangibles, the stuff of which true greatness is constructed; the greater the stress on the concrete, the less opportunity for the child's imagination. The children's own colors of fantasy, they contend, are always brighter than the so-called real ones. Whether one agrees or not, such professional and philosophical argument should be respected and pondered, not condemned.

The truth is probably somewhere in between the two opposing philosophies. Certainly, however, the teacher must use every teaching tool that contributes in any way to the full education of his pupils. He will use books and serials, maps and pictures, and projections and sound as vicarious media of learning, and he will use the direct-experience, three-dimensional objects in their many forms.

KINDS OF OBJECTS

Any classification of things in the world would tax the best system yet devised by man. Even the more restricted grouping of things used in learning has its hazards of overlapping. Nevertheless, for the purpose of broad identification, the following forms of realia are considered: (1) objects, specimens, relics; (2) models, mock-ups, replicas; (3) panoramas, cycloramas, dioramas; (4) displays and exhibits; and (5) boards of all kinds.

Objects, Specimens, Relics

The term "object" is so inclusive that it has been used to identify the entire class of Instructional Materials often referred to as "realia." Any differentiation between objects and specimens, for example, is strained. An object has been defined as any teaching thing complete in itself, and a specimen as one part or unit of a teaching thing. But, obviously, a specimen of Florida sand, or rain water, or mahogany wood, or stainless steel is also an object. The same can be said of a relic, even though relics are distinguished as objects related to the past rather than the present. A Revolutionary War cannon, though a relic, is also an object in its own right. Object, specimen, or relic, each has its place in the Materials Center if it relates to the educational needs of the school.

Models, Mock-ups, Replicas

A model is a representation of an object. Usually the model is smaller or larger than the original. Even if it is the same size, it differs from the original in appearance, material, or operation. Movement is not necessarily a characteristic of a model, but the presence of motion adds realism, fixes attention, and explains function.

Movement is much more an element in mock-ups, which are imitations of the real thing. They were conceived by the armed forces during World War II to explain how equipment works. A simulated telephone switchboard showing connections or a battery, wire, and bell on a panel, revealing cause and effect, are examples of possible mock-ups. The armed forces also had another device called a "breadboard," which illustrated a schematic on a board without necessarily showing how it worked. One other difference between a model and a mock-up is that the mock-up may be distorted to emphasize complex parts while the model is always exactly like the original.

A replica is an exact reproduction of the original, used when the original is precious or rare. Strictly speaking, a replica is made by the maker of the original. The replica has the same relationship to an object that a facsimile has to a rare manuscript.

Cycloramas, Panoramas, Dioramas

A panorama is a picture revealed a part at a time by being unrolled before the viewer. The diorama was said to have been invented by Louis Daguerre, originator of the daguerreotype. As conceived by him, it was a two-dimensional pic-

The Atlanta Cyclorama. *Courtesy Cyclorama, Parks Dept., City of Atlanta.*

ture painted on transparent cloth and looked at through a small opening. Today the diorama, as used in our schools, is a three-dimensional miniature scene showing figures in their native environment. Objects are seldom prepared to scale, but are arranged in perspective to obtain an illusion of depth. For example, buildings at a distance are made to look smaller than those nearby.

The cyclorama is a much larger pictorial representation, partially three-dimensional and encircling the spectator. Perhaps the most famous example in the United States is the cyclorama depicting the Battle of Atlanta which can be seen in Atlanta. The dimensions of this cyclorama are 50 feet high and 400 feet around.

In terms of school possibilities, many subjects lend themselves to dioramas—a fishing village or a log camp, a feudal castle or a circus, the westward movement of the pioneers, or colonial life in America. Dioramas are inexpensive to construct; they produce many of the team values that go into a mural; and they can be made collapsible and portable so that the best of them may become a part of the Materials Center collection.

Displays and Exhibits

There is a distinction made between displays and exhibits. The display emphasizes the two-dimensional and includes layout in newspapers and magazines, posters, painted signs, merchandise arrangements, and window views. Flat materials dominate, and they are intended to interest, influence and inform. The exhibit is primarily composed of three-dimensional materials and is educational in its interest. Although this differentiation between displays and exhibits is made professionally, most dictionaries use the words interchangeably. Basically, both displays and exhibits, as well as dioramas, are the consummation of teaching with objects. To accomplish their purpose of focus on things, displays and exhibits include generous use of a variety of boards—bulletin, peg, magnetic, flannel, and even the chalkboard.

Boards of All Kinds

Schools today come equipped with a great variety of boards. The blackboard, or chalkboard as it is now called because many of them are green, is a classroom indispensable, although it is hardly used to its full potential in most instances. Nor is the chalkboard sufficiently recognized in its relation to other Instructional Materials or to the Materials

Center. It is hardly expected that the library will procure and handle erasers and chalk, although conceivably it might stock colored chalks—and perhaps the recently developed fluorescent kind. But the Materials Center or library can contribute mightily to the more effective use of the chalkboard by the teacher. Chalkboard tracing patterns, stencils, templates, grids, and opaque and transparent projections are a class of materials that will be receiving increased attention by the librarian. More will be said about them later.

Similarly, display or bulletin boards are a vital part of classroom teaching. In the hands of a skilled teacher, they will communicate to all the individual differences in his class. Bulletin boards also have possibilities as display mediums for outstanding pupil work. But their principal potential relies on the selection and procurement of pertinent materials, and in this matter a good school library or Materials Center is important.

Flannel, magnetic, and peg boards have the advantage of supporting objects more effectively than bulletin boards. The flannel board is usually covered with a black flannel, to provide contrast, although a sky-blue flannel is also effective. The objects that adhere to flannel are usually made of felt suede or rough paper. Many of the materials used, available from the library or created in the classroom, are silhouettes, printed pictures, and paintings, all backed with sandpaper or suede felt. One definite advantage of the felt board is the possibility of build-up; an outline map on a felt board, for example, can be developed by progressively adding physical and cultural features to it. In physical education the felt board has been used effectively to teach football plays, moving the player indicators freely in and out of positions. The magnetic or magna board enables the teacher to display three-dimensional small objects on the chalkboard. A large sheet of soft iron is mounted on the chalkboard, and magnets are glued to little figures of people, animals, things, giving them the same mobility on the board as on the flannel board. Figures for the magnetic board should be available in the Materials Center as they relate to a lesson in progress. Finally, laminated wood, pressboard, or pegboard is used for display. By means of bent wire or wooden pegs, three-dimensional objects can be displayed.

SELECTION AND UTILIZATION OF OBJECTS

Evaluation

In place of the museum within or without the school, or as a supplement to it, the library or Materials Center is doing a different job of selecting and organizing realia for teaching purposes. Since there can be no suggestion that these objects are to be mere dust gatherers, the same principles of selection that apply to other classes of Instructional Materials are also applied to realia. To the teachers and pupils who offer collections of stamps, coins, fish, rocks, machine parts, ancestral relics, models, knocked-down dioramas, exhibits, bulletin boards, and other objects of art, science, etc., the librarian today opens his doors of welcome. But at the same time he makes it clear that the Center can house only so much of this material. What has outlived its school usefulness must be returned to the donors unless there is continuing or recurring evidence that a need for this material is perennial. Then and only then will objects become a permanent part of the center, to be classified, cataloged, stored and maintained. Here, again, is the first criterion for all teaching objects—*relevancy*. Are the materials related to specific curriculum needs?

A second criterion pertains to the *three-dimensional quality* of the teaching object. Is the subject one that is more effectively taught through a medium that has depth and substance? If so, does the object in hand communicate these attributes more effectively than other materials—two-dimensional pictures, for example, or the words of a book or a motion picture?

A third criterion relates to the *multisensory quality* of the teaching object. If touch, smell, and taste, or any one of these senses is necessary to an understanding, then the object has an inherent advantage over the book or picture which obviously can communicate only through sight. In that case, are the necessary other senses adequately stimulated?

A fourth relates to *accuracy*. Any model, replica, or mock-up is not necessarily the object itself. There may be differences in size, material, quantity, and quality. This may not affect the usefulness of the simulated object. Accuracy in models is not always necessary. Children's abundant imagination will fill details. We know that children tend to exaggerate what appeals to them—the ears of a donkey, the wings of a plane, the smokestack of a ship. The purpose of the grade and unit may not be fidelity as much as general impression, in which accuracy of detail can be subordinated. But the object should communicate as accurately as the teaching purpose requires.

A fifth criterion is *size*. Few school libraries can afford the space needed to house a Model T Ford, despite its increasing rarity and its pertinence to a study of the history of the automobile. Neither is it desirable to set up a Procrustean bed for all teaching objects, requiring them to fit into a predetermined area. Rather, it would be well to consider all candidates that could be accommodated by the available facilities in the school library—shelves, vertical files, exhibit cases, tables, drawers, cupboards, files, lockers, film racks, etc.

Evaluation Checklist for Objects

Relevancy: Is the object related to specific curriculum needs?
Three-Dimensional Quality: Is depth effectively communicated?
Multisensory Quality: Are all senses stimulated that are necessary for learning?
Accuracy: Is adequate general impression conveyed?
Size: Does the object fit available housing?

Standards for the Collection

Certain standards must be applied to the collection as a whole. In the first place, the ultimate size of the collection must be determined. This decision can be made by teachers, pupils, and librarians together. The value of a collection is not always determined by its size. Nor are duplications advantageous in all cases. Only if the duplicates can be housed in individual classrooms that have a frequent need for them should duplication be considered.

Labeling and indexing policies should be established. All objects should be adequately identified, using not only a short—one word if possible—label, but a few words of description covering place, time, purpose and operation. All labels should be legible, attached to their objects, and protected by shellac or a transparent covering. Items of importance should be given catalog consideration, with subject entry, along with related books, pictures, and other Instructional Materials.

A program of care and maintenance should be established early. Cleanliness and neatness invite use. Periodic inventory along with stock-taking of books and other Instructional Materials will insure availability of items when wanted.

Selection and Use of Objects and Specimens

The only justifiable approach to selection of objects and specimens is from the standpoint of school needs. Area by area, here are some representative objects for the major subjects.

For the biological sciences, live plants and animals of all kinds are important. White mice, fish, rabbits, and birds can be candidates, but their care is something beyond the call of duty of a Materials Center. Interested teachers and pupils will want to keep live specimens near them in their rooms. But mounts of all kinds, pressed flowers and leaves, and shells and rocks kept in exhibit cases, if not in the laboratories, can be located in the Center.

Physical science objects, including radio sets, storage batteries, and dry cells, will probably be in the laboratories associated with them, but they can also be located in the Materials Center for loan to particular classes. In general, most of the science materials will tend to find homes in the laboratories.

For the social studies, the Materials Center should have collections of coins, stamps, relics, and toys.

Mathematics could use examples of slide rules, micrometers, the abacus, compass, scales, and different kinds of rulers.

In the language arts, it would be helpful to know that stage props, printing type and forms, a hornbook and a battledore, were handy.

Examples of fabrics, textiles, threads, and wallpaper, while more properly belonging in the home economics laboratory, have a place in the Materials Center as specimens of things met in many subjects.

Perhaps these are enough illustrations to indicate the broadening concept of the Materials Center and the potential such a resource unit in the school has for the teacher who wishes to supplement his limited selection and procurement facilities with those of a school agency organized to acquire materials on a somewhat grander scale.

Selection and Use of Models

As previously defined, models are three-dimensional representations of objects. If the object is very large—an ocean liner, for example—the model may be very much smaller, but representative enough to give a good idea of what the full-size object is like. On the other hand, if the object is very small—an amoeba or a human hair—the model may be considerably larger. And then there are models that are exact in dimensions but differ in the materials. A model of the human brain may be scaled exactly but, of course, need not be constructed of living tissue. The point to be remembered here is that the relative size must be indicated in order to guard against misconceptions.

There are also cross-sectional models, revealing internal structure. Such cut-aways consist of a collection of parts that can be assembled into a whole. Sometimes the same purpose is accomplished with transparent materials that reveal the inner as well as the outer surfaces.

Models with working parts, such as a working cut-away model of an engine, perform additionally by illustrating objects in action. Better understanding is aided by simplifying and by accenting the essential elements. Often color is used to highlight key parts.

Assembling a model develops skill and knowledge. *Courtesy Models for Industry, Inc.*

The working model differs from the mock-up in one important respect. Models fairly closely resemble the objects, while mock-ups do not. A rigged-up sending and receiving apparatus to demonstrate wireless equipment may, in the case of a mock-up, look nothing at all like the equipment, but it will reveal clearly how the components function.

Selection of models should be based on certain obvious criteria. First of all, models are three-dimensional, so thickness as well as length and width must be considered. The size should be such that the model is suitable for study, large objects being reduced and small ones enlarged. Essentials are emphasized and nonessentials subordinated so that observation may be concentrated. If the model is a cut-away or cross section or if it has working parts, it should be so constructed that it can readily be taken apart and put together again. These are general criteria for selection.

Models to be assembled are available from innumerable supply houses and can also be found in drug and grocery stores. But the value of constructing them in the school must not be overlooked. Model planes, ships, and automobiles are common enough hobby interests to provide a source of supply.

The use of models must never neglect the important element in teaching objects—the appeal to more senses. Touch must be encouraged, and where taste and smell are involved, those senses also must be stimulated.

Selection and Use of Dioramas

The tragedy of school dioramas is so often that much of the creativity is lost once the diorama has served its purpose. True, much of the educational value of a diorama is in its planning and staging. But it is equally true that there is enough inspiration in a diorama to stimulate succeeding classes to emulate and surpass what they have seen produced before. Reconstruction of the good ones from time to time, possibly for location in the Materials Center, might act as an inducement to other classes. Certainly many of the diorama ingredients can be filed and stored somewhere in the Materials Center.

The diorama is the true little theater. It can be set up on its own stage anywhere in a room. Its subject can be anything in history, depicting life in a community or home of any period or place; or it can be a scene out of a literary work, complete with characters, costume, and incident; or it can depict a discovery or an invention, with the inventor and his apparatus dramatically displayed; or it can be pure fantasy aboard a space ship or on the planet Mars. Whatever the choice of subject, the diorama offers an opportunity for creative work.

It is imperative, when the class decides to embark upon such an exciting undertaking, that there be enough encouragement in a central resource center to provide a minimum number of accessories. Increasingly the good Materials Center is prepared to assist the creation of a diorama with information and components, and afterward to provide storage and dissemination for its subsequent use.

Selection and Use of Exhibits

The school exhibit is in many ways the synthesis of teaching with objects. It sums up the learning with real things, acts as an evaluation, and in its own way rewards the efforts of teachers and pupils. To be effective, the exhibit must observe certain principles and enlist many objects and accessories.

A good exhibit, like a good picture, has a central idea or theme. It is dramatic and colorful. If possible, it is planned so that pupils may be working during as well as before and after the exhibit period. This can be accomplished by such processes as weaving, clay modeling, tape recording, picture painting, or any one of a number of learned skills which can be under way in connection with the show. Involving all or as many of the pupils as possible and awarding them all by-lines for their work is psychologically effective in giving everyone a feeling of participation. Especially important is adequate labeling and a sufficient number of signs and posters. These are often the critical elements in exhibit communication. In this connection, boards play an important part. The array of boards now at the disposal of the teacher is worthy of special consideration here.

Selection and Use of Board Materials

Among the boards frequently used by teachers to communicate with pupils, five are of extreme importance:

Chalkboards. Characteristically, the chalkboard is for spontaneous work in the classroom. When so used by the teacher, it is well for him not to forget the techniques that will enhance the chalkboard as a teaching tool. One of the first requirements is legibility. If a teacher's script is difficult to read, then he should print. If he has a tendency to write lightly, then he must bear down on the chalk sufficiently so the student farthest away can read it. Simple drawing can be learned with a little practice, and catchy, pithy phrases can be developed to sharpen points.

At some time before the class begins, the teacher should survey the board from all angles in the room. From this survey he should decide how low or high on the board he may write; how large the letters should be, and just where a glare obscures vision. To accompany board writing, the teacher should always remember to talk to the class and not to the board, and to erase material as soon as possible so that too much will not remain on the board at one time. Screeching chalk detracts. Color attracts.

But important chalkboard work can be done before class. With the help of the Materials Center, the teacher can welcome his class to a chalkboard that will communicate brilliantly to every pupil. There are at least four classes of chalkboard materials that may be borrowed from your library or Materials Center.

On roller shades or in files, the Materials Center may have paper *tracing patterns* of maps, symbols, objects, and diagrams used frequently by certain classes. Examples are maps of the home state, the region, the United States, North America, the Western Hemisphere, and the world. Triangles, squares, circles, pentagons, etc., may be in constant demand for chalkboard work. All of these things, and more, are already prepared on heavy paper stencils perforated with small holes that outline the desired shape. With one of these stencils, the teacher has only to rub a dusty eraser over the holes and connect the resulting dots into the desired outline. Commercial patterns of this type already made up are available from various firms (8–1).

Templates are stiff cardboard, plywood, or sheet metal cutouts of various objects and symbols, such as Bunsen burners, triangles, squares, circles. They are placed against the board with one hand and traced with chalk on the board with the other hand. Templates, too, may be found filed in the Materials Center available at any time for loan to the teacher.

The next chapter will say more about *opaque projections.* Here it is enough to indicate that many pictures and objects housed in the Materials Center can be borrowed, together with an opaque projector, and projected on the chalkboard for tracing.

The next chapter will also describe the overhead *transparency projector* and its advantages. Suffice it here to indicate that Materials Centers also house transparencies that can be projected by the overhead projector and that the projection can then be traced on the chalkboard.

Bulletin Boards. The variety of materials that can be displayed on the bulletin board is almost as great as the individual differences among children: drawing, illustrations, clippings, posters, post cards, holiday materials, cartoons, comics, and on and on. The one characteristic they have in common is that they are two-dimensional. (Three-dimensional materials have been tried, but other boards described below, are more suitable for that purpose than bulletin boards.) Good examples of all of these classes of materials, as we have already discovered, are part of the regular stock of a Materials Center. The problem of selection is most important.

Perhaps these principles will be helpful. A center of interest is as important on the bulletin board as in other media. It should be directly related to the teaching the teacher wishes to accomplish. The first thing the bulletin board must do is stop the passer-by with an eye-catcher. That element, too, will influence choice of materials for the bulletin board. Having been stopped, the viewer will want a simple, clear, pleasing message. It must have balance, unity, and perhaps a dash of color. Captions, legends and explanations will be helpful. With all these considerations in mind, the teacher should be able to weed and choose from the rich collection in his Materials Center.

Flannel Boards, Magnetic Boards, and Pegboards. Flannel boards, magnetic boards, and pegboards are used in display-

A pegboard display. *Courtesy Demco Library Supplies.*

ing three-dimensional objects. Appropriate objects can be selected from the Materials Center collection. To begin with, the felt, suede, and rough-paper objects suitable for the flannel board will as often as not be two-dimensional. They will include silhouette cutouts, printed pictures, various flat symbols, and pictures. But the flannel board will also take cardboard objects, and even pencils, books, and rulers, if they are backed with sandpaper, suede, felt or flocking. Felt boards and cutouts can be obtained commercially from several firms.

The magnetic board has greater possibilities with three-dimensional objects. If powerful enough magnets are attached, even fairly heavy objects can be posted.

Most effective for three-dimensional display is the pegboard. By means of bent wires and pegs, it is possible to support vertically three-dimensional objects of considerable weight. Heavy books, figures, bits of equipment, pieces of art, all are shown to advantage by means of the pegboard.

COMMUNITY RESOURCES

The limited number of objects possible which can be stored within the walls of the Materials Center can be augmented by harnessing the resources of the community. Every locality in the United States is blessed by a number of natural, human, and social resources. Mountain, desert, sea, lake, river, sand dune, forest, wildlife, or whatever other environmental feature nature has bestowed upon the community provides learning opportunities. The citizens themselves in almost any town will include doctors, lawyers, engineers, travelers, military personnel, hobbyists, and specialists of all kinds who may contribute not alone through talk about their unique experience, but with exhibits, demonstrations, and performances. Within the community are social institutions created by these citizens—governmental (the courts), recreational (the playgrounds), protective (the police and fire departments), health (the hospitals), transport (the air terminal), communication (the radio station), and cultural (the public library).

All of these resources within the town or county, and sometimes accessible even in distant places, are at the school's disposal, more generously than many teachers suppose. Their potential has only begun to be tapped in the classroom. Comparative neglect of them can be attributed in part at least to the lack of organization for their use. In part, community resources have probably not played a greater role in classroom teaching because of educational philosophy. There is still considerable inertia in the intermingling of study with life. Yet we accept as one of our cardinal principles the responsibility of preparing youth for citizenship. Certainly some of this responsibility should include guided study of the pupils' own community. What better way can such study be furthered than through first-hand experience with the resources of the local scene?

Approach to Community Study

The purpose of community study is to provide learning opportunities through first-hand experiences with nature, people, and culture. Such opportunities are provided either by taking the school out into the community or by bringing the community into the school. The vehicle in the first instance is the "school journey." Bringing the community into the school involves classroom visits by individuals, or deposits in the school of sample local resources.

The school journey is now a recognized teaching device. It is variously called field trip, excursion, tour, school visit, school-sponsored expedition, and what not. Terminologists will make a sharp differentiation between an excursion and a field trip. The former, they will insist, has for its purpose merely an over-all view, such as a visit to the Grand Canyon. But the field trip, they contend, concentrates on learning specific facts. It is probable, however, that all trips—no matter what they are termed—encompass some concentrated attention to specifics along with over-all views.

The field trip, as it will be called here, involves a number of activities and all of the senses. In the course of excursions, tours, or school journeys, pupils will undoubtedly see, hear, smell, and, where not prohibited, touch objects. On occasion there will be tastes of food and other materials. In addition, pupils may, from time to time, participate in demonstrations, processes, or enterprises. They may interview individuals, photograph subjects, record sounds, and sketch items of interest.

When the community comes to the school, almost the same number of activities and senses may be enlisted. Individuals who talk will be listened to, may be recorded, sketched, photographed, and interviewed. Collections of objects may be viewed, touched, smelled, and even tasted. Whether through field trip or bringing the community to the school, community resources as teaching tools await only proper selection and utilization to become at once a powerful augmentation of the teacher's own teaching efforts.

Community-Resource Targets

The number of community resources available in even the smallest locality is very large. These educational "targets" can be grouped broadly around the headings "natural," "social," and "human."

Natural Resources. In a high school history class, pupils had been studying about erosion in China. Yet just outside the bluff on which the school had been built, erosion had worn gullies of ominous proportions. The variety of natural resources available for study in any locality will vary with the topography, climate, and other environmental features of an area. Most areas will offer opportunities for learning about flora and fauna, and rocks and minerals, and perhaps about streams and waterfalls, forests and timber. Towns located near the sea offer treasures of shells and fish, and opportunities to study sand and water and storms. Inland towns on plains and in deserts, and along lakes and rivers, provide other natural sights and objects. With the help of naturalists and sportsmen, campers and hikers, foresters and sailors, the alert librarian can catalog the natural resources of the locality that relate most closely to curriculum units and call these opportunities to the attention of the teachers concerned.

Social Resources. There are man-made resources worthy of study in almost every town or county. A checklist of these can be developed by grouping the targets around the principal enterprises of the community:

Commercial and Industrial

Banks
Hotels
Department Stores
Office Buildings
Stock Exchange
Factories
Utility Plants (power, light, water)
Dairy
Laundry
Farms
Nurseries
Lumber Yards
Stock Yards

Government

Courts
City Council
Post Office
Weather Bureau

Transportation and Communication

Air Terminal
Railroad Station
Bus Depot
Bridges
Tunnels
Telephone and Telegraph Offices
Newspaper
Radio and Television Station

Recreation and Health

Youth Clubs
Community House
Parks and Playgrounds
Stadium
Sanitation and Health Departments
Hospitals

Cultural

Public Library
Museum
Theaters
Music Programs and Lectures
Churches
Zoo

Human Resources. The talent stockpile in almost any community is potential teaching material. The Metropolitan School Study Council of New York has dramatically opened the door to human resources in its potent pamphlet "Fifty Teachers to a Classroom," by indicating how the teacher can call on this hidden "treasure trove" and augment all of the many materials now used. All that is needed is a systematic plan for discovering these resources and enlisting them at the critical learning point.

In any community men and women in the professions and business, travelers, inventors, baseball players, musicians, painters, actors, military men, collectors, and hobbyists need only an invitation to come into the classroom and share their experiences. Often they bring their collections for exhibit, set up demonstrations, or perform on instruments.

Planning the Field Trip

The teacher who contemplates a community study does so with certain purposes in mind. There is the hope that a field trip, or a school invitation to some person or group in the community, will arouse and interest the class in the subject under study. By providing first-hand experiences, new understanding of the abstractions encountered in reading may be given. Desirable by-products, also, may come from increased community awareness and possibly even participation. Finally, observation at a vocational area may eventually lead to the choice of a career.

If the community study is to take the form of a field trip, then preliminary planning is essential. The steps in such planning must include target selection, administrative clearance, and class preparation. In discussing these steps, let us assume that the planning involves a fifth-grade class studying weather.

Target Selection. If the school has a well-organized Materials Center, target selection might well begin there. The card catalog will reveal materials available in the Center—books, pictures, maps, objects, films, filmstrips, transparencies, etc. But the card catalog, also, should indicate what community resources can contribute to the subject. In this instance there is a local weather bureau, and that fact had been recorded, with a reference to a "target folder" on the shelves. An examination of the target folder should reveal such basic information as location, telephone number, contact, and hours. If another class has previously visited the bureau, there will be a chronicle of the students' experiences and possibly suggestions on how to improve the next field trip.

Administrative Clearance. Having selected the weather bureau as the target, the teacher proceeds to clear the trip with the school principal. With such approval, the teacher alone may then visit the bureau, checking with his contact on time and other details, and previewing for himself the facilities that will be available. In some instances the contact may be invited to the classroom as a preliminary "human resource" to arouse the children's interest in the field trip.

Dear_____ (Parent's Name) _____

    We are planning a class visit to_____ (target) _____

on_____ (date) _____ _____ (time) _____ to study

_____ (purpose) _____. We believe this will be a valuable learning experience for_____ (pupil's name) _____, who has already expressed a desire to go and a willingness to abide by the code of conduct and safety developed by the class, signing his name along with other members of the class. _____ (pupil's signature) _____

    If you concur in your child's desire and agreement, will you please sign here, authorizing participation in this field trip.

                          _____ (Parent's Signature) _____

Thank you.

                    Yours sincerely,

                          _____ (Teacher) _____

After that the teacher has at least two important administrative obligations. First, transportation must be provided.

School buses covered by insurance are preferable. Conveyance in private cars increases the hazard and makes each auto owner personally liable. Second, the parent's consent is essential. Standard forms have now been developed by school systems. A possible form is shown on page 239.

Class Preparation. Lesson plan and Instructional Materials will have played their parts before the field trip is undertaken. If the contact, too, has appeared before the class, readiness for the trip will be at a high pitch. Such preliminaries as letters to the parents, principal, and contact requesting permission will have been attended to if such letters are part of the plan.

Class discussions should center around what the pupils already know about weather and what they want to find out in the weather bureau. In this connection, a list of questions to be asked at the bureau, if they are not answered by what they see, should be compiled. Technical terms that are at present understood only in dictionary definitions should be noted for further amplification on the visit. Material to take along should be considered; notebook pads and pencils for everyone may be desirable, and a camera and a tape recorder might perhaps prove helpful. Individual assignments can be given to various class members.

It is desirable for the class to draw up its own code of conduct for the trip. Discipline self-imposed is always preferable. Into the code, which may take the form of army "general orders," can go orders relating to safety, conduct, respect for guides, and plans for letters of appreciation to those who made the trip possible. A "buddy" system comparable to that employed by the army in group swimming, where two individuals are responsible for one another, may be adopted, or the group may be divided into squads of four with a reporting squad leader.

On Target. At the scene of the field trip it will be important for the teacher to watch out for several possible learning failures. One of these may result from the diffidence of certain class members who hang back too far and never see operations or equipment at the moment of demonstration or description. Another may be caused by the overly aggressive few who monopolize the guide's attention and succeed in closing out the view for others. A third type of failure occurs when pupils overlook important details or exaggerate trifles, and at such times the teacher must try to restore balance. Conflicts with information previously obtained from readings or viewings should be reconciled or corrected if possible.

Follow-up. After the field trip a number of activities will serve to clinch the experience. Discussion and comparison of notes taken will resolve differences and bring a consensus of understandings. Some of these understandings will be reported in letters to parents and friends. But most of them should be organized into a report that will be placed in a target folder—the chronicle of this class' field trip to the local weather bureau.

The Target Folder

Some school systems have developed field trip guides for their teachers. These are helpful as far as they go, but they can be supplemented if each class will record its experiences on a field trip not only for the purpose of clinching its own learning, but to provide information for succeeding classes that undertake similar trips; in just such a manner, the Air Force provides its pilots with target folders about various areas. Field-trip target folders can be organized according to a standard outline, such as the following:

1. *Place:* Plainville Weather Bureau
2. *Reporting:* Miss Katherine Jones' 5th grade field trip, April 5, 1958
3. *Address:* 2065 Ellis Ave.
4. *Telephone:* 2–8849
5. *Contact:* Henry Hurricane, chief meteorologist
6. *Visiting Hours:* Monday–Friday 9 A.M.–5 P.M.
   (visited, 9–11 A.M.)
7. *Conveyance:* School bus
8. *Traveling Time:* 25 minutes each way
9. *Travel Route:* Hamton to Main, to Lake Shore Boulevard, to Ellis, and north
10. *Admission:* free

11. *Guide Service:* Mr. Hurricane and his assistant, Mr. Sunshine
12. *Maximum number:* 30 (27 made the trip)

Chronicle at Target

   a. text, including observations and remarks by pupils and teacher
   b. handouts by weather bureaus (samples)
   c. photos, taken by class
   d. tapes recorded by class
   e. objects given to class

Readings

BYE, E. C. *How to Conduct a Field Trip.* Washington, D.C.: National Council for the Social Studies, 1952. 8 pp.

COLLINGS, M. R. *How to Utilize Community Resources.* Washington, D.C.: National Council for the Social Studies, 1952. 7 pp.

COMMITTEE ON HUMAN RESOURCES OF THE METROPOLITAN SCHOOL STUDY COUNCIL. *Fifty Teachers to a Classroom.* New York: The Macmillan Co., 1955. 44 pp.

JENKINS, J. W. "Let's Make a Diorama," *See and Hear* (November, 1948), 36–37; (January, 1949) 35.

RYAN, MARION L. *How to Use a Bulletin Board.* Washington, D.C.: National Council for the Social Studies, 1953. 6 pp.

WITTICH, W. A., and SCHULLER, C. F. *Audio-Visual Materials: Their Nature and Use.* New York: Harper & Bros., 1957. Pp. 211–42.

Viewings

"*A Field Trip.*" Virginia Education Department. (Film, 10 min., sd., b & w)

"*The City.*" *Curriculum Films, Inc.* (Filmstrip, 25 frames, si., color)

Part III

The World of Sight
and Sound

9

STILL PROJECTIONS

An image reflected at some distance, usually on a screen, is a projection. In psychology the verb "to project" means to externalize thoughts and feelings so as to give them objective reality and that is literally what a projection does. When the images move, the projection is a motion picture; when they remain stationary, the result is a still projection.

Still projections as teaching tools have a distinct advantage over nonprojected graphic materials. A picture or an object that is not projected can be seen only with difficulty by pupils in the back row. When projected on a screen, the same picture or object may be enlarged sufficiently to be visible in detail to all members of the class.

Still projections also have some advantages over motion pictures. Their stationary nature permits greater deliberation in viewing. Furthermore, except in the case of filmstrips, still projections may be presented in different sequences and brought back with great ease for a second look.

There are, of course, some limitations to the use of all projections. They are not as ready for use as are nonprojected materials. Equipment and preparation are necessary before projections can begin to communicate. Skill in projection, although easily acquired, is also a prerequisite. A screen, too, must be obtained if the walls are not light enough, and darkening of the room is necessary for some types of projection; in warm weather, darkening also entails consideration of proper ventilation.

Despite these limitations, however, the still projection brings drama and newness into the classroom. It arouses, lures, and approaches individual differences in a unique way.

A wide range of projections is now available on all subjects, graded for the needs of every age and grade level.

A major division of all still projections can be based on whether they are opaque or transparent. Opaque materials require different equipment, lighting, and often location of the projector from what is needed for the projection of transparencies. Light cannot pass through materials that are opaque. All books, magazines, serials, and pictures and most objects are potentially opaque projections. They can be projected through an opaque projector, which will be described.

Transparent materials are those that transmit light rays or can be seen through. These include glass slides, filmstrips, and other transparencies. They may be projected through one of several types of transparency projectors, also described later.

In this chapter, still projections are treated in the following order: (1) opaque projections and the projection equipment; (2) transparent projections and projection equipment; (3) individual classes of transparencies, including (a) slides (2- x 2-inch and 3½ x 4); and (c) filmstrips; (4) stereographs; and (5) microprojections, which may be either opaque or transparent.

OPAQUE PROJECTIONS AND PROJECTION EQUIPMENT

Opaque Projections

Anything opaque and within the dimensions of 8½ by 11 inches can be projected for viewing by a whole class or group. Larger opaques can also be shown in parts. Among the kinds of materials suitable for opaque projection are book illustrations and text. The opportunities here are almost unlimited. A single copy of a book can be read together, with every pupil following the text on the screen. Illustrations, which normally must be displayed by holding the book up to the class, so that the back row has to strain to see, can now be projected very large. The same applies to flat pictures of all kinds—drawings, photographs, charts, diagrams and graphs, cartoons and comics, post cards, and parts of posters.

But even more helpful is the fact that objects can be projected—not only two-dimensional ones, such as stamps

Using the opaque projector. *Courtesy American Optical Company.*

and leaves, but such three-dimensional ones as coins, rocks, shells, keys, watches, and other small and not too thick realia. Innumerable opaques of all kinds are available in the Materials Center. Items of which there are only single samples can be projected whenever it is desirable for the class to see them at one time.

In addition to the fact that materials can be shown to an entire class at the same time, opaque projection offers certain other advantages. It provides a means of protecting materials of value. One showing or even several to a class is easier on materials of high quality than individual handling by 30 or more pupils.

More important, however, are the teaching possibilities with the opaque projector. As was indicated in the section on graphics, it is possible to reproduce a small map on the board in whatever dimensions are needed for total viewing by the class. An 8½- x 11-inch map in an atlas, for example, can be projected on the chalkboard at a distance of 25 feet to produce a map image 10 feet wide. The map can, of course, be made smaller if desired. With chalk the teacher can outline the map on the board and use it to fill in whatever detail he wishes to build up during the class period. Such use of opaque reproduction need not be limited to maps; objects, figures, and forms of all kinds can be traced on the chalkboard by projecting them in the desired size.

One important class of opaque materials is the students' own work. Papers and drawings of all kinds lend themselves to opaque projection. A theme can be read and corrected as a class project by casting the paper on the board. The same can be done with problems in mathematics and science, with designs and sketches of clothing, interior decoration, typing exercises, and indeed, with almost any individual student's assignment that could be viewed by others with profit. These examples merely suggest the teaching potential of the opaque projector.

Subject by subject, and level by level, the opaque projector offers learning opportunities. A service bulletin for classroom teachers called *Opaque Projection Practices*, published by one of the manufacturers of projectors, the Charles Beseler Co., is replete with tested suggestions for teaching with the opaque projector in all subjects. Reading readiness, penmanship, spelling, composition, literature, and library skills have all been taught effectively with the aid of the opaque projector.

Opaque Projection Equipment

Opaque projection is simple despite the formidable look of one of the heavier projectors. Needed are a projector, a screen, and darkening facilities. Skill in using these can be acquired by the teacher quickly and easily. Better yet, pupils can be taught by the teacher to operate the projector from the back of the room while the teacher is free to teach from the front or side.

An opaque projector. Crank (a) moves the platen (b) for inserting opaque materials. Switch (c) turns on the light and fan. The lens cover (d) is opened and the lens focused by the knob (e). By manipulating the lever (f) an arrow of light can be pointed at any spot on the material projected on the screen. *Courtesy Charles Beseler Company.*

The opaque projector (9–1) is based on the old magic lantern principle. A strong light is directed on a picture or object which is reflected by a tilted mirror through a lens onto a screen. Important parts of the opaque projector are the housing, the lens, the aperture or opening, the lamp, the cooling system, and the feeder. Housings have been streamlined, lightened, and improved for handling. They include handles for carrying and tilting devices for raising and lowering. Lenses on most standard models are 4 to 5 inches in diameter.

The aperture is the projection opening; usually it is 10 x 10 inches in an opaque projector to permit horizontal or vertical projection of 8½- x 11-inch pages. Illumination of the copy is accomplished by the projector's 1000-watt lamp. A cooling system which consists of a fan and a motor also frequently performs the second duty of producing the vacuum for holding down the copy. The feeder is a sort of conveyor belt that eliminates the necessity for raising and lowering the platen on which the material is placed. Copy is fed in on one side and released on the other.

It is unnecessary for the teacher to become an expert to operate an opaque projector. All that is necessary are these steps: (1) the projector is wheeled into place, or placed on the stand or table in the position from which projecting is to be done; (2) it is connected to the floor plug, and the switch is turned on; (3) the copy is inserted by raising or lowering the platen, if it is that type, or it is rolled into place; (4) the focus is adjusted so that the image is clear by turning the focusing knob. Opaque projectors are now equipped with pointers—a little arrow with which you can point to the specific part of the image—also controlled by a knob. One added suggestion: if a book is to be projected a piece of window or other heat-resistant glass should be used to hold the page flat.

Other elements necessary to projection are a screen (9–2) and proper darkening. There are three principal types of screens. The matte or flat white screen is almost any surface

—chalkboard, bulletin board, plywood, fabric, celotex, plaster board—covered with several coats of flat white paint. A bed sheet, put up on the wall, can also be used, or just a light-painted wall. There is a justifiable aversion to this latter type of improvisation by the audio-visualist, because such surfaces often do not have adequate reflective power and because it is considered false economy to do without as important a bit of equipment as a screen. Silver, aluminum-coated, and other metallic screens are especially suited for three-dimensional projection, and, of course, do well with two-dimensional material. The glass-beaded screen reflects the most light and is therefore the most satisfactory unless the room is of the shape that requires pupils to sit at a wide angle to the screen.

There are also translucent screens which transmit rather than reflect light. These work with the projector behind rather than in front of the screen. Because this type of projection is suitable only for small groups seated near and directly in front of the picture, the screens have limited classroom use.

The best location for the screen in a classroom is where it is darkest and at a height where the bottom level is eye-height for the seated viewers. The projector then should be about 4 feet high so that the light will pass over the pupils' heads. Screens are constructed in the shape of oblongs, with a height-width ratio of 3:4. They range in size from 18 x 24 inches to 15 x 20 feet. A screen 30 x 40 inches is estimated to be suitable for showings to as many as 23 viewers. Screens permanently assigned to a room can be mounted on the wall, roller-shade fashion. Portable varieties are also available on tripods or on stands for desks.

Despite improvements and innovations, it is still unsatisfactory to project opaques in daylight. For best results, therefore, the classroom should be darkened. The best way to darken a room is with opaque shades designed for that purpose. If the classroom is not equipped with them, then a black duckcloth can be hung in such a way that it can be drawn across the entire side of the room. If there is considerable wall space between windows, drapes can be hung on curtain rods over each window instead.

TRANSPARENT PROJECTIONS
AND PROJECTION EQUIPMENT

Transparent Projections

Slides and filmstrips are the two principal classes of transparencies. They have all the advantages of projected materials in general—they are dramatic, eye-catching, instructive, and attention-focusing, and provide enlargement and reproduction assistance. But they have some special features of their own which make them superior to opaques in some respects and inferior in others.

Transparencies generally require less darkening. The overhead transparency projector, for example, can be operated in full daylight. It can also be placed in front of the room, enabling the teacher to face his class while projecting his transparencies.

Opaque projection has the advantage of greater availability of materials. Almost anything opaque can be projected. But transparencies have to be prepared, and such preparation involves time and money. However, the number and variety of transparencies, both noncommercial and commercial, are very much on the increase.

To begin with, camera fans are producing 2- x 2-inch slides in color, mounted on cardboard called "Readymounts," in such quantity as to constitute almost a major supply of transparencies in themselves. Also, the preparation of 3½ x 4 glass slides has reappeared as a hobby, offering a revived opportunity for projecting art work. Finally, filmstrips are being produced, both commercially and in schools, in enormous volumes. The result is that the total supply of transparencies is now quite adequate for subject and level needs. A final booster for transparency projection is the series of recent innovations in equipment for producing transparencies. These will be mentioned again later.

Transparency Projection Equipment

The most common equipment for the projection of transparencies is the filmstrip projector. Despite the variety of models and the variation in devices, the filmstrip projector is really very simple to operate. Essentially it consists of these parts: housing, lamp, series of lenses, fan and motor, and film channel and knob. The housing is smaller and lighter than the opaque projector's, and has a tilting device and focus mechanism. Near the film channel is the knob which is turned by hand in order to draw the filmstrip through the projector. This knob is connected to a sprocket wheel that engages the sprockets of the filmstrip.

Filmstrip-slide projector—shown with the filmstrip attachment that permits showing both single- and double-frame filmstrips. This attachment can be removed easily by turning a setscrew; then the slide attachment (not shown) can be inserted. *Courtesy Viewlex, Inc.*

Filmstrip projectors usually can project slides also. Such projectors come with 2- x 2-inch slide carriers which have two compartments that permit loading and unloading of slides while one is in projection. There are also 2 x 2 slide viewers, as well as projectors which range widely in price.

The Society for Visual Education offers an inexpensive film-strip viewer called the E-Z Viewer that weighs only one and a half pounds and can be used at a desk. Hand slide viewers are also available.

Usually used for 3¼- x 4-inch slides, this horizontal projector also handles 2¾- x 2¾- and 2- x 2-inch slides. *Courtesy Charles Beseler Company.*

As in the case of the opaque projector, the power of the lamp, the focal length of the lens, and the size of the aperture are important. For classroom projection, the 500-watt lamp is desirable, although 300-watt lamps are still common. With large groups in an auditorium, the 1000-watt lamp is a necessity.

Most filmstrip projectors come with a lens which produces at a distance of 20 feet a single-frame image of approximately 32 x 43 inches. For larger classrooms a lens of 7-inch focal length is preferable, because it can produce at 50 feet an image approximately 58 x 77 inches. Such a lens also has the advantage of projecting a 2 x 2 slide at that distance so that the image is about the same size as a 16-mm motion picture projected the same distance with a standard motion-picture projector.

Horizontal and Overhead Projectors. The 4-inch slide (3¼ x 4) is most commonly projected by the so-called horizontal projector. It is operated from the rear and has a slide carrier. It provides greater brilliance than the overhead projector, but its superiority ends there.

A most serviceable teaching projector is the overhead. It is so called because the instructor can stand in front of his class beside the projector, which projects overhead onto the screen. The overhead can handle any size of transparency, beginning with the 2 x 2 slide and going on up to the 10-by-10. It also comes equipped with a 100-foot cellophane roll which is pulled across the light field with a small crank; on this roll teachers and pupils can write or sketch with a wax pencil. Above all, it is unnecessary to darken the room.

One of the fine features of the overhead is the opportunity for overlay. It is possible, for example, to have a series of transparencies placed on top of the other to build up a complex subject from its simplest elements. The study of anatomy, for example, can be developed by presenting in succeeding overlays various parts of the anatomical structure.

There are various combinations of transparent projectors and also transparent-and-opaque projectors. The most common combination is filmstrip and 2 x 2 slide. The Beseler "Slide King" handles 2 x 2, 2¾ x 2¾, and 3¼ x 4 slides. Projection Optics Co., Rochester, N. Y., has announced the "Transpaque II" with one projection for overhead and opaque. Optional equipment includes slide holders for 2 x 2 and 3¼ x 4 slides and filmstrips, and a tachistoscope. (The tachistoscope is a mechanical flashboard, an apparatus for testing recognition, attention, and memory, which flashes images on a screen for measured periods of time, usually from 1/100 of a second to one second.) Audio-visualists, as a rule, are not enthusiastic about combinations and urge separate projectors for different purposes.

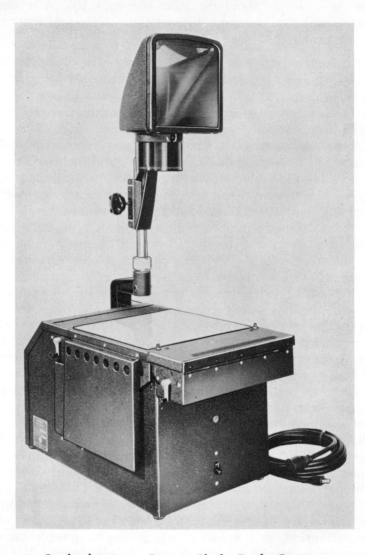

Overhead projector. *Courtesy Charles Beseler Company.*

INDIVIDUAL CLASSES OF TRANSPARENCIES

Slides

The slide materials now available both in 2 x 2 and 3¼ x 4 are plentiful. Many of these can be obtained in sets like those issued for subjects from art to transportation by the Keystone View Co., Meadville, Pa. A great many other slides are available free and can be located in the *Educators' Guide to Free Slidefilms*. Some of the agencies that produce 2 x 2 slides include the American Council on Education, America Dental Association, American Museum of Natural History, Coronet Films, Encyclopaedia Britannica, Society for Visual Education, and the U.S. Office of Education. Among the agencies that produce 3¼ x 4 slides, the National Geographic Society and the National Audubon Society should be noted. Firms like Denoyer-Geppert and Keystone produce both kinds of slides.

Supplementary to all of these commercial offerings are the school-made slides. Teachers and pupils with their own cameras can take all of the 2 x 2 slides that can be shown during any unit. In black and white or color, the 35-mm film is the basis for the slide. Selection from among these productions for inclusion in the Materials Center is in itself an educational lesson.

Even more economical to produce are the 3¼ x 4 slides. These can be made with plain or etched glass, cellophane, binding tape, and colored pencils and inks. Etched glass has been treated with an acid or slightly roughened on one side so that the crayons or inks may be directly applied without danger of running. If plain glass is used, a thin gelatinous coating is applied on one side, or it is treated with a dilute shellac, glue dissolved in water, or cooking gelatin. Directions for making ten kinds of slides are described in J. S. Kinder's *Audio-visual Materials and Techniques*.

Larger transparencies for the 10 x 10 overhead are also beginning to appear in greater volume. But more important are improved and economical ways of producing these. In

(1)

(2)

(3)

(4)

(5)

(6)

Vu-Graphics, "a manual of Vu-Graph Projection," Allan Finstad, educational director for Charles Beseler Co., has written an excellent section on "Making Your Own Transparencies" by hand, the dry-ammonia method of reproduction, the direct positive reproduction, and color transparencies and overlays.

An inexpensive technique of transferring printed matter from a magazine to a more permanent and usable acetate base is known as "lifting." The steps of the process are shown in the accompanying illustration. It was first developed by Professor Frye at Indiana University and subsequently refined and simplified by Charles Gidley and Mary Alice Hunt at Florida State University. The magazine paper must be of a clay-coated type to be usable for lifting. Since nearly 90 per cent of the library-recommended periodicals qualify, here is an economical method to convert opaque pictures in magazines to transparencies that can be projected in an undarkened room with the overhead projector.

Transparency production and reproduction have also been greatly improved recently. A photo-copying process that uses the chemical diazo and is identified by the trade name Ozalid (diazo spelled backward with an *l* inserted between *a* and *i*) provides an inexpensive method for producing transparencies. In another process, using the so-called Projecto Printer, a transparency is produced in four steps: (1) the

---

The lifting process (*left*): (1) Dipping frosted acetate into the rubber cement. (2) Completing the dipping of the acetate. Excess cement runs toward the bottom. After dipping the acetate, the picture is dipped in the same manner and both are hung to dry. (3) When both the acetate and picture are dry, they are sandwiched together. A rubber roller may be used to make sure that the two surfaces coated with rubber cement are in close contact. (4) The "sandwich" is then placed in straight vinegar or a vinegar rinse to soak for 5 to 10 minutes. When the paper begins to loosen at the edges, it may be peeled away from the acetate, leaving the inks (and some paper fibers) on the rubber cement. (5) The paper fibers and clay residue are rinsed away in cool water. A cotton swab may be used to help remove the residue. Then the transparency is allowed to dry. (6) When the transparency is dry, it may be sprayed with a clear plastic, which protects the surface and tends to clear any remaining haze on the transferred picture. *Courtesy Florida State University.*

drawing is traced on translucent paper; (2) the paper is exposed to a violet ray; (3) the paper is placed in contact with film for two minutes; and (4) the transparency is developed in an ammonia developer. It was estimated at the

A transparency photo-copying machine. *Courtesy Ozalid.*

Florida State University workshop that an 8 x 11 transparency could be produced at a cost of 26 cents and an opaque of the same size for ½ cent. A Polaroid Land camera could also produce such a transparency, but at a somewhat higher cost. The principal point is that the obstacle to the use of transparency projectors—namely, the cost of transparencies—is steadily being overcome.

Filmstrips

A filmstrip is also a transparent projection, but it differs from slides in that it is a fixed sequence of related stills on a roll of 35-mm film. Variations of the term "filmstrip," such as "stripfilm," "slidefilm," and "filmslide," have created considerable confusion. It now appears that the word "filmstrip" is on the way to universal acceptance.

Each of the stills in a filmstrip is called a frame. In single-frame filmstrips, the pictures are connected vertically; in double-frame, the pictures "run" horizontally. A typical filmstrip contains 20 to 50 frames, is several feet long, and is rolled up in a cylindrical metal container.

Sound filmstrips are accompanied by recordings with record speeds of either 78 or 33⅓ revolutions per minute. These recordings carry the narrations and sound effects for the filmstrips. An audible signal indicates when the next frame is to be shown.

Compared with the other types of transparencies, filmstrips have both advantages and limitations. The filmstrip, because of its fixed sequence, is not as flexible for individual stills as are slides, which can be shown in any order. Since it is a still medium, the filmstrip cannot represent motion as effectively as can the motion picture. The filmstrip is easily damaged and not easy to repair. It is, however, noninflammable, since the base is cellulose acetate, a material which is resistant to ordinary wear and tear. When damage does occur, it is because the sprocket holes tear easily from faulty threading. Rubberized rollers provide some protection.

On the positive side, filmstrips have definite advantages over both slides and motion pictures. Because of their fixed sequence, they provide a plan of subject development that is often lacking in scattered slides. The fact that the filmstrip is a series of stills offers an opportunity for deliberate study not found in the motion picture.

The history of the filmstrip goes back to just before 1920 when Underwood, of New York, put their large photo library on 55-mm film. Later Slidefilm Co. took over these film rolls for distribution to schools. When the 35-mm became standard, the filmstrip's popularity increased. A decline set in during the 1930's but once again the filmstrip is on the upgrade. This is undoubtedly due to specific teaching potentials in this medium.

For a detailed stationary examination of a subject, the filmstrip is an excellent teaching tool. It can reveal step-by-step developments as deliberately as the slowest learner requires. Motion can be reduced to a slower pace than even the slowest-motion movie.

In evaluating a filmstrip, several criteria must be considered: (1) Relevance to the teacher's purpose is paramount. Does it help the teacher teach what he wants his pupils to learn? (2) How good are the pictures? Do they meet the standards of center of interest, drama, clarity, and other features expected of any good picture? (3) Is the sequence logical and psychological? Will pupils be able to follow it? (4) What about the photography? Is it clear or fuzzy? (5) What of the treatment? Is it balanced or is it biased and distorted? (6) The legends and captions must come in for consideration. What about the vocabulary level in relation to the grade, and how much do the words help the pictures?

There are now many good filmstrips from which to choose, and some excellent selection sources are available. Vera M. Falconer's *Filmstrips—A Descriptive Index and User's Guide* (9–4) describes 3000 filmstrips produced prior to January, 1947. The H. W. Wilson Co. issues the monthly *Filmstrip Guide* (9–5) which began where Falconer left off. It follows the Wilson method of cumulation and of listing filmstrips under subject as well as title. Other selection aids include the *Educators' Guide to Free Slidefilms* (9–6) already mentioned in connection with slides, and the Library of Congress list issued now in connection with the union catalog. Film catalogs of rental libraries administered by universities and ex-

Some suggestions on using a filmstrip are shown in these six frames selected from the filmstrip *Teaching with a Filmstrip. Courtesy Society for Visual Education, Inc.*

Gauge the screen time of each frame by the interest and needs of the group.

Show again any part of the filmstrip needing more study.

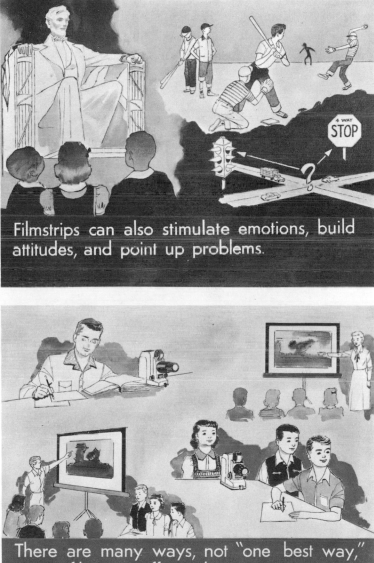

Filmstrips can also stimulate emotions, build attitudes, and point up problems.

There are many ways, not "one best way," to use filmstrips effectively.

tension agencies also list filmstrips available for rental, but most of these libraries urge schools to purchase rather than to rent filmstrips.

Three-dimensional slide projector. *Courtesy Bell & Howell Co.*

Increasingly, school libraries and Material Centers are stocking filmstrips and classifying and cataloging them with books and other Instructional Materials. This is especially true now that so many filmstrips are being produced to accompany books. A notable recent example is the Yale University Press *Chronicles of America* filmstrip series to accompany its famous set of books.

An important producer of filmstrips and filmstrip projectors is the Society for Visual Education, a business firm. Its filmstrips relate to every level and subject of the school curriculum. A monthly *Filmstrip Forum* issued by SVE contains many suggestions for successful filmstrip use.

There is considerable agreement on basic principles for filmstrip use. In the first place it is always good practice for the teacher to preview the filmstrip and fit it into his lesson plan. Presentation of the filmstrips should be preceded by some introductory remarks by the teacher intended to arouse interest. This introduction might well include such points as what the filmstrip is about, why it is being shown and what the class should get out of it.

The filmstrip itself should be shown during the beginning of the period. Legends may be read out loud by the teacher or by a pupil. Discussion during the showing of a silent filmstrip should be encouraged. Repetition of individual frames or of the whole filmstrip may sometimes prove highly desirable. Relating the filmstrip to other Instructional Materials is most important—to reading, to a field trip, to other still pictures, or to teaching objects. As a follow-up, a quiz or theme offers review opportunities.

Evaluation Checklist for Filmstrips

Relevance: Does the filmstrip help teach what pupil needs to learn?

Quality: Do individual frames meet picture standards of center-of-interest, drama, clarity?

Sequence: Is it logical and psychological?

Photography: Is it clear?

Treatment: Is it balanced and objective?

Verbal: Are legends and captions adequate?

Stereographs

In the opinion of some, the three-dimensional picture is the most realistic of all. As previously indicated, the stereograph consists of two pictures of the same scene taken from slightly different angles by a camera with two lenses set about as far apart as the human eyes. The two pictures are viewed separately but simultaneously through a projector known as a stereoscope. Both stereo photos and stereo transparencies provide an illusion of depth.

Because stereoscopes in the past have permitted only one person at a time to view the stereograph, there has been a tendency not to consider this medium a projection. However, stereographic transparencies are now being projected on a screen and the viewers are being provided with special glasses designed to make the three-dimensional image stand out. Despite limitations imposed by the necessity for a special screen and glasses for the viewers, and a tendency toward exaggeration of depth in close-ups, the three-dimensional picture remains the most forceful projection yet discovered. Material Centers are now stocking stereographs as never before, and providing stereoscopes in quantity reminiscent of the presence of a stereopticon in many 1890 homes. Also, stereoscopes and commercial stereographs are being produced at low cost.

Microprojections

Micromaterials, often referred to as miniatures, have introduced another revolution into learning. By means of various types of microprojectors, microscope slides (called microslides) are made visible to an entire class at the same time. The advantages of these microprojectors are many. There is an immediate economy in eliminating the expense of individual microscopes. Pictures are greatly enlarged. Every pupil sees precisely what he should see, and the instructor is sure of it. Among the phenomena effectively shown through microprojectors are fibers, fingerprints, blood smears, optical principles of light, crystals, foods, minerals, chemicals, and bacteria. An example of a microprojector used in science is the "Bioscope," manufactured in Tulsa, Okla.

An equally exciting development in miniatures is the appearance in libraries of microtexts. There are now four types of microtexts, two transparent and two opaque, with projectors or readers to fit the materials. The two transparent microtexts are microfilm and microfiche. The former is a roll of 35-mm film that looks much like filmstrip. Each frame can cover a large part of a page of newspaper text. The latter is a single 35-mm frame mounted on cardboard, not used much in the United States but popular in the libraries of Europe.

A microfilm projector, or "reader." *Courtesy Eastman Kodak Company.*

The two opaque microtexts are the microcard and the microprint. The former is a 3- x 5-inch celluloid card that contains a 60-page issue of a magazine, including advertisements as well as articles and pictures. The microprint is 6 x 9 inches and includes 100 pages of a book. Each of these materials has a reader designed specifically to accommodate the size and form of the microtext. Libraries are now stocking microfilm, microcard, and microprint as a means of saving storage space and protecting rare or expensive materials.

Readings

ANDERSON, PAUL. *Short Outline of Tachistoscopic Technique*. Meadville, Pa.: Keystone View Co. (n.d.).

BROOKS, MARY ESTHER. "Lantern Slides and How To Make Them," *See and Hear*, 1946: (April), 65–73; (May), 70–79; (October), 48–50; and (November), 29–31.

CROSS, A. J. F. "Three-D in the Elementary School," *Instructor*, LXIII (January, 1954), 17.

CYPHER, IRENE F. "Filmstrips to Use in the Classroom," *Instructor* Supplement, LXIII (June, 1954), 31.

FINSTAD, ALLAN. *Vu-Graphics, A Manual on Vu-Graph Projection*. Newark: Charles Beseler Co., 1952.

HAMILTON, G. E. *How to Make Handmade Lantern Slides*. Meadville, Pa.: Keystone View Co., 1952.

———. *The Stereograph and the Lantern Slide in Education*. Meadville, Pa.: Keystone View Co., 1946.

KINDER, J. S. *Audio-visual Materials and Techniques*. New York: American Book Co., 1950. Pp. 575–78.

SIERGIEJ, E. J. "Using the Opaque Projector in Tool Subjects," *Instructor*, LXII (June, 1953), 92–93.

Slides. Rochester, N. Y.: Eastman Kodak Co., 1949.

TAYLOR, J. Y. *Opaque Projection; A New Frontier in Teaching*. Buffalo: American Optical Co., 1941.

WIMMER, M. "Microscopic Projection and Micro-photographic Slide Making," *Educational Screen*, VIII (January, 1939), 8–9.

Viewings

"Enriching the Curriculum with Filmstrips." Society for Visual Education, Inc. (Filmstrip, 59 frames, b & w)

"How to Make Handmade Lantern Slides." Indiana University. (Film, 22 min., sd., color)

"Slidefilm in Teaching." Young American Films. (Filmstrip, 46 frames, b & w)

10

MOTION PICTURES

To a large number of teachers all over the nation the motion picture is the medium that symbolizes the term "audio-visual." Audio-visual experts would prefer teachers to consider motion-picture films just one class of many good Instructional Materials. But it is natural for teachers to place the movie in a special category.

The motion picture can communicate through sound and sight simultaneously. It blends words, pictures, objects, motion, and color to make an indelible impact on children's minds. Through a series of techniques it brings reality into pupils' experience almost first-hand.

Consider animation. By photographing a series of literally thousands of drawings, each showing a progressively slight change of movement, the figures come to life and move when the drawings are projected in rapid succession. Or think about "photomontage" in motion pictures, where several scenes appear on the screen at one time to present a lightning whirl of objects. Or look at the marvel of "time-lapse" photography, which enables a viewer to see the petals of a flower open up before his very eyes. If the increasing marvels of "Cinerama" and "Todd-AO" on the commercial screen are also considered, one can understand the awe with which the teacher watches this miracle of man's inventive effort enter the classroom as a teaching tool.

The motion picture can be defined as a rapid sequence of pictures projected on a screen to create, with the help of human persistence of vision, an optical illusion of moving figures and objects.

The invention of the motion picture cannot be attributed to any one individual or even to a single year. Although the United States Post Office by its commemorative fiftieth anniversary stamp set the year as 1894 and by implication made Thomas A. Edison the inventor, a motion picture device was exhibited at the Chicago World's Fair in 1893; and two California inventors, John D. Isaacs and Edward Muybridge, experimented with the possibility of moving pictures for several years before. In fact, the discovery of "persistence of vision" and the phenomenon that images appear to move can be traced at least as far back as Ptolemy in 130 A.D.

The motion picture today, both 16-mm in the classroom and 35-mm in the theatre, is an instructional medium of as yet unlimited potential. Alone or in combination with other teaching materials, the film has provided the teacher with another device for arousing pupil interest, for re-creating the past, for demonstrating the complex, or for condensing the information that frequently requires a considerable portion of a lifetime to experience first-hand.

A conservative estimate of the number of 16-mm motion pictures available for educational use is well over 16,000 titles. This number does not include many films now out of print nor those produced by individuals—teachers, pupils, parents, and others—that have been used in one way or another in the schools. The problem that confronts the teacher is very much like that which faces him with books and other classes of Instructional Materials. He must somehow select from this proliferation the small number of films he can use in any class during a given school year. Likewise, he must make some decisions that do not confront him in selecting other materials.

The initial expenditure for a film is at least ten times as great as for a book. This does not mean, necessarily, that the per pupil cost is higher. On the contrary, a $50 film shown to as many as 1000 students in 40 sections of a college biology class costs only a fraction of one cent per pupil. But the fact remains that the individual teacher cannot, because of financial limitations, select as many films as book titles. This enforces even more strict application of selection criteria for films than for almost any other class of Instructional Materials.

Storage for projectors and screens. *Courtesy Alameda County (California) Schools Materials Center.*

Furthermore, the teacher as selector has an additional selection decision to make in the case of films: shall he recommend purchase of a title for about $50 or rental for about $1.00? There are a great many film libraries located in state universities, extension divisions, and commercial agencies that rent to schools. Rental rates are usually based on length of film and whether color or black and white. A typical rental scale in use at these various libraries is that published in the film catalog of Flordia State University, which is given on the following page.

Length (minutes)	B & W	Color
5–8	$1.00	$1.50
9–14	2.00	3.25
15–19	3.00	4.50
20–24	4.00	5.75
25 and over	4.50	5.75

For the rentals above, schools may use a film for from one to five days, exclusive of week ends. Postage at the reduced educational materials rate is paid one way by the school. In general, it might be suggested that a film be rented and tried first. If the frequency of its use subsequently increases, purchase may prove to be more economical.

As in book selection, study of announcements and reviews is helpful as a prelude to selecting films. Even more useful is the preview. Many school systems conduct film previews for teachers as an aid to selection. Florida State University has offered four new films for preview every Tuesday night for a number of years. Usually the films in any one preview night are devoted to one teaching area, such as science, literature, or government. Discussion leaders stimulate the audience to express opinions and vote for or against the purchase of an individual title.

Classifications of Motion Pictures

Films can be classified in a variety of ways: by length, color, sound, technique, producers, content, grade level, and perhaps from the standpoint of other considerations. At least the first three listed are included in the bibliographic entry for a film; the others are usually part of the annotation.

Length. Length is always indicated in terms of minutes, rather than in number of feet of film. One standard reel of 16-mm film is approximately 400 feet long, and the running time is 10 to 11 minutes.

Color. The letters "B & W" that appear in a film entry indicate that the film is in black and white. Color usually costs a Materials Center twice as much. What the teacher must consider with the librarian is whether to spend money for one film in color or two in black and white. A nature film teach-

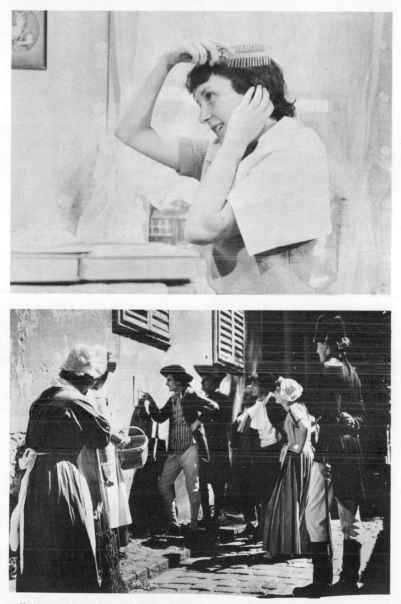

Stills from the 16-mm educational motion pictures. *Personal Health for Girls* and *The French Revolution. Courtesy Coronet Films.*

ing the color of plants and animals is obviously shortchanged by black and white. But an etiquette film on dating for teen-agers may do very well without color.

Sound. There are comparatively few silent films now. Nevertheless, they have a place and are used effectively in studying football games and other athletic activities, lands and travels in geography, and art reproductions. Sound some-times adds little to a picture, especially when the narrator pontifically points out the obvious. The term "sync sound" (synchronized sound) describes sound that accompanied the action of the scene rather than sound—usually music or the voice of a narrator—that was dubbed in after the picture was taken. Sync sound, although more difficult and expensive, should be used where it will do the job better than a narrator in the background. At a preview there may be considerable difference of opinion as to whether a particular film could be improved by sync sound. Coronet's *Johnny Appleseed,* for example, stirred heated debate at one preview session, be-cause a number of teachers felt vehemently that an oppor-tunity for a realistic film was lost by not employing sync sound and dialogue.

Technique. Many techniques are now used in film pro-duction. Only a few of those met in school films are men-tioned here. Direct photography records audio-visually things as we normally hear and see them. But some impres-sive variations have been developed to aid learning.

One of these relates to changed-speed photography. "Slow-motion," so-called, is motion-picture recording by a high-speed camera that can take pictures of action too rapid for the human eye to catch. Instead of photographing at the usual rate of 24 frames per second, the high-speed camera shoots many times that number. When a film so taken is then projected at the normal rate, the human eye can detect details that would otherwise be unnoticed. For example, the movement of every muscle of a pole vaulter as he clears the bar can be studied. "Time-lapse" photography is the reverse of slow motion. By setting a camera to take still pictures at a rate of one frame every fifteen minutes, the growth of a plant over a period of days or weeks can be seen in a matter of a few minutes, simply by showing the stills at the normal rate of 24 frames per second.

Animation is the process by which the appearance of motion can be imparted to drawings. This is done by photographing a series of drawings in which the position of the figure or object is gradually and progressively changed and then projecting the film at the normal speed of 24 frames per second. Morton Schindel of the Weston Woods Studio has used a technique somewhat akin to animation to produce the stories of children's books with the original illustrations. By means of clever camera work, he achieves a semblance of movement. The sound track includes an unpatronizing reading of the text by a narrator, simple sound effects, and some background music. Animation is, of course, symbolized and personified by the work of Walt Disney. Within this technique there is a great range of movement, from the extreme animation of the cartoon to the relatively static motion of art masterpieces used in some educational films. In the latter case, the question might well be asked whether the filmstrip is not the more natural and economical medium.

Microphotography is the technique of photographing things unseen, or of reducing things to the point where they can be seen only through a microprojector. Mention of this technique was made in the last chapter in connection with still projections such as microtexts and microslides. But amoebic and other invisible specimens of life can also be photographed and projected. Coronet has produced a motion picture, *The Cell,* showing the growth and division of this element of life. Small insects like the ant and the bee can now be watched in their many activities through the microphotography.

Other techniques employed with effective teaching results are "X-ray," "telescopic," and "close-up" photography. X-ray photography undertakes to film internal parts of the body. In telescopic photography distant or dangerous views are brought close to the viewer by means of a special telescopic lens. The close-up is a scene taken at close range so as to bring out small details on a large scale.

Motion pictures are sometimes classified, therefore, by the camera techniques employed or stressed.

Producers. Films are also classified by their producers. There are several broad classes of films that can be established on the basis of their origin. A great many teaching films are now being produced by schools themselves, by colleges and universities, and by nonprofit associations and foundations. The National Education Association, for example, is the producer of the dramatic *Freedom to Learn* and the Library of Congress of its counterpart *Freedom to Read.*

Government agencies represent another class of educational film producer. The Department of Agriculture and the Office of Education have issued motion pictures of classroom value. State agencies—and, with increasing frequency, local governments—are producing not only promotional films which have value in geography teaching, but motion pictures with effective lessons in conservation, safety, government, health, and a score or more potential school areas.

The big sources of classroom films are the companies which produce instructional films. There are many of these, ranging from large corporations, like Encyclopaedia Britannica Films (EBF) and Coronet, to individual enterprises that may produce no more than a single film. A noticeable trend is the production by book publishers, of films that are correlated with textbooks.

Commercial entertainment film companies, which in this country mean Hollywood, have also contributed 16-mm motion pictures to the classroom, although not in the quantity and quality which might be desired. An interesting phase of Hollywood's classroom relations is the films that resulted from Teaching Films Custodians (TFC), founded in April, 1938, as an outgrowth of a stated purpose of the Motion Picture Association of America (MPAA), "to develop the educational as well as the entertainment value and general usefulness of the motion picture." In furtherance of this purpose, MPAA had as early as 1922 surveyed with the National Education Association the theatrical films adaptable for classroom use. A pioneer series of 16-mm silent films for school use was produced by Eastman in 1926. By 1937 some 75 excerpts from Hollywood feature pictures were receiving experimental consideration in the classrooms. An appropriation of $50,000 made possible a review of some 2000 Hollywood films, from which 364 were chosen for school use. Out of this activity came TFC, charged with the custodianship of the films owned by the participating companies. Eight motion picture companies co-operated in this enterprise, which received the enthusiastic endorsement of educators. But in 1956 two of the companies—Loew's MGM and Warner Brothers—withdrew, apparently to establish their own 16-mm services.

Finally, there is a class of motion picture known as the "sponsored" film, offered free to educational agencies by industry and business as a public relations device. Many of these films are highly professional in form and educational in content. Most of them avoid advertising their product directly. An example is the animated cartoon produced by Johnson & Johnson on baby care. The only reference to their products occurs toward the end of the film, and then only indirectly when the mother reaches for a can of Johnson's talcum powder. Films of this type are produced by automobile, oil, airline, telephone, and other concerns.

Form Classifications

To the teacher-selector the primary classification of films is one based on form, content, and level. Three fundamental educational film forms are recognized by most authorities.

The Documentary Film. The "documentary" film is a realistic, factual presentation of a problem. Origin of the term is credited to the British producer John Grierson, who applied it in his review of Robert Flaherty's South Seas film *Moana.* Flaherty, considered the greatest of the documentary producers, also produced *Nanook of the North,* on Eskimo life, and *The Louisiana Story,* about the development of oil fields in the swamplands. Grierson also produced many documentaries, including *Drifters,* about the herring fishermen of England. R. H. Watt's *Night Mail,* another famous British documentary, is the story of the English postal system.

But perhaps the motion picture that best represents "documentary" in the American viewer's mind is Pare Lorentz's famous 16-mm *The River.* No matter how often one sees this motion picture, the painful lesson of reckless dissipation of our natural resources is always there as the mournful voice of the narrator chants, "down the Yazoo—down, down the great rivers of the Mississippi system our rich soil was washed." More recently the work of Julian Bryan has added to the stature of the documentary.

Some contemporary documentaries worthy of any teacher's previewing time are:

Boundary Lines. McGraw-Hill. 10 min., sd., color. A powerful plea for tolerance of differences among peoples.

Brotherhood of Man. Brandon. 10 min., sd., color. Animation that proves all races are part of one human race.

Picture in Your Mind. McGraw-Hill. 16 min., sd., color. A symbolic presentation of the roots of prejudice and the ways to create truer mental pictures.

As an impelling teaching tool the good documentary is almost without equal for presenting a pressing social problem.

The Expository Film. What is called the "expository" film usually explains a process. It is the "how-to" film. Numerous excellent and too many poor expositories have been produced. They deal with all kinds of subjects, from farming to swimming. There are expositories on how to type, take shorthand, keep books. There are others that teach long division, first aid, grooming, etiquette, courtship, carpentry, home repair, weaving, reading, how to use a library, and citizenship responsibilities. There are differences of opinion about individual expositories, perhaps even more so than about other film forms.

Too many expositories seem to be pitched at the lowest intellectual quotient. As a result they drag unbearably for even the average pupil and drive the bright youngster to intolerance of classroom "movies." Perhaps the element of greatest exhaustion for some is the platitudinous recapitulation that some educational advisers deem indispensable at the end of an expository film. Summaries less obvious and more creatively designed accomplish the purpose more effectively.

Expository films should be critically previewed by the teacher before class use. Explanations in motion pictures are always hazardous. Unless the approach is exactly right for the age level and background of the viewers, a feeling of wasted time and money will overcome the teacher. A patronizing narrator, the laboring of the obvious, and duplication of what the teacher himself can do on the chalkboard are some of the common faults in expository films. To insure selection of an adequate film, preview by the teacher himself is most important. Where that is not possible, critical review by others should be studied.

Some examples of expository films are:

Accent on Learning. Ohio State University. 30 min., sd., b & w. Acquaints teachers with audio-visual techniques and materials.

Advanced Typing (shortcuts). United World Films, Inc. Government Films Department. 35 min., sd., b & w. Demonstrates efficient use of tab stops, tab bar, decimal tabulator and shows how to make erasures, insert missing words and letters, type cards, envelopes, and labels, and perform better as a typist.

Ball Handling in Basketball. Encyclopaedia Britannica Films, Inc. 11 min., sd., b & w. Teaches stance, grip, fingertip control, and other techniques.

Personal Health for Girls. Coronet. 10 min., sd., b & w. A high school girl shares with the audience her cleanliness routines, exercise, complexion care, and diet.

The Entertainment Film. Most people usually associate the "entertainment" film with Hollywood. But educationally speaking, this classification includes all imaginative films, or story films. Perhaps there is a Puritan holdover in the reluctance of some classifiers to recognize the educational value in these films. Experience has shown that viewers are much more intent during a motion picture that carries narration and action than during a didactic film that tries to concentrate and condense the textbook on the screen. Certainly, the filmed classics and the dramatizations of history appear to teach English and social studies as effectively as any medium.

Although details may be criticized by historians, the dramatic telefilm series "You Are There" brings such history subjects as Grant and Lee at Appomattox, D-Day, the Boston Tea Party, and the Emancipation Proclamation into the classroom with impact. Kinescopes of Shakespearean plays involving casts of notable actors give life to literature that is sometimes difficult. Children's classics, like *Three Fox Fables*, which brings Aesop to the screen, *Goldilocks and the Three Bears, Heidi*, and *The Night Before Christmas* correlate with the picture books children read. Whether these are called entertainment films or imaginative films, they deserve a place among Instructional Materials no less conspicuous than that accorded imaginative literature on the library shelves.

Motion Picture Evaluation

Film selection by teachers can be systematized through the use of a card or sheet form bearing the evaluative criteria which appear in the checklist at the end of this topic. Some teachers prefer to keep a notebook of half or full sheets in preference to maintaining a 3 x 5 or 4 x 6 card file. It has the advantage of being more easily carried to the Materials Center or to selection meetings.

The card or sheet should begin with a number of production facts. Title of the film, name of the producer and his address, and date of production are essentials. Other facts should include color or black and white, sound or silent, length in minutes, and price. Then should follow the equivalent of a book annotation in the form of content analysis, and perhaps a critical note.

In succession these criteria should be applied to a motion picture at a preview before class use with pupils:

Authorship of the film should be approached first from the standpoint of the producer's possible aim. Although the best commercially sponsored educational films no longer sell their products with sledge-hammer obviousness, the possibility of indirect selling lurks in every frame. Consequently, the teacher must consider whether the sponsor's message serves a particular teaching purpose. Films produced by educational agencies have the initial psychological advantage of not being suspect, but carry no further advance assurance of success. Such commercial producers of educational films as book publishers bring a reputation based on their output. Along with the producer's name must be considered the standing of the authors, educational advisors, and others participating in the production of the film.

Content must be related to the teaching purpose of a curriculum unit or an over-all course of study or an activity. The degree to which the film furthers the teacher's objective will largely determine his selection.

Presentation, too, will influence the teacher's decision to select a film. Since any given unit must be covered in a specified number of class periods as planned by the teacher, he must weigh a class hour of viewing with a similar or shorter period of time to be spent in reading, discussing, demonstrating, listening, visiting, or experimenting. If the film duplicates or is less effective than any of these other approaches to learning, then the teacher may decide against the motion picture. For example, a motion picture which presents a series of stills may be less economical than a lecture supplemented by a filmstrip or a series of slides or opaque projections, which can accomplish the same results at less expense. Or a film which merely photographs a teacher working fractions on the chalkboard in the usual way might well be replaced by the teacher's working fractions on his own chalkboard.

Level is a tricky criterion. Many films pitched for a certain grade or age range overshoot or undershoot the mark. Besides, age levels vary in actuality and in older folks' estimations of the next generation. A British film on magnetism viewed recently at a preview elicited the response from a physics professor that "this is too advanced for our high school students here," and an almost immediate retort from a seventh-grader that "it's too elementary." This underestimation of the younger generation is not confined to teachers. In a showing to college freshmen of the McGraw-Hill film on "Human Reproduction," students were asked: "Should this film be shown coeducationally, or separately to boys and girls?" The overwhelming response was "coeducationally." But when the identical question was put to high school seniors, they replied in chorus: "separately." Level can only be hazarded, except for the obvious, but in general the same criteria advocated for other materials should be considered. When in doubt, it is better to overestimate than underestimate the age level of your viewers.

With regard to *technical quality*, there are more tangible measures. The photography and sound can be rated on a scale from "poor" to "excellent," as they are on the EFLA (Educational Film Library Association) evaluation sheet. Specifics to look for include lighting, focus, and exposure. Dark pictures are frustrating, and images out of focus, eyestraining. Subjects should be exposed to the viewer in proportion to their complexity or interest. The technical handling of such devices as fadeouts (slow disappearance of a scene), quick cuts (abrupt shifts), and dissolves (merging of the end of one scene with the beginning of another) is another measure of the film's photographic quality. Clear sound and articulate voices are other elements.

There are many evaluation guides for rating motion pictures. The EFLA sheet has already been mentioned. Individual scales have been prepared by various school systems.

Evaluation Checklist for Motion Pictures

Authorship: Are producer and editor qualified?
Content: Related to what school subjects or units?
Presentation: Does the film communicate with the usual force of the motion-picture medium?
Level: Is the film challenging to age or grade for which intended?
Technical Quality: Is photography adequate? Sound? Color?

Aids to Selection

There are now many listing and review sources for 16-mm films. Perhaps the most important and comprehensive list is the *Educational Film Guide* (10–1) issued by the H. W. Wilson Co., monthly and cumulated. It is basically a subject list and provides Decimal Classification for each film. Full production facts are supplemented by an annotation. Films can also be located by title. The *Educators' Guide to Free Films* (10–2), published annually by the Educators Progress Service, Randolph, Wisc., gives production facts, including the address of the source and a brief annotation for each film. The comprehensive Library of Congress Catalog of Films (10–3), usually found in large libraries, is a careful listing but without annotation. There are many other lists of films published, some selective and others aiming at comprehensiveness. More selective than the lists mentioned are the catalogs of film libraries issued periodically by state universities and extension agencies. A Materials Center should be on the mailing lists of several rental libraries to achieve a wider range of selection.

Among the review sources, the Educational Film Library Association, better known as EFLA (10–4), does a major job. Its membership is composed of schools, libraries, audio-visual centers, and other institutions, and their individual faculty and staff members. A major purpose of EFLA is to encourage the production of better films. It does this through critical evaluations which are issued on cards to all of its members.

Other review sources include the audio-visual and library journals, particularly *Educational Screen, Library Journal, Audio-Visual Instruction, Teaching Tools*, and *Film World*. Among the general periodicals that include reviews of 16-mm films, the *Saturday Review* should be cited.

Blurbs from the producers, and teachers' guides, provide synopses and production facts. Some of the producers are now putting their announcements of new films on 3 x 5 cards which can be used to build up a request file.

Utilization of Motion Pictures

As in the case of other kinds of Instructional Materials, the first step in using films effectively is "keeping up" with film literature, especially in your teaching area. Materials Centers now are routing announcements of new films to the teachers most concerned. Files of these announcements or records of them should be kept by the teacher and followed up in several ways. Also, reviews of new films should be watched for in the review journals. If possible, arrangements should be made to preview any promising film, and then evaluate it in terms of a place in the school's teaching plan.

All films have teaching guides. Materials Centers differ in procedures of handling them; some automatically enclose the teaching guide with the film, and others keep it filed separately to be requested by the teacher if he wants it. Teaching guides are useful, but all of them stress the fact that the teacher should work out for himself how best to use the film in a particular learning situation.

Two teacher's guides will be described here as illustrative of the aid which such guides offer. Encyclopaedia Britannica Films has produced for primary and intermediate grades *The Hare and the Tortoise* based on the Aesop fable. In order, the teacher's guide gives in boxes "Suggested Use" and "Facts About the Film," including length. This is followed by a short synopsis and suggestions for the use of the film. These suggestions are grouped around a plan for introducing the film, presenting the film immediately after the objectives have been formulated, and following up, which may include talking together, playing the story, planning a play, reading, and answering review questions. "Vocabulary Growth" lists those words introduced by the film which are worthy of study and discussion. The rest of the teacher's guide is the continuity, which includes film sequences and narrations.

The particular Coronet teachers' guide to class preparation selected for description here is that accompanying the motion picture *The Cell*, recommended for use in junior high through adult level in such areas as general science, biology, health, clubs, and general groups. Film facts are given succinctly and include running time as well as color and sound. The section "Behind the Scenes" gives the purpose and place of the film and acknowledges the photographer. This is followed by sections headed "Preparing to Use the Film," which introduces the subject of microscopes and magnification; "What You Will See in the Film," which is the nearest thing to a continuity included in the Coronet teachers' guides; "Additional Suggestions on Effective Use . . ."; and a list of "References" to books. The last is helpful but could be more so if other kinds of materials also were included.

These two teacher's guides are representative of these aids and suggest an approach to film utilization. In general, the teacher's own preparation should include three steps: (1) reading of film reviews, (2) previewing of the film itself, and (3) study of the teacher's guide that accompanies the film. This should probably be followed by some careful thought about such decisions as when, where, and how to show the film. Pupil preparation may take a number of directions. It may be accomplished by preliminary reading and examination of other materials on the subject, or by a field trip or by an opening talk from the teacher. But preparation may also be strikingly achieved by introducing a unit with the showing of a film first. The impact of one of the CBS "You Are There" television programs might well launch the introduction to an American history discussion of Grant and Lee, the conclusion of the War Between the States, and, indeed, the entire war. This television series is available in 16-mm film.

The showing itself, first of all, should not be marred by operational difficulties. To accomplish this smoothness of operation, the projector, screen, and speaker should all be set up in advance and all arrangements for speedy darkening rehearsed. Despite the most careful preparation, however, projection is subject to imperfections. It is well, therefore, to be prepared with an alternate plan for the period—just in case. These exigencies are reduced almost to impossibility as the supply of projectors grows and operators increase their proficiency. The teacher should never permit frustrations to blunt his enthusiasm for a teaching medium that has so much support for learning.

It is better also for the showing not to be interrupted by comment or discussion. Such interruptions inevitably lose sequences for the audience.

Attention to the comfort of the viewers is important. All chairs should be placed in such a way as to insure vision and to prevent awkward viewing angles. Darkening must be adequate; the right temperature and ventilation should prevail, even though this is sometimes difficult with improvised shades, especially on a hot day. Air conditioning will eventually overcome such difficulties.

The follow-up may take several forms. Discussion should come immediately after the showing. Encourage differences, because defenses and challenges are good stimulants to learning. Let the discussion lead to further investigation through other materials. It is evident that any film must be based on facts drawn from books and other sources. Let these facts be checked and documented. Encourage supporting evidence or refutations drawn from textbooks, reference books, trade books, periodicals, pictures, and objects.

Projection Techniques

Because the motion picture communicates through both sight and sound, two techniques are involved. The teacher can learn as much or as little of the details of these techniques as interest him. Minimum understanding of operation, however, is necessary.

Standard-speed motion pictures are taken by cameras as a series of still pictures at the rate of 24 exposures per second. When they are run through a projector, they are flashed on the screen as a series of separate pictures at the same rate of 24 per second. This is accomplished by a start-and-stop motion which brings each frame of the film between the lens and the light for a fraction of a second. For $\frac{1}{50}$ of a second, when one picture is moving out and the next is moving into the position between light and lens, there is darkness on the screen, but the human eye is such that "persistent vision" sustains the mental image of the previous picture, creating the illusion of motion from a series of still pictures.

A 16-mm sound projector with magnetic-sound attachment. *Courtesy Victor Animatograph Corp.*

The first sound in talking pictures was accomplished by synchronizing a disk record with a film. But the discovery of the photoelectric cell in 1928 made it possible to record sound right on the film. Consequently, when a film moves through a motion picture projector, a constant light directed through the sound track converts the variable intensities into corresponding diaphragm movements in the loud-speaker. Thus picture and sound are presented in synchronized relationship.

A magnetic-sound film projector is now available, which enables the teacher to create his own sound either on a silent film or on a commercially produced sound film. This is accomplished by sending the film to a laboratory to be "sound striped." A thin stripe of magnetic material is painted on half or all of the sound track. When the film comes back from the laboratory it is projected and the sound is recorded on the sound track, much as it is done on the tape recorder. If the sound track is half-striped, the film can be projected either with the original sound or with the recorded sound, merely by flipping a switch. The teaching possibilities of this device are important but the cost is still quite high.

The projection of motion pictures can be reduced to simple elements. Modern 16-mm projectors for the classroom have been so simplified that manufacturers now vie with each other on the number of seconds necessary to set up for projection. In terms of operation, the steps to be taken with almost any projector can be grouped into three stages. The first stage is placing the projector on a stand or table in the back of the room at a height sufficient to permit projecting above the heads of viewers; the second, setting up the screen in the front of the room; and the third, preparing the projector for operation. This third stage usually consists of (a) attaching the two reel arms (the feed reel on which the film is placed, and the take-up reel to which the film goes as it is being unreeled), (b) making electrical connections by plugging in for both the projector and the speaker to wall and projector outlets, and (c) threading the film. The speaker can be left in the projector or placed in front of the screen.

The operation calling for the most effort is probably film threading. Diagrams indicating the route the film will follow from feed reel to take-up reel are indicated both on the projector itself and in the accompanying manual. Although threading varies in complexity, all of it is much easier than it seems at first. The film gate, at the point where the film passes between lens and light, and the various sprocket tabs act as guideposts to the threading process. Once the film has been connected with the take-up reel, the show can be started.

It is a good idea to check threading by hand or to try by hand or by motor the leader (a bit of blank film) which precedes the actual film itself. Then in succession turn on the amplifier for sound, the film-moving mechanism, and the lamp. Focus the lens and adjust volume and tone. Close up as much of the housing as you can to reduce mechanical noise.

Post-operation techniques include rewinding, repacking, and maintenance.

Selection of a projector (10–4) is frequently influenced by habit and previous experience. Most projectors on the market are quite satisfactory. Whether or not service is available locally should be an important factor. The librarian or coordinator is the best person to select a projector and assist the teacher with its operation. In many schools, pupil operators are doing a creditable job of operation for all classes. Certainly the operation of a projector should be no obstacle to the teaching use of motion pictures.

Readings

ARNSPIGER, V. C. *Measuring the Effectiveness of Sound Pictures as Teaching Aids.* New York: Teachers College, Columbia University, 1900. 56 pp.

DALE, EDGAR. *Audio-Visual Methods in Teaching.* New York: Henry Holt & Co., Inc., 1954. Pp. 218–68.

DEKIEFFER, ROBERT, and COCHRAN, L. W. *Manual of Audio-Visual Techniques.* Englewood Cliffs, N.J.: Prentice-Hall, Inc., 1955. Pp. 85–95.

HARTLEY, W. H. *How To Use A Motion Picture.* ("How To Do It Series," no. 1), Washington, D.C.: National Council for the Social Studies, 1951. 8 pp.

WITTICH, W. A. and SCHULLER, C. F. *Audio-Visual Materials: Their Nature and Use.* New York: Harper & Bros., 1957. Pp. 362–427.

Viewings

"Facts About Projection." International Film Bureau. (Film, 11 min., sd., b & w)

"Facts About Films." International Film Bureau. (Film, 10 min., sd., b & w)

"Film Tactics." *United World.* (Film, 22 min., sd., b & w)

"Instructional Films: The New Way to Greater Education." Coronet. (Film, 25 min., sd., b & w)

"Using the Classroom Film." EBF. (Film, 21 min., sd., b & w)

11

RECORDINGS

Learning through listening is both one of the oldest and one of the newest forms of education known to man. When the earliest pupil copied what his teacher said, he relied almost entirely on his sense of hearing. In today's school the child at the "Listening Post" in a Materials Center receives from the earphones clamped to his ears the sounds that will give him the theme of a great symphony or the nuance of a Spanish idiom. And that is not all.

Within the curriculum subjects, area by area, there is hardly one that does not offer opportunities for learning through sound. In the language arts how much more meaningful are the classics, adult and juvenile, when heard aloud as they are read by a great actor or reader, with the pupil's eye following the text? Who can measure the child's thrill at hearing the children of Cuba speak the Spanish vocabulary he has painfully memorized from a grammar? With what motivation will the student strive to improve his diction when he hears his own voice saying things not quite as he had imagined it?

A whole new world of history and the social studies are spread before the student as he hears "The Day of Infamy" address before Congress in Franklin D. Roosevelt's own voice. Here in the classroom is a meeting of the state senate conducted by the speaker in parliamentary fashion as legislator after legislator arises to debate an increase in the sales tax. Assembled on one recording are all the sounds of modern transportation—plane, train, bus, steamship, auto—in a realistic identification study for a primary unit.

Science takes on a new vitality through the sounds of birds and fish and four-legged creatures all over the world. A class in typing undertakes shorthand from a dozen different voices dictating at varying speeds. And as for music, in what better way can appreciation, instrumentation, and vocalization be stimulated than by recorded great performances of the masterpieces of all time?

Students listen while they read. *Courtesy Board of Education, City of New York.*

In the vast and growing collections of disk and tape recordings, there are now an infinite number of approaches to individual differences through sound. All that is needed by the teacher is acquaintance with the recordings available and confidence in the operation of the simple equipment. What is needed by the pupil is adequate listening skill. Judging solely by the relative amount of time Johnny devotes to listening during each school day, it would seem even more important for him to know how to listen than how to read. Investigations reveal that more than half of the school time spent by children in grades one through seven is spent in listening. This being the case, what better opportunity for sharpening Johnny's listening acumen than through the concentration which the recording encourages?

Kinds of Sound Media

Both direct and recorded sound constitute an important medium of teacher-pupil communication. Recorded sound has the advantage of permanence over direct sound. Recorded sound can be brought back again and again in identically the same manner as the first time it was produced. In that one advantage is a tremendously important teaching aid.

Recorded sound may be defined as sound which has been transferred by electrical or mechanical means to the groove of a phonograph record or the magnetic track of a tape and which can be reproduced continuously and at will. Recorded sound that accompanies visualizations is best represented among school media by still and motion pictures that carry sound and by television. Teaching tools depending solely on recorded sound include radio and disk and tape recordings. Still and motion pictures with sound have already been considered; radio and television are reserved for the next chapter.

The two major forms of recording for school use are disk and tape. Disk recorders convert sound waves picked up by a microphone and store them in grooves inscribed on the surface of a blank or plastic-coated record. Tape recorders convert the sound waves picked up by the microphone and store them magnetically on a metallic-coated tape. Both kinds of recordings have the advantage of perpetuating teaching sounds, but each has its peculiar features. There is a broader and more distinguished collection of recordings available on disk than on tape. But the tape offers greater flexibility in recording specific parts of a program and of locating them later.

The term "transcriptions" is applied to recordings for radio or of radio programs. They offer unlimited possibilities for reproduction of desired parts of broadcasts which may be conveniently heard at any time. This is particularly important for school use, since so many of the better radio programs are scheduled outside the school day. Furthermore, by recording only what is wanted, objectionable parts of broadcasts can be eliminated. Transcription is possible both on disk and tape.

DISK RECORDINGS

The Teaching Potential of Disks

School libraries have long collected disk recordings. Most of these have included music classics, instrumental and vocal demonstrations, and a few readings of excerpts from literary masterpieces. Such recordings have been principally of assistance to music and English teachers. But in recent years record production has been extended to include the entire range of the curriculum. Foreign languages are being taught so that the student can learn to speak as well as to read and write, thanks to the recordings of native teachers' conversation. The songs and sounds of birds and animals are being reproduced so faithfully that nature expeditions to capture these songs and sounds are almost second-best learning experiences. Into today's classroom come the voices of contemporaries who are making history—the President of the United States and the governor of the state; the foreign delegate to the United Nations and the local councilman. These are the curriculum possibilities of disk literature.

But what gives the disk recording its great potential is how the teacher uses it. First of all, recordings can be preauded. (The verb *to aud* has now been accepted professionally. See John Caffrey's article, "Auding Ability at the Secondary Level," in *Education*, v. 75, pp. 303–10, and see also the California Auding Test.) This enables the teacher to prepare the pupil for active listening. Second, there is strength in the independence of scheduling this listening period for the classroom instead of fitting into a radio schedule.

A recording can be stopped at any place and played over as many times as necessary. In the case of foreign language pronunciation, for example, even the most patient teacher cannot repeat a word frequently enough to satisfy the slow imitator. But a record can be played over and over again until the finest nuance penetrates the auditory sense.

The recording gains reinforcement from alliance with other materials. Keyed to books, disks add another dimension to reading. There is no more attentive look on a child's face than when he is following the printed word while a recorded voice is reading it. The sound filmstrip, too, is augmented by the synchronized disk record that accompanies it.

These are only a few advantages which encourage more teachers today to go to the Materials Center for disk recordings. Not, however, until more teachers have become aware of the range of disk literature and gained greater confidence in the operation of disk record players can the Materials Center be expected to stock better collections of recordings.

Disk Recording and Playing Equipment

Most of us own or can operate a record player. But most of us also are aware of the fact that a social, if not a professional, distinction has developed between the owner of a "bourgeois" long-playing record player manufactured by one of the commercial companies and the person who has assembled "Hi Fi" components into a true high fidelity instrument. There can be no question that in most instances the latter is a superior reproducer of all the tones and overtones necessary to differentiate various instruments and sounds. The assembled components constitute, in fact, a closer approach to high fidelity than the average ready-made console. However, if such insistence on high fidelity reaches the fetish stage, it will discourage schools and teachers from using disk recordings because of their diffidence toward technicalities and because of the unavailability of such equipment in the school. In that case it would almost be better for the teacher to use an Edison cylinder phonograph.

There is no great mystery about the basic equipment needed to utilize disk recordings in teaching. The player or playback must as a minimum today be equipped to play records of three speeds and three diameters. The speed at which records formerly were played, almost exclusively, was 78 rpm (revolutions per minute). The speed at which modern LP (long-playing) records are played is 33⅓ rpm. There is also a 45 rpm record, and many record players are equipped with variable speeds so that any number of rpm's

Disk player and speaker. *Courtesy Newcomb Audio Products Company.*

may be used. Sizes of records have not undergone any changes comparable to speeds. The 10-inch and 12-inch disks are as standard in 33⅓ rpm records as they were in 78 rpm. There is, of course, a difference in the playing time. Whereas the old 78 rpm 12-inch recording provided only five minutes of playing time, the 33⅓ rpm 12-inch disk gives 22 minutes. Also available is a 45-rpm 7-inch disk, presumably for "juke box" service, which has not been popular in schools. One of the objections to this speed and size is that it reduces the advantages of LP by forcing more frequent record changes. Another objection is to the increased size of the center hole from the standard $\frac{5}{16}$ of an inch to 1½ inches. As a result, schools must purchase either an extra spindle or center post as an attachment to the player or buy individual inserts, called "spiders," for each record.

A high fidelity system usually consists of four basic components: (1) the tuner, which is used to receive radio broadcasts; (2) the record player, which can be operated either manually or automatically; (3) the amplifier, which increases the electrical energy received from the program source— tuner or record player—to the point where it will activate the loud-speaker; and (4) the loud-speaker, which converts the amplified electric energy into sound.

As to the record player, the teacher should know four important components. The first is the "turntable" on which the record is placed. Because of its flywheel action, the turntable should have proper weight and balance, and it is better driven from its center drum than from its rim. If these elements are not right, a rumble and "wow" will develop to interfere with listening. The second is the "tone arm," which consists of the arm itself and the cartridge. This cartridge is the unit which holds the needle. The weight of the tone arm should not exceed four to seven grams.

Pickup cartridges, often called "pickups" because they pick up the sound, are most often, on home and school sets, either crystal or magnetic. The crystal pickup has limited frequency range and is therefore unsuited for "Hi Fi." Magnetic pickups have proved highly satisfactory. The stylus or needle is made of one of the following materials: (1) osmium, a bluish-white amorphous, metallic chemical element of the platinum group; (2) sapphire, a hard, translucent variety of corundum; (3) diamond. The comparative wearing qualities of these three kinds of needles are indicated by the following table:

Maximum Number of Record Plays Recommended

Needle	On Microgroove	On Standard
Osmium	35	100
Sapphire	75	250
Diamond	1,000	2,000

The record changer on automatically operated players is the motor that operates the turntable, tone arm, and mechanism that changes the records. On three-speed players this changer must provide speeds of 33⅓, 45, and 78 rpm; accommodate three record diameters—7-, 10-, and 12-inch; and have spindles for two center holes—⁵⁄₁₆ and 1½ inches.

Other components are the amplifier and the speaker. An amplifier is required because the amount of electrical energy or output that comes from a record player is very small, and the electrical signals must be amplified to audibility. Without going into the technical aspects of amplification, it can be stated that a good amplifier not only amplifies desired sounds but suppresses unwanted noises.

The speaker is so important that without a good one it is impossible to have high fidelity. A good speaker consists of two parts: a very large cone, professionally known as the "woofer," which is the low-frequency reproducer covering a range up to 2,000 CPS (cycles per second); and a small cone, known as the "tweeter," which is the high frequency reproducer, covering a range from 2,000 to 18,000 CPS. The average human ear responds to frequencies or vibrations ranging from 16 to 20,000 CPS. (Frequency is determined by the number of vibrations per second of a tuning fork, piano string, or vocal cord.) Some human ears can detect sounds as low as 15 CPS and as high as 30,000 CPS. A good loudspeaker should therefore reproduce as much of this human range as possible.

Record Player Operation

Opportunities for record playing occur in the classroom and in the Materials Center. When the teacher operates a record player in the classroom for the entire class, certain procedures should be followed. The speaker should be set up in the front of the room, higher than the pupils' heads. If the speaker and turntable are separate, it is possible to place the turntable at the side of the room where the operator can sit. This has the advantage of removing him from the pupils' line of vision. It is well to remember that a 33⅓ rpm record will take 22 minutes on one side. If only part of this record is wanted for the class period, it is better to tape that part than try to fumble for the exact spot on the record. Pupils should be taught not to touch the groove surface of the record, but to handle the disk by its edges.

In the Materials Center two types of disk record-playing facilities may be found. Little listening rooms or booths, each equipped with a record player and sound-proofed, will provide individual and private listening opportunities. Listening Posts, often placed right out in the reading room on tables, will enable groups of as many as eight to listen to the same record without disturbing anyone else.

The Listening Post consists of a three-speed record player, a multiple phone box, and up to eight sets of earphones. Specifications for a Listening Post were drawn up by the director of audio-visual instruction in the public schools of Houston, Tex., where outstanding work has been done with this equipment, as follows:

Three-speed 78, 45, 33⅓ rpm. Amplifier output 5–7 watts; turntable and arm to accommodate 16-inch transcriptions. Output jack for external speaker and input for microphone; speaker size not less than six inches. Shall include a variable reluctance, or ceramic cartridge with two sapphire needles in pickup arm. Complete with 10-inch power cord and portable case. With four sets of quality earphones and one multiple phone box or equal.

Evaluation of Disk Recordings

If the Materials Center is to stock an adequate collection of disk recordings, teachers must be in a position to evaluate the output and make strong recommendations. As in the case of other classes of Instructional Materials, there are criteria that can be applied.

The first criterion is *relevancy*. In pre-auding a recording, the teacher must ask first, "Is it related to my teaching purpose?" Part of the answer is in the teacher's conviction that he can motivate his class to listen to a particular recording and motivate a desire to emulate the performance or go on to investigation through other media.

Closely related to the criterion of relevancy is the criterion of *maturity*. A recording can err in two ways—by being either too much above or too much below a particular age or grade level. Story telling is a particularly sensitive kind of performance to evaluate by grade level. But the same is true of music, poetry reading, and dramatization of plays. Often a decision on this point cannot be made by pre-auding alone, but only after a trial in class. The recording of "The Bear that Wasn't" has held adult and child spellbound, and yet has been pre-auded on occasion as unsuitable for both.

Performance by the artist, whether musician, speaker, or reader, is another criterion. Application of this criterion, however, will require adjustment. A recording of the songs of birds will involve an appraisal of the recorder's success rather than the performance of any single blue jay or bobolink.

Technical quality of the sound is another element for evaluation. Unless the voices and instruments are clear and differentiated, some of the teaching value will be lost. There are two recordings of Paderewski's performance of the Paganini-Liszt *La Campanella*, one made before World War I, when the virtuoso was at the peak of his vigor and technique but when the techniques of recording were still in their infancy, and the other after World War II, when record-making was much improved but the pianist had retreated before advancing age. Such contrasts in recordings inevitably present the music teacher with the dilemma of desiring to select both.

Finally, another basis for selection must be *correlation*. The extent to which the recording relates to other materials and spurs pupils to read and view and perhaps experience first-hand will certainly be one measure of its desirability.

Evaluation Checklist for Disk Recordings

Relevancy: Is the recording related to the teacher's teaching purpose?

Maturity: Is the recording at the age and grade level of the pupils?

Performance: Does the artist, reader, or director present the content adequately?

Technical quality: Are the sounds, voices, instruments adequately differentiated?

Correlation: Is the recording related to other Instructional Materials?

Selection Aids for Disk Recordings

Numerous sources can be checked systematically for new and old disk recordings of value in the classroom. But as yet there is no one selection aid that covers the entire range of educational recordings. Some lists are strong in music, others in readings, and still others in special phases of the curriculum.

The most comprehensive list is the Library of Congress catalog of music and phono records. It includes cylinder, disk, tape, and wire recordings. There are also good books on record collecting which include basic lists for the home and for school and hobby needs. Examples are such volumes as those by Irving Kolodin. Philip Eisenberg and Krasno Hecky compiled in 1948 *A Guide to Children's Records* (11–1), and A. S. Leavitt and M. S. Freeman published *Recordings for the Elementary School* (11–2) the following year. All of these, if in the Materials Center, can be of assistance in discovering older recordings.

Among current selection aids, the Music Library Association's *Index of Recorded Music* (11–3) and the *Educators' Guide to Free Tapes, Scripts and Transcriptions* (11–4) will prove helpful. Henry C. Hastings has compiled a bibliography of *Spoken Poetry on Records and Tapes,* "an index of currently available recordings," and Lillian Baldwin has brought together *Musical Sound Books for Young Listeners*, a selected and annotated library of recorded music. These two are evidence of increasing attention to bibliographic work with recordings (11–5).

A number of current professional and general periodicals feature reviews of recordings. Among these, both the audio-visual journals, such as *Educational Screen, Audio-Visual Instruction*, and the *Audio Guide*, and such library periodicals as *Library Journal, Wilson Library Bulletin*, and *ALA Booklist* feature listings and notes on recordings.

The catalogs of all of the major recording companies are worthy of examination as they appear annually and periodically. Both RCA Victor and Columbia have educational divisions concerned with school use of recordings. RCA Victor issues an *Educational Record Catalog*, which includes, among other items of information, graded and classified lists of Victor records suitable for school use. Columbia has issued a four-page leaflet which includes a page on "How to Use Records to Help You Teach," by Louise Whaley, and three pages of classified lists of Columbia educational recordings.

The record dealers' catalogs, too, are particularly useful for bargain hunters. The *Gramaphone Shop Encyclopedia of Recorded Music* was long a helpful guide to the record producers' output. Now such catalogs as those of Sam Goody and Chesterfield Music Shops offer price opportunities in record purchases. The Schwann catalogs are basic (11–5).

Representative Disk Recordings

The recordings to be mentioned in this section are by no means the basic recordings for a school. They are suggestive of some of the rich opportunities that await the teacher who sets out to teach through recordings.

First, in the field of the social studies and history a cavalcade of famous voices and historic incidents has been pressed into the phono-disk. The voices of most of the Presidents of the United States since Theodore Roosevelt can be heard in the RCA Victor album called *Cavalcade of the United States Presidents, 1901–1940*. Then, the Enrichment

Record series, already mentioned, has produced 16 significant events in American history based on the Landmark Books, each event available either on two 78-rpm records or, combined with another event, on one 33⅓ rpm record. Among the subjects are *Voyages of Christopher Columbus, Landing of the Pilgrims, California Gold Rush, Paul Revere and the Minute Men, Daniel Boone,* and *Monitor and Merrimac.*

Other recordings of interest to the social studies are Bruce Eell's transcriptions of commercial radio programs, such as *Captains of Industry, Strange Adventures in Strange Lands,* and *Frontier Fighters.* The study of World War II, its causes and results, can be made real through the various series of available recordings: the voices of Hitler, Chamberlain, and Daladier tell why in *Then Came War: 1939,* and these voices and many more are tied together in a story of the period between the two World Wars, by Edward R. Murrow, *I Can Hear It Now.* For an understanding of America's part in the war and what was in many ways the most unusual presidential administration in our history, no teaching tool can have quite the classroom effect of the two albums *Rendezvous with Destiny,* the excerpts from Franklin D. Roosevelt's radio addresses.

For literature and the language arts, Columbia has recorded the voices of many eminent writers reading their own works. Among them are Aldous Huxley, Edna Ferber, Somerset Maugham, William Saroyan, and John Steinbeck. There are the dialogues and dramatizations of Eva LeGallienne, Charles Laughton, and Orson Welles, among others, as recorded by Bowmar. The National Council of Teachers of English is responsible for poetry readings by Robert Frost, Vachel Lindsay, and others, and for masterpieces of English literature. A rich literature for children illuminates such folk tales as Paul Bunyan and Pecos Bill and those of the Scandinavian and French people in the American Library Association series called "Folk Tale Records." Decca has produced such children's stories as *Goldilocks, Little Red Hen,* and others, and there are recordings for children that cover a wide range in the library offered by the Sound Book Press Society.

Some recordings for other fields should be mentioned. For the study of foreign languages, the Linguaphone and the Holt series have long been outstanding. There is a series of unusual nature recordings by Comstock, including *American Bird Songs,* that will be useful in science, and two collections by textbook publishers—*Let's Listen,* by Ginn & Company, and *Sounds Around Us,* by Scott, Foresman & Company— which contribute both to early science training and to developing listening skills. The number of records in music appreciation and training is legion.

This brief catalog of recordings in some of the school areas is only a fraction of the examples that await the teacher adventuresome enough to explore this medium for possible lesson approaches.

Utilization of Disk Recordings

To begin with, the very presence of a record player put into position for class action has its element of suspense, drama, and motivation. There must be no letdown. The charge in the classroom air must be sustained throughout the playing, as well as before and after.

Pre-auding by the teacher is a prerequisite. Enthusiasm of the teacher for a particular disk is half of the pupil conversion that will follow. The teacher should be sufficiently committed to the recording to provide the necessary motivation that must precede the playing of the record in the classroom. So teacher pre-auding and pupil motivation are the first two steps in using recordings.

But these two steps, almost universally agreed upon in audio-visual literature may be qualified. It is probably not good practice to play records "cold," hoping that in some way passive learning will occur merely through the pupils' presence amidst the sound waves. Certainly every advantage can be gained by creating anticipation and by alerting the listeners to watch for certain theme passages or for definite critical points, or to challenge statements and interpretations in the recordings. This active listening is certainly purposeful utilization of a potent teaching medium.

But so-called passive listening, too, may make its educational contribution. In the Florida State University Materials Center Reading Room there is continuous soft music. An LP record changer in the librarian's office is stacked with records three or four times a day, and the sound is carried out among the students working on assignments, reading, or viewing. When this service was first inaugurated, only two people out of hundreds of patrons found anything objectionable in it, and one of them was among those who later came in to remind us when the records ran out and there was an accidental period of silence. The important point, however, is that here was passive listening, music beamed in as background only. And we know of students who had little interest or knowledge of music but gradually and subconsciously became aware of melodies and themes and eventually asked about particular recordings. We heard these students hum tunes that have been played as background, and we came to the conclusion that even passive listening must contribute something to the learning of students.

But consider also the possibility of classroom listening without teacher pre-auding and pupil motivation. Under two circumstances at least this may prove effective. One, a frank statement by the teacher, "This brand new record has just arrived. I haven't had a chance to hear it. Have any of you? I wonder if it is any good?" Of course, there is a type of motivation here. Together, teacher and pupil are going to undertake pre-auding and critical evaluation.

Another procedure can be used—pre-auding by pupil and motivation of the teacher. Students are encouraged to bring their favorite records from home. They play and advocate them—"This is why I liked this record." There is anticipation in this exercise, of course, and enough challenge to prevent passivity. If carefully planned, student record playing can result in an effective period of critical evaluation.

An important part of good utilization is provision for a good listening climate. This includes placement of the speaker in front of the class, if possible. Forming of a shallow arc around the speaker is sometimes also recommended. To prevent interruptions and disturbances, some teachers place signs outside their room reading "We Are Listening," or "Please Do Not Disturb—This Is a Listening Period."

Audio experiences should inevitably be followed by reading, viewing, dramatizations, student broadcasts, and other activities. But these follow-ups should not be stilted or forced. Always with teaching envy we must watch how children voluntarily follow radio space ship or Lone Ranger programs with excited emulation. If some of this spontaneous imitation occurs after a listening period, something certainly has taken hold.

TAPE RECORDINGS

The Teaching Potential of Tapes

Perhaps the chief advantages of the tape over the disk lie in the fact that recording is easier and less expensive. That in itself makes for a teaching potential that has only begun to be realized. It gives magnetic recording the possibility of assisting learning through creation, excerpt, and reproduction that is unique to this medium.

One of the disadvantages of the disk recording is the difficulty of finding and playing a pertinent excerpt; this is even more difficult on the LP recording, with its greater coverage on one side. Here the tape can help by excerpting the portion wanted. The tape's excerpting possibilities can be further used with radio programs desired for classroom use, omitting commercials and other irrelevant parts. An example of this type of excerpting is the taping of radio returns on election night. Dramatic moments were captured in the Truman-Dewey election count, including Mr. Gallup's explanation of why the poll went wrong, the candidates' final statements of victory and concession—the whole edited into a talking book that would fit the time limits of a class period. How better to teach the facts and the intangibles of the American election system!

Reproductions of all sorts of sounds and talks inside and outside of the school offer unlimited teaching possibilities.

A part of the assembly program, a teacher's lecture, a pupil recital, square dance calling, the school band and orchestra at their best—all can be reproduced on tape and placed in the Materials Center as a permanent part of the school collection, to be classified, cataloged, and filed. In the community, sounds and speeches, recitals and lectures, and bird songs and animal calls can be taped.

There is also plenty of opportunity for pupil creation via tape. Speech correction and instruction can be aided by progressive recording of pupils' voices. The same can be done for both instrumentation and vocalization in music. Interviews set up in the community between pupils and leading citizens to establish certain facts about local political, economic, or social conditions bring lessons in social science close to home. The use of a portable tape recorder on field trips will aid review and follow-up besides providing other teachers with a record in the Materials Center.

One of the most dramatic uses of the tape is in foreign language exchanges. For several years now, Florida school children have been recording on tape for pupils in Latin America. This good neighbor venture has resulted in reciprocal activities by Latin American children. It is not difficult to imagine what the learning of Spanish means to Florida children as they listen to the children in the Spanish-speaking nations talk to them idiomatically. Nor can the similar effect in Latin America be overlooked. Exchanges among children on tapes have spread everywhere and include all of the modern languages taught in our school.

Tape Recording and Playing Equipment

Recording, playing, and erasing are all provided for in the compact tape recorder which is fast becoming standard school equipment. Components include a microphone, one or two recording heads, amplifier, and speaker. A magnetic head for recording consists of a magnet coil wound on an iron core. The sound waves picked up by the microphone are converted into a series of electrical impulses that reach the small magnet. When the metallic-coated paper or plastic tape passes through the magnetic field, it receives and retains these magnetic impressions corresponding to the sound waves set up by the voice or other stimulant.

Tape recorder. *Courtesy Ampex Audio, Inc.*

The tape can now be rewound and played back at once. As it passes the playback head, the magnetic field on the tape excites the magnetic core, creating sufficient voltage to feed the amplifier and affect the speaker. Erasure is accomplished by demagnetizing the tape. During recording, the tape always passes through the erasure head to insure a clean tape.

One of the important considerations in recording and playing is tape speed. The frequency range of a tape recorder is largely determined by tape speed, which is stated in terms of inches per second (ips). Frequency response is roughly 1,000 times the ips. Thus, a tape speed of 15 ips will

permit an upper limit of 15,000 CPS, whereas a tape speed of
7½ ips imposes an upper limit of 8,000 CPS. However, economy is another factor. At the higher speed, a reel of tape
will give only half the recording time that it will give at a
lower speed. Some economy can be effected by dual-track
recording, in which only half of the width but all of the
length of the tapes is used. To do this, a dual-track head is
required on the tape recorder. Some idea of the relation between tape reel dimensions and playing time can be gained
from the following table. For dual-track recording, double
the playing time in each case.

Reel Size	Reel Length	Playing Time At	
		7½ ips	15 ips
(inches)	(feet)	(minutes)	
5	600	15	7½
7	1200	30	15
10½	2400	60	30

In the operation of a tape recorder, only a few simple
steps must be mastered. The first of these is threading, and
that is simpler than the comparable operation on the motion-
picture projector. Load the desired length of tape on the
supply reel and pull some of it through the guide post in
front of the take-up reel. Fasten that end to the take-up reel
and, after removing any slack left in the tape, the recorder
is ready to operate. Next select the desired speed and turn
on the mechanical function control. This sets the tape in
motion from the left past the erasure head and on to the
recording head. When the desired recording has been completed, it can be played back at once by rewinding to the
place in the recording wanted and switching to playback.
(The simple technique of splicing tape should be learned,
also, for both mending and editing.)

There are many good tape recorders on the market
(11–8). For a comparison of specifications and features on

most well-known makes, the *Audio-Visual Equipment Directory* (9–9) is most helpful. Periodic reviews of magnetic tape recorders appear in articles and advertisements in such audio-visual journals as *Educational Screen* and *Audio-Visual Instruction.*

Tape Selection and Aids

Whether the tape will ever replace the disk entirely will depend largely on whether the tape can overtake the disk in the number and variety of ready-made recordings.

There can be no question that the tape already surpasses the disk in the field of school and community-produced recordings. Economy and flexibility are working to the advantage of the tape, as are the educational agencies and movements which have turned to the tape rather than to the disk. For example, during the academic year 1949–1950, the Minnesota Department of Education published a catalog of some 700 tapes available to teachers on an exchange basis. Schools wanting these tapes merely sent a blank tape on which the desired recording could be reproduced. The service was later offered by other states and agencies, including Cornell University, Kent State University, and the University of Washington. What is more, this service has taken on a real exchange aspect as schools in each state have tended to send their recordings to an agency acting as a clearinghouse (11–9).

Mention has already been made of the foreign language exchanges being carried on between schools of this nation and other nations. The "pen pal" is being replaced by the "tape pal." Tapes of radio and television programs are increasing in number and desirability. So also are tape recordings of plays, speeches, interviews, and sounds. The Marine Biological Laboratory at Florida State University has been taping fish sounds for years. The variety of taping efforts described by these activities suggest additional sources for tape recordings and an aspect of selection that is concurrent with and sometimes even ahead of the actual production of a tape recording.

The best aid to selection of ready-made tape recordings is the *National Tape Recording Catalog* (11–10) sponsored jointly by the Department of Audio-visual Instruction, the NEA Association for Education by Radio-Television, and Kent State University. The second edition, issued in 1957, lists over 1000 selected programs, classified by subject areas. Any of these tapes can be obtained from Kent State University, Kent, Ohio, on the exchange blank plan, with a small service charge for copying.

There are other aids to selection, several of which, like the *Educators Free Guide to Tapes, Scripts and Transcriptions* (11–4), were mentioned in the previous section on disks. The possibility of developing a collection of tapes in any school system is almost unlimited as far as scope is concerned. By exchanging with other schools and with state and national agencies, the tape recording collection can soon grow to the proportions of a major class of Instructional Materials.

PUBLIC ADDRESS AND CENTRAL SOUND

Classroom and school focus on sound is often accented by public address equipment. A central sound system in a school serves to organize and integrate the various sound media available for learning. PA equipment in the classroom or auditorium provides voice reinforcement and increased listening range.

The three parts of a public address system are the microphone, amplifier and loud-speaker. Whether portable or fixed, it is important that these components be flexible enough to be capable of integration with all kinds of sound facilities—radio, tape, and disk recorders and playbacks, and television.

Microphones of good quality are essential. Crystal microphones are inexpensive and sensitive, but they lack fidelity, especially for music, and are usually unidirectional; i.e., picking up sounds from one direction only. Velocity microphones, which are bidirectional and dynamic microphones, are usually nondirectional and have greater fidelity. Since microphones are subjected to rough treatment, sturdy equipment is desirable.

Amplifiers and speakers must be large enough to do the job. Since the amplifier reinforces the electrical impulse, one test of its adequacy is the amount of volume required. If it is necessary to turn the volume all the way for normal use then the amplifier is probably not adequate. Classrooms should be fitted with 8-inch, or in the case of large classrooms, with

A central sound system for schools of a hundred rooms or more. It includes amplifier, intercom, control panel, AM-FM radio, and four-speed automatic record changer. *Courtesy Du-Kane Corporation.*

10-inch speakers. Auditoriums require dual speakers. The number of speakers that can be hooked to a PA system depends upon the amplification.

Central or school sound systems integrate the various audio media in the building. The functions of such a system may be grouped around three purposes—administrative, instructional, recreational. Administratively, the central sound system offers instantaneous interclass and interunit communication for announcements, conferences, and conversation. It may also provide automatic bell ringing for class periods.

Instructional and recreational needs can be served by the central sound system in a number of ways. Radio, disk, and tape transmissions can be directed to any part of the building as needed. With the addition of closed circuit television, visual material can also be so provided. Cocurricular activities in drama, debate, and lecture, can be shared, whether they originate in the auditorium, gymnasium, athletic field, music room, or other classrooms.

Central control for the school sound system, usually located near the principal's office, but also possibly part of the Materials Center, provided personnel are added to the Center's staff, serves as the distribution point. Equipment generally includes a control panel with provision for two or more input channels so that more than one program at a time may be distributed. For two or more microphone and recording attachments to be used simultaneously an input-mixer is needed. Switches to permit piping of sound to individual or groups of rooms or to all rooms at one time are very important. Furthermore it should be possible to pick up programs regardless of where in the building they originate.

BINAURAL SOUND

Developments in sound engineering during recent years have brought continuous improvement in reproduction. Most recordings are made through one microphone and heard through one speaker and are known as monaural. So-called binaural recordings, tape or disk, are made with two microphones placed apart like the human ears, and the sound from each microphone is recorded on a separate track or area. When played back through binaural equipment, the sound from each track comes through a separate speaker, thus producing the highest fidelity yet known. Although binaural equipment is available for school use, expense and complexity have delayed general adoption. Nevertheless, it is to the advantage of the teacher to keep up with these developments and request new equipment somewhat in advance of their perfection.

Stereophonic sound, which reproduces sound recorded from two or more sources, is rapidly gaining in popularity and is found in many commercial motion-picture theatres and in some schools.

Readings

BROWER, R. C. *Tape Recordings for Teaching.* St. Paul, Minn.; Minnesota Mining and Manufacturing Corp., 1952.

DALE, EDGAR. *Audio-Visual Methods in Teaching.* New York: Henry Holt & Co., Inc., 1954. Pp. 294–304.

DARRELL, R. D. *Good Listening.* New York: Alfred A. Knopf, Inc., 1955. 206 pp.

DEKIEFFER, ROBERT, and COCHRAN, L. W. *Manual of Audio-Visual Techniques,* Englewood Cliffs, N.J.: Prentice-Hall, Inc., 1955. Pp. 141–61.

HEILMAN, ARTHUR. "Listening and the Curriculum," *Education,* LXXV, (January, 1955), 283–87.

SIGGELKOW, R. A. *How to Use Recordings.* Washington, D.C.: National Council for the Social Studies, 1951. 8 pp.

WITTICH, W. A., and SCHULLER, C. F. *Audio-Visual Materials: Their Nature and Use.* New York: Harper & Bros., 1957. Pp. 271–321.

Viewings

"Ear and Hearing." EBF. (Film, 10 min., sd., b & w)

"Nature of Sound." Coronet. (Film, 10 min., sd., b & w)

"Tape Recording for Instruction." Indiana State University. (Film, 15 min., sd., b & w)

"The Magnetic Recorder." State University of Iowa. (Film, 22 min., sd., b & w)

12

RADIO AND TELEVISION

Five centuries ago mankind experienced a communication revolution only slightly less sensational than the one now transpiring. Then the invention of printing was the cause; today it is the invention and development of radio and television transmission. So widespread is this latest transformation in communicating that already dire predictions of the replacement of print by transmission have found expression in all of the media. Some evidence of this is manifest.

Radio and television have unquestionably taken a huge slice out of the advertising budgets formerly allocated to newspapers and magazines. As a result, several major publications and many minor ones have ceased to print. Various studies of leisure-time activities by both adults and children have shown a declining devotion to reading and a catapulting attention to listening and viewing. It is estimated that 100 million radio sets are at the disposal of the American people, and the number of television sets is increasing so rapidly that almost any figure given today will be unrepresentative tomorrow. Analyses suggest that teachers average 12.2 hours each week in front of their home television sets, high school students 14.3 hours, and elementary school pupils 23.5 hours. Although these figures appear high as averages, they seem low in the face of housewives' admission that TV sets are turned on almost continuously every day from morning to midnight, and that evening viewings for the whole family extend from supper to signoff several times each week.

Such a communication transformation has inevitably affected classroom learning. Not to the extent that the pessimists would have us believe, however. There is no evidence that all of the other classes of Instructional Materials are antiquated. The facts continue to point to the interdependence of all media. Radio depends on scripts and the book reading necessary to document them. It cannot do without the tape or disk recording. Television has similar dependence and a few additional reliances. Graphics of all kinds create the necessary props for staging, and still and motion-picture projection fill a major portion of both the video and the audio telecasting time. Therefore, rather than viewing with alarm these media of radio and television that have introduced new dimensions of communication and education, farseeing educators are exploring ways and means to harness this new learning power in the interest of better teaching.

Radio and Television Potentials

Many broadcasts and telecasts have certain learning disadvantages. One of these is the nature of the programs. Overwhelmingly the content of both radio and television is pitched at the level of the lowest common denominator—or lower. Programing seems to have been aimed only at those with an elementary education, with utter disregard for those whose schooling, formal or otherwise, has gone beyond.

Another disadvantage is the inflexibility of broadcast timing. Many of the best programs for educational purposes occur outside school hours. Even such radio and television casts as come within the school day can hardly be expected to coincide with the different curriculum sequences found from coast to coast in the nation's schools. As a consequence, much, if not most, of the learning power in radio and television is lost to the schools.

Finally, such material as is used by the schools is often surrounded by extraneous and useless matter, inevitable impositions by sponsors and inanities by performers. For reasons of programing, timing, and irrelevancies, therefore, broadcasts and telecasts direct from their program sources are not as effective learning media as when they are selected, directed and converted by the teachers themselves for classroom use.

The nature of this conversion is two-fold. Careful screening of advance announcements of program schedules can result in a selected list of curriculum-related programs. These programs can be assigned by the teacher for homework as listening or viewing periods. Specific questions to be an-

Television adds a new dimension to education. *Courtesy National Education Association.*

swered, points to watch for, or skills to observe can be outlined in advance. In this whole approach to using broadcasts as they originally appear, the Materials Center can help in many ways. It can compile annotated lists of advance programs of promise, attaching any preview notices that might help the teacher. It can also post these programs on a bulletin board with encouragements to the teachers to aud or view them.

The second type of conversion is the recording: radio transcriptions, or television programs recorded on film, which are referred to as "kinescopes." The advantages the transcription or kinescope have for schools over the original radio or television program are several. First, the kinescope can be previewed or the transcription pre-auded. Second, either can be scheduled for any time that fits in with the teacher's plan. Third, audio or audio-visual recordings can be repeated as often as the teacher thinks desirable. Fourth, the disk, tape, or film lends itself better to organization and dissemination by the Materials Center as an Instructional Material. Finally, the fact that a radio or television program has merited recording is in most cases evidence of its relevancy to a learning need.

EDUCATIONAL RADIO

The Broadcast Potential

For the first two decades after Marconi's invention of wireless telegraphy, only code messages were transmitted. But in 1915 Dr. Lee DeForest invented the audion, and the United States became the first nation to transmit and receive the human voice by radio. The first two commercial stations, KDKA in Pittsburgh and WWJ in Detroit, began regular broadcasts in 1920. By 1926 some 600 local radio stations had been activated and in that year many of them were joined up in national networks. Commercial radio had come of age.

But what about educational radio? As early as 1919, systematic classroom use of radio began when the state-owned University of Wisconsin radio station WHA undertook to broadcast to schools and communities within the state. Other states established similar facilities, calling themselves either "school of the air," as in Wisconsin, Texas, and Indiana, or "school broadcast services," as in Minnesota and New York. City curriculum-coordinated radio programs were also established, many of them, like Chicago, Cleveland, Cincinnati,

Los Angeles, Houston, Detroit, Flint, Indianapolis, and Omaha, pioneering innovations of note. Also, commercial stations devoted a percentage of their time to educational broadcasts and offered their facilities for school and college use.

Despite these advances, however, radio had to undergo periods of regulation by the government. This responsibility was early placed with the Secretary of Commerce and subsequently in a Federal Radio Commission and in the Federal Communications Commission (FCC). One of the major government responsibilities was for the assignment of frequencies to stations. Since the broadcast band was limited to the range from 500 to 1500 kilocycles, there was considerable jockeying for favored places on the dial. Up through World War II, radio was an expanding industry. With the rise of television, commercial radio steadily declined in popularity. But educational radio took on new life through the activation of FM (frequency modulation) stations that used higher frequencies and gained through clear, static-free transmission what they lost through limited distance.

Some Technical Considerations

Radio can be defined as a system of wireless communication by sound. In the process through which such communication is accomplished, sound waves are converted into electrical waves which are radiated into space, picked up by a receiver, and then reconverted into sound waves. Since electrical waves can travel only short distances, "carrier" waves are used to transport them. It is these carrier waves that are measured by frequencies of vibrations. A radio beam of 700 kilocycles has a frequency of 700,000 vibrations per second.

The frequency range of 550 to 1600 kilocycles has been reserved for what is called amplitude modulation (AM) radio. Frequencies for AM radio stations are fixed and assigned by the Federal Communications Commission. Because of these fixed frequency assignments, AM radio carrier waves never vary from this frequency. But, because of overtones, sound waves vary considerably in quality or harmony. Because of the inflexibility of the AM station's frequency assignment, it is not possible for it to transmit the full range of tones and overtones that the human ear can hear.

Discovery of the ultra high frequency range's possibilities led to the introduction of frequency modulation radio (FM) with assignments in the frequency range of 42,000 to 50,000 kilocycles (42 to 50 megacycles). In this broader and less crowded frequency range, frequencies may vary by 200 kilocycles, or plus or minus 100 from any given frequency. With such a variation, an FM station can broadcast a full range of sound frequencies without interfering with the frequency of another station.

Because FM radio is more economical to install and to operate, it has become the favorite of educational institutions. It also has other advantages over AM. As already indicated, it provides higher fidelity and is also static-free. Several school systems, like Cleveland, Chicago, New York, and San Francisco, that have changed over from AM to FM radio, report the reception is so much better that as a result there has been a marked increase in radio teaching in the classrooms. But it has one disadvantage, too. FM radio can broadcast only between the antenna and the horizon—no farther.

Evaluation of Radio Programs

Despite the decline in radio listening, the number and variety of programs have probably never been greater. Thus, selection presents the teacher with the first problem in utilization. In the case of radio programs, selection is complicated by the fact that the choice must be made in advance and without the opportunity, in the case of originating broadcasts, for pre-auding. This is a case where co-operative selection through the Materials Center can be particularly helpful.

In general, radio programs can be grouped into major big classes—those that emanate from commercial stations and those that are broadcast by educational stations. Of the former, differentiation is generally made between sponsored and sustaining programs. In the case of sponsored programs, a commercial firm is paying for the time and using part of it to advertise its product. There are plenty of teachers who will have nothing to do with sponsored radio programs because of the commercials. But it is also true that many sponsored programs are superior in their classroom possibilities, and an increasing number of the sponsors are restricting their commercials to a simple statement of sponsorship.

Sustaining programs are those paid for by a network or local station without advertising. These are often programs produced by educational agencies, civic clubs, and organizations working for the education and betterment of a community. There is considerable classroom material in many programs emanating from commercial stations. But scheduling is a deterrent to convenient use. In general, commercial station broadcasts fall into three time-schedule groups as far as their school usability is concerned. First, there are programs during school hours that are curriculum-correlated. These often do fit in with the schedules of some classes. But it is too much to expect all schools in the nation to have a sequence of teaching units that will enable every teacher to arrive at the exact point of time to utilize a specific radio program. Rather, if the teacher can partially anticipate a program of promise, he can so adjust his schedule as to provide some preparation for the broadcast.

Then there are programs that come during school hours that, although not specifically planned for the classroom, have considerable educational value. These also can be prepared for by the teacher. An obvious example is a White House message to Congress which a civics class might want to hear.

Another time-schedule class of programs includes the great number of broadcasts outside school hours, many of which are of real educational significance. There is no way to take advantage of them except through homework assignment.

Of the programs broadcast by educational stations, certain advantages can be listed unreservedly. No part of the time is absorbed by advertising. There is likely to be no con-

tent unsuitable for children and young people, and, on the
positive side, most of the communication will have some cultural and educational value. Time-schedule difficulties will be
somewhat reduced because the programs will be directed in
many instances toward specific classroom requirements and
because the length of the broadcast day may be limited. The
chances are that where a school system has its own radio station selection procedures will probably favor consideration of
its offerings first.

As in the case of other classes of Instructional Materials,
radio programs should comply with certain criteria. The first
criterion is *authority*. To insure accuracy of content, a subject
specialist should have some responsibility for the program, as
should a teacher. The collaboration of a subject specialist
with an educator on a radio program often produces good
results. It goes without saying that the authority team will be
incomplete without technical assistance from the station's
program and engineering staff.

A second criterion concerns *relevancy* to the teaching purpose. In the case of radio programs, there is an aspect of im-
mediacy involved. Special events, current developments,
coinciding interests, and timely observances may particularly
contribute to a teaching unit. A civics class beginning its
study of state government would be helped by tuning in to
an opening session of the Legislature. If the Beethoven *Eroica*
happened to be scheduled for performance during a class
hour in music appreciation, this program might be a priority
selection.

Since radio broadcasts *music* as background even more
often than as a separate program, the quality of the *music*, a
third criterion, should come in for separate evaluation. This
can be prejudged only by the reputation of the musicians
who will be responsible and by the direction if the work
has not been performed before.

A fourth criterion concerns listener *participation*. To what
extent does the program encourage preparation for listening
by providing guides or other teaching aids in advance? Is
there likely to be participation by the listener during the

broadcast and stimulation to follow up with investigation in other media?

Evaluation Checklist for Radio Programs

Authority: Is there a balance between "what" and "how" competence in the personnel responsible for the program?

Relevancy: Does the program promote the desired teaching purpose?

Music: Are the selection and performance likely to be high in quality?

Participation: What guides and listening aids are available, and how much listener participation is provided for?

Selection Aids for Radio Programs

Daily newspapers are now more than ever listing a week's radio programs in advance. It is possible, therefore, to select from the local stations' offerings broadcasts of promise. All of the four major networks issue complete program lists which will be sent to schools on request. Columbia Broadcasting System publishes its own *Listeners Guide.* From the National Broadcasting Co. comes a monthly bulletin which classifies all of its programs under such headings as news, public affairs, music, education, the arts, religion, and special features. Newsletters and bulletins are issued by the other two networks—American Broadcasting Co. and Mutual Broadcasting Service.

There are, besides, good listings and reviews of radio programs in general periodicals and school periodicals. *Scholastic Teacher,* for example, lists selected, approved programs from all parts of the networks every month. The librarian will have access to many sources (12–1) of advance information about radio programs and will send notifications to teachers concerned, or post general schedules on the radio bulletin board.

But the more promising prospect of selection aid with radio programs is in recordings. An increasing number of the better and more lasting broadcasts are now being transcribed both on disk and on tape. The Bruce Eells venture has been referred to in the previous chapter. Networks are transcribing programs of lasting value for school use. Many of these are listed in the bibliographies of disks and tapes mentioned previously, such as the *Educators' Guide to Free Tapes, Scripts and Transcriptions* (11–4).

The time is coming, however, when individual school systems and in co-operation with other school systems and agencies will undertake regular monitoring (critical listening) and taping of promising radio programs. There is a risk involved, of course, in recording a program of promise that turns out to be a disappointment, but that risk is not even the cost of the tape, since that recording can be erased and the tape used over again. What is called for is a co-operative division of work among the schools, each assuming responsibility for monitoring and taping a portion of the selected programs. Once taped, the exchange program can go into effect, with the master being placed on deposit in the state, regional, or local service agency.

Radio Utilization

Adequate use of the radio medium begins with selection. A method of informing pupils of worth-while radio programs is essential. This can be done in a number of ways. The radio bulletin board in the Materials Center is effective. It should include not only a time schedule of selected promising programs, but arousing announcements, reviews, published controversies, or pictures of personalities relating to the programs. Notification to teachers is another way. A third possibility is listing of promising programs in the school paper.

Once a radio program has been selected, the assignment should point toward specific objectives. Exposure to good spoken English, with attention especially directed to diction, sentence structure, and pronunciation, should have implication not only for language arts classes but for other subjects. Teachers should be on the lookout for storytelling, book review, dramatization, author interview, and book forum programs as allies in literature classes. The social studies will find rich lesson materials in newscasts, interviews with statesmen, and on-the-scene reports by commentators for such events as legislative sessions, political conventions, natural disasters, dedications of government, and cultural centers, and pageants like the Tournament of Roses, the Gasparilla, and Mardi Gras. Forums, election nights, and campaign speeches are other opportunities for social studies listening.

Science is receiving increased attention on the air. The program with the "What's New" theme is deservedly popular. Visits to laboratories, museums, and industrial plants, and interviews with the personnel directing these operations, are always instructive. Medical forums on health and disease, usually enhanced by question-and-answer features, are an asset to hygiene classes.

The only problem for music teachers is selection. During any one day there is enough good music and talk about it to crowd a term of music lessons and assignments. Programs of music appreciation, and of symphonic, operatic and chamber music, and talks about music programs are abundantly produced. Some of these are directed for children.

After selection and auding, utilization may take a number of forms. The program heard by an entire class will provide content for an exhilarating discussion. Points of difference will sharpen learning. Variations from facts gathered from other sources will stimulate further search in other Instructional Materials. Here the transcription will prove most valuable for checking what was heard.

In all of this consideration of radio as a teaching medium, one fact must be underscored: radio is a listening approach to learning. As such, the importance of repetition must not be overlooked. The very nature of the radio broadcast prevents or limits this repetitive element in learning. Transcription offers a way to overcome this limitation. Inevitably more recording of worth-while radio programs must be undertaken if the radio medium is to be used to its full potential. This becomes daily more feasible with the increase and improvement of recording equipment.

EDUCATIONAL TELEVISION

The Telecast Potential

Television began probably in General Electric's radio station WGY, Schenectady, N.Y., in 1928. But these telecasts were only the culmination of a century of contributing discoveries, such as the discovery of selenium in 1817 and of its light-sensitive propertics in 1873, the successful development of cathode ray by Sir William Crookes in 1873, and the introduction of the electric light in 1878 by Thomas Edison. During the decade 1920–1930 the greatest advances in the development of television were made with supersensitive tubes and the study of scanning. Flickering pictures were transmitted. In 1931 RCA telecast experimentally from the Empire State Building in New York City, and in the next few years television as a medium of communication was once and for all established. The opening of the New York World's Fair in 1939 was telecast. Research made steady advances during World War II, but telecasting itself stood still while giant corporations, belying the force of competition, struggled with each other for control.

At the close of World War II, nine TV stations were in operation. By 1948 the number had increased to 64. A total of 2053 outlets had been provided for by FCC and by 1957 the number of applications for commercial stations was steadily increasing. In the meantime the number of TV sets owned by Americans had passed 40 million. Commercial television, flexing its muscles, was about to put every other medium out of business, or reduce them to impotence.

But if commercial television has arrived, the educational branch has not. Here and there in the nation's schools, isolated examples of successful programs can be cited, but there is a sense of over-all frustration and impasse. One receives the impression from all of the conferences and councils, all the symposiums and workshops, all of the special meetings called to consider the future, and all of the legislation passed that here is something so big that it is presently impossible to take hold of it. The potential of educational television, both closed-circuit within the schools and commercial, is still largely on the horizon.

The principal obstacle to harnessing the television teaching power is money. Fantastic figures—at least fantastic ones viewed from the background of school budgets—seem to be involved in the activation of even a small television station. As a result, there has been nothing like a stampede to apply for the 242 outlets reserved by FCC for noncommercial and educational telecasting. As a matter of fact, considering that the date April 13, 1952, when the reservation was made, has been hailed as a red letter date on the educational calendar for many years, the response has been somewhat disappointing. This has not, however, been due to lack of planning.

In 1950 the National Education Association and six other national groups formed a committee on educational television. Largely through the efforts of this committee, the FCC set aside 12 per cent of all the TV outlets (80 very high frequency—VHF—and 162 ultra high frequency—UHF) for educational telecasting. Aided by grants from the Ford Foundation Fund for Adult Education, committees to study, advise, and encourage local applications for outlets have been active. A National Citizens Committee for Educational Television is investigating all possibilities for this medium in our society. Out of all this effort, one day, there will unquestionably come a learning force as big as television itself.

What the nature of this force will be can only be surmised. In a nation of pupil surpluses and teacher shortages, it is only natural for layman and educator to look to television as a possible equalizer, if not an outright panacea. The possibility that one teacher can now teach many classes through telecasts has appealed to school boards and administrators. But the danger of stereotype and automation has not escaped the thoughtful. The warmth of personal contact through a screen has not been entirely established.

A more likely direction for television use will be exploitation to the full of its "close-up" feature in relation to experiences and learning that are normally remote. Educational television, as a living showcase or exhibit of all the phenomena of living, has within its scope the possibility of presenting every experience and concept significant for life, in an unforgettable way. And it can do this by marshaling the force of all of the other classes of Instructional Materials so as to give each medium more strength than ever.

A glossary of instructional-TV terms is included on pages 330–31.

Some Technical Considerations

Television can be defined as a system of wireless communication of sound and sight. The process through which such communication is accomplished sends sound and pictures over the air simultaneously by radio waves. In its simplest aspects, a television camera records light patterns and converts them into electrical impulses. These impulses are sent to a target and then swept off in single file at the rate of four million a second by a scanning or sweeping beam. These impulses are amplified and sent into space, where they are intercepted by an antenna which leads them to the receiver. There they are selected or tuned, amplified, and directed to the small end of the picture tube. The impulses are then scanned or sprayed on the inside surface of the large, flat end of the tube, which is coated with a chemical like that used in fluorescent light; thus they strike the kinescope screen at the same rate of four million a second, forming 30 completed pictures. These 30 pictures a second can be compared to the 24 frames a second of the motion picture, accomplishing the same effect of motion.

Of particular interest to schools is so-called closed-circuit television. As compared with broadcast television, closed-circuit television is limited to a restricted audience usually within a small area such as is encompassed by a university campus or a school. But some recent court interpretations indicate the area is less of a defining element than the audience. Consequently, subscription television might presumably be considered closed-circuit, since it is not broadcast but limited in audience to subscribers.

GLOSSARY: INSTRUCTIONAL TV

Audio Frequency Signal. An electrical signal whose frequency lies within the limits of audibility, that is, 20 to 20,000 cycles per second.

Audio Pair. A pair of wires used to interconnect audio equipment such as microphones, speakers, etc.

Audio-Video Mixer. A miniature television transmitter which may be fed video and audio signals from separate sources for purposes of combining them into a signal which can be transmitted on a cable at radio frequencies. These radio frequencies usually fall in a standard television channel and are fed to a conventional television receiver.

Camera Monitor. A video monitor that is an integral part of the control unit for a television camera. It is electrically interconnected with the camera circuits and includes a wave-form oscilloscope.

Carrier Frequency Signal. An RF signal with which an audio or video signal may be combined for transmission.

Coaxial Cable. Special cable consisting of a center conductor concentrically positioned within an outer shield used to provide low loss transmission of video and/or radio frequency signals.

Distribution Amplifier. An amplifier used to connect a number of receivers or monitors to a source of a television signal.

Image Orthicon. A camera pickup tube in which the granular elements of a photosensitive screen generate a current when activated by light source and these currents are then internally amplified by electron multipliers within the tube.

Instructional Television. Television when used in formal classroom instruction on any educational level. The term is suggested to avoid confusion with possibly conflicting terms such as "wired television," "captive television," "closed loop television," "industrial television," "vidicon television," etc. This is also in contrast to the generally accepted term "educational television" which emphasizes broad non-credit cultural or educational programs of both commercial and educational telecasters. Instructional television is generally distributed throughout the campus or building by means of coaxial cable. Under certain conditions, it may be delivered to distant areas by micro-wave or low power transmitters; this possibility does not, however, alter the basic differentiation between instructional and educational television.

Line Amplifier. An amplifier used to boost the strength of video signals that have been attenuated by traversing long coaxial circuits.

Master Monitor. A video monitor employed in an originating studio which includes a wave-form oscilloscope to permit previewing any picture of several picture inputs supplied by different cameras and simultaneously observing the electronic trace of the waveform which forms the picture.

Patch Panel. A device on which incoming cables terminate in connectors in order that the various circuits may be interconnected at will by patching short lengths of cable between connectors.

Radio Frequency Signal. An electrical signal whose frequency lies above the limits of audibility, that is, greater than 20,000 cycles per second.

RF Amplifier. An amplifier that boosts the strength of a radio frequency signal.

Synchronizing Generator. A device which generates precision electrical timing pulses used to coordinate various functions throughout a television system.

Video Frequency. An electrical signal containing picture information derived from a television camera. The range of video frequencies commonly lies between 20 cycles per second and 6 million cycles per second.

Video Monitor. A television picture tube (kinescope) actuated by a high definition electronic circuit. If permanently connected to a program line, it is often referred to as a "line monitor."

Video Switcher. A device used to interconnect a desired video signal with an output circuit while retaining the electrical balance of all of the circuits connected to it. If specially adapted to fade one picture into another or to replace or superimpose pictures, it is called a "switcher-fader."

Vidicon. A camera pickup tube in which the outward flow of current is proportional to the amount of light falling upon the particular granular particle in a photosensitive screen upon which the scanning beam is focused.

From *Instructional Materials,* June, 1956 (by the editors). Reprinted by permission.

From the school's standpoint, the important aspect of closed-circuit is its economy and simplicity. It is now possible to buy the components for a complete television system, with as many receivers as are desired, well within the limits of school equipment expenditures. Furthermore, the Louisiana Educational TV Commission has pioneered a mobile television production and teletranscription unit capable of producing a complete recorded television program. The unit includes broadcast cameras, film pickup facilities, kinescope recorder, lights, and sound facilities. This ETV-Mobile was produced by the Dage Television Division of Thompson Products, Inc. It has been successfully demonstrated not only in Louisiana but during two summer workshops in Florida State University and elsewhere. Its mobility permits on-the-scene telecasts.

One of the most valuable features of this unit is the equipment for producing permanent recordings. Combined with mobility, which permits televising live programs directly from the program resource, the retention of the telecast for more than one showing adds the dimension necessary for harnessing the full power of education television.

Evaluation of Television Programs

The kinds of telecasts available for classroom use can follow approximately the classification set up for radio programs. Programs produced by commercial stations specifically for schools during school hours have already reached significant proportions. But both in quantity and quality the telecasts available outside school hours constitute the major potential.

Educational television stations, too, are increasing in number and output. The teacher, therefore, is already confronted with as large a selection problem as in the choice of radio programs or other classes of teaching tools. Furthermore, the same lack of previewing opportunities confronts the teacher as does the comparable lack of pre-auding of radio. Consequently evaluation must be based entirely on announcements, descriptions, and any teaching aids issued by the telecasters, plus such previous reputations as the participants and subject have earned.

As in the case of radio broadcasts, telecasts should meet certain standards of quality. The first criterion is *relevancy*. Does the program give promise of providing a desirable learning experience related to the teaching purpose? It is too much to expect the telecast always to be timed for the strategic day in the course of study, but if the content supports the curriculum adequately, a kinescope or even an off-schedule viewing will justify the use of the television medium in preference to other Instructional Materials.

The next criterion, *authority*, is of more importance in radio and television than in any other instructional medium. Since there is often no way to preview and evaluate in advance a telecast for classroom use the reputation of the personnel and the sponsoring agency frequently furnish the only basis for selection. On past performance certain sponsors, musicians, performers, directors, and authors can be counted on to produce nothing substandard.

Technical quality in telecasts increasingly involves more elements. To evaluate the video quality, criteria of several of the major classes of Instructional Materials may be involved—pictures, graphics, and still and motion projections. To judge the audio some of the criteria applied to disk and tape recordings may have to be called in. Briefly, the question can be asked, were the necessary details seen and the sounds heard by everyone?

Finally, the promise of viewer *participation* as evidenced in advance information, guides, and preparation will influence the teacher in deciding whether assignment of a telecast will benefit the pupils as much as reading in the library. Some participation may be direct, as in the teaching of a foreign language, where viewers are asked to repeat with or after the teachers. In some cases indirect activity will occur when viewers struggle with a problem posed on the screen or take action afterward.

From the attempts to evaluate both radio and television programs, it is evident that the learning potential of both radio broadcasts and telecasts is considerably reduced by the lack of an opportunity on the part of the teacher to pre-aud or preview. Both television and radio are further handicapped as classroom media by the absence of opportunities for repetition. Both of these handicaps, however, exist only in relation to the raw or original programs. Once recorded, the cast is exactly on the same educational level as print, eligible for the same preview and review consideration as all other media. It is evident that the recording is the device needed to convert the power of these two great media of learning. Fortunately such transformations are on the way.

Evaluation Checklist for Television Programs

Relevancy: Is the program curriculum related and better support for the teaching purpose than other media?

Authority: Can the sponsors and performers, based on past productions, be counted on to produce a quality program?

Technical Quality: Does video show vital details clearly, and is audio audible to every one?

Participation: How much participation by how many in the class is created?

Selection Aids for Telecasts

As has been intimated, kinescopes are to telecasts as transcriptions are to radio broadcasts. The kinescope, or "Kine," is mounted on a 16-mm motion-picture reel and can be projected on a 16-mm sound projector. It differs from a regular motion picture primarily in the fact that it is a recording of a live program exactly as it was telecast. Kinescopes can frequently be seen as rebroadcasts over educational television stations, or purchased or rented from film libraries.

In 1954 the Ford Foundation Fund for Adult Education established the Educational Television and Radio Center. Its purpose is to arrange for the recording of the best educational telecasts offered by commercial and educational television stations. Recently the Center has been obtaining foreign telecasts of educational promise. In this undertaking is the beginning of one of the most important future developments.

Because kinescopes are included in most of the motion picture selection aids previously described, a ready library for selection assistance is at the disposal of the teacher in the Materials Center. Most film libraries also are beginning to stock kinescopes, and titles will be found in the catalogs of state agencies which have a rental service for schools.

One of the earliest kinescopes produced was of the Kefauver committee's investigations of crime in cities. The CBS "You Are There" series has already been mentioned. In 1956 the Ford Foundation Center chose several TV program series for kinescopes, among them *Understanding Numbers*, a sequence of 30-minute telecasts on mathematics; *Talking Sense*, on speech correction; and *Friendly Giant*, which featured visits to a castle.

As the kinescope literature grows, the power of television in the classroom will take on new proportions.

Readings

AMERICAN COUNCIL ON EDUCATION. *Credit Courses in Television.* Washington, D.C.: American Council on Education, 1952. 49 pp.

DEKIEFFER, ROBERT, and COCHRAN, L. W. *Manual of Audio-Visual Techniques.* Englewood Cliffs, N.J.: Prentice-Hall, Inc., 1955. Pp. 163–71, 179–88.

GOLDENSON, R. M. "How to Get the Best Out of Television." *Parents Magazine,* XXXI (November, 1956), 44–45.

LEVENSON, W. B., and STASHEFF, EDWARD. *Teaching Through Radio and Television.* New York: Rinehart & Co., 1952. 553 pp.

LEWIS, PHILIP. "Closed Circuit TV," *Educational Screen,* XXXV (September, 1956), 270 ff.

UNITED STATES OFFICE OF EDUCATION. *Jobs Ahead for Educational TV.* Washington, D.C.: Government Printing Office, 1953. 2 pp.

Viewings

"Air Waves." Radio Corporation of America. (Film, 11 min., sd., b & w)

"Lessons from the Air." British Information Services. (Film, 14 min., sd., b & w)

"Television: How It Works." Coronet. (Film, 11 min., sd., b & w)

"The Television System." The McGraw-Hill Book Co. (Film, 14 min., sd., b & w)

Part IV

The Teacher
and Instructional
Materials

THE TEACHER
AND THE MATERIALS CENTER

A boy was performing an experiment of his own. In the physics lecture the day before, he was told that some metals conduct heat better than others. He encountered the subject of conductivity again that evening in his textbook, which listed the relative conductivity of all metals. In the morning he stood before a Bunsen burner. In his left hand was a foot-long piece of copper wire. His right hand held an equal length of iron wire, and both wires were of identical thickness. Deliberately he placed the ends of both wires into the flame of the Bunsen burner. The result was inevitable. He had to drop the copper wire in his left hand suddenly. The copper wire was red-hot, because of copper's greater conductivity, and it burned his fingers, while the iron wire was still relatively cool and did not produce such an unpleasant reaction.

The teacher who observed the experiment chuckled inwardly. Copper's greater conductivity had been indelibly impressed on the boy's mind—and fingers. But the teacher's chuckle was followed almost immediately by sober, professional reflection. What was his own "conductivity" in relation to the boy? That is, how was the light from his flame of knowledge and experience being conducted to the boy seeking knowledge?

The Teacher as Communicator

That the teacher's relation to the pupil has been changing

in recent years has been equally remarked about by layman and pupil. Many elements of change have been noted. But perhaps none has been more often decried than the apparent lack of subject specialization among those who teach. Comparisons have often centered on the scholarship of yesterday's teacher as contrasted to the methodology of today's pedagogue. In some academic circles, the product of our teacher education institutions has been scorned for knowing better "how" than "what" to teach. And subject specialists of the old school have been excoriated for their inability to share their knowledge with the pupils they undertake to teach. Without entering into this debate, which will continue unconstructively until both sides are willing to consider the merits of the case for their antagonists, the indisputable fact remains that neither "how" nor "what" can be taught without communication between pupil and teacher. The ancient adage of scholarship, "Half of knowledge is knowing where to find it," is as true today as it was in the past. Indeed, because of the acceleration in discovery and invention, the adage may be even more true today than in the past.

Consequently, whether the subject specialist, the child specialist, or a little of both are important to the teacher of the very young, it is apparent that special knowledge of the media of communication is of paramount concern. The variety and quantity of teaching tools are now so vast that mastery of the tools can no longer constitute merely an incidental aspect of teacher preparation. Nor can the teacher hope to keep pace with either his subject or his pupils unless a systematic contact with the universe of Instructional Materials is established.

The best approach to teaching tools is undoubtedly through a library or Materials Center. Early and continual relationship with the resource center of the school, and of the school system, and with libraries in the vicinity will insure adequate appraisal of teaching tool developments. Such relationship can be successful only if the teacher understands what these centers are and gains the acquaintance with them that is necessary to use them with confidence.

THE CLASSROOM-LEVEL MATERIALS CENTER

As indicated in the opening chapter, a Materials Center begins and ends at the classroom level. This must be understood at the outset. All of the Instructional Materials of a school system are selected, procured, organized, administered, maintained, and disseminated for the sole purpose of supporting the teacher's effort in the classroom. Consequently, the classroom itself is basically a Materials Center for the pupils who occupy that room, and the teacher must in his own way be somewhat an expert in Instructional Materials as well as a specialist in a content field and in dealing with a particular grade or age level of children and young people.

The responsibility of being an administrator is thus also placed on the teacher. He must plan with his pupils for his classroom collection of materials. In the process he must perform on a smaller scale many of the duties undertaken on the building level by the librarian or coordinator, and on the system level by the supervisor.

A look at the modern classroom suggests at once that the teacher must be prepared to carry on with at least three basic library functions for his classroom. He must first of all be able to select and procure Instructional Materials and equipment that will best augment his teaching effort. In the second place, he must see that adequate housing, organization, and maintenance of this equipment and material are provided while they are in the classroom. Third, he must be prepared adequately to utilize or to direct the use of these materials and equipment so that maximum educational use will be made of them.

These three functions constitute basic elements in librarianship. The teacher who performs them successfully on the classroom level and is convinced of their importance to learning will inevitably teach better.

Selection and Procurement

What is emerging is a recognition of the need for two collections of classroom materials. One of these is a rotating

The modern classroom: light for reading, shade for viewing. *Courtesy Research Laboratory Classroom, University of Michigan.*

collection of materials borrowed from the building Materials Center, and sometimes from the System Materials Center through the building center. The other is a permanently or semipermanently deposited collection of items which are needed so continually or periodically throughout the year that the school is justified in duplicating or purchasing them specifically for one classroom out of the Instructional Materials budget. In all cases, Instructional Materials that belong to the school system should be inventoried centrally, in the building and system centers.

Permanent Classroom Collection. Itemization of the permanent classroom collection of materials will vary according to a number of factors: grade level, subject, funds, and duplications available in the building center. Nevertheless, there would appear to be certain items nearly as important as the classroom tables, chairs, and chalkboard, and these constitute an Instructional Materials core.

In the way of equipment, certainly bulletin and pegboards are very important. So also is a screen for projections. The time is coming when radio and television receivers, and possibly disk and tape recorders, will be permanent equipment for each room. For the present, nothing quite as ambitious as permanent projector equipment has been proposed. In 1948, L. C. Larson's study for the 48th Yearbook of the National Society for the Study of Education showed that the frequency of average use in a school of 30 teachers for the more common projection equipment would permit one motion-picture, filmstrip, and 2 x 2 projector for every ten teachers, and one 3¼ x 4 projector and one opaque projector for every 15 teachers. It is probable that today the opaque and overhead projectors are used frequently enough to warrant one for every classroom.

When it comes to materials, we can begin with the textbook adoptions for the grade and subjects and certain alternates that might well be permanently represented on the classroom shelves. Some reference books are essential throughout the year. It is inconceivable that a classroom would be without at least one dictionary for its grade level —and perhaps several—so that the levels below and above might be interested. One standard school encyclopedia per classroom will earn its keep a hundred times during the school year. But this may be too large an investment for the average school. Compromises are effected in some buildings by duplicating standard sets in sufficient number so that single volumes or whole sets may be rolled into classes for extended periods of time. An atlas or two seem worthy of permanent classroom location. Few if any Reading books belong in the permanent collection. Their strength is in frequent rotation, and nothing can quite match the lure of new covers brought in from the library at frequent intervals.

The supply of classroom magazines will include at least one copy of the pupil subscription and any copies that students and teacher bring from home. Many free periodical subscriptions can also be duplicated in the classroom. The same is true of pamphlets and government publications, but any involving expenditure of school funds should probably be requested through the building library. Minimum globe and map requirements were indicated in the chapter on place media. A 12-inch globe belongs in each classroom above the second grade. Wall maps of the state, the United States, and the world belong there, too.

A picture collection is obligatory in nearly every classroom. If a vertical file is not provided, an orange crate will do. The rich sources of pictures have already been described. Scissors and paste will help in picture collection. Odds and ends of graphic materials gathered by pupils and teachers will enhance the permanent classroom collection. These include photos, cartoons, comics, posters, broadsides, graphs, diagrams, and charts. The same can be said of objects—specimens, models, dioramas, etc. Teacher-and-pupil-produced glass slides (2 x 2), transparencies, and other still projections can become a part of the classroom collection. But they can also be exchanged and shared with other classes through the building Materials Center.

Rotating Classroom Collection. The rotating collection will change as curriculum units require. Selection will result from teacher-pupil planning. In some cases the first contingent of materials will arrive after a teacher conference with the librarian. More often, student committees or individuals will investigate the resources available in the Materials Center and sponsor certain selections. Equally important will be the exposure of shortages and the stimulation of locating desirable wants for purchase by the Materials Center. Any of these student selection efforts will be superior in learning opportunities to a teacher selection based on the teacher's own investigation or college notes.

Classroom Utilization

Selection of the rotating collections during the school year may become the heart of Instructional Materials utilization. Upon the introduction of a curriculum unit, the teacher will want to take several steps to provide Instructional Materials in quantity and range sufficient to meet the individual differences in the class. A preliminary conference with the librarian should be held in advance to review the scope of the materials available. At this time the teacher should go over his outline or plan for the curriculum unit. He should also review his list of materials and wants. The librarian should be encouraged to make additional suggestions. If motion pictures are involved and especially if they are to be rented from an outside agency, the librarian will need time to make bookings. All of the materials relating to the subject of the unit can then be assembled on a table or in one section of the shelving. Or the materials can be left in place for the purpose of giving the pupils the opportunity to discover them.

What library skills the pupils will have to master in order to use any new kinds of materials, and what old skills will have to be reviewed, should also be discussed during the conference. For example, if the periodical index is to be used for the first time, some instruction in Wilson index entry form will have to be undertaken.

Scheduling of Materials Center or library work for the whole class or on an individual basis, or both, is usual practice. Successful procedures under all three have been seen in many schools.

Regularly scheduled library periods for a whole class at a time are more common in elementary than in secondary schools. An example of a library schedule is this one in a Florida elementary school:

Period	Hour	Mon.	Tues.	Wed.	Thurs.	Fri.
1	8:30– 9:00	Collecting Materials Requested by Teachers				
2	9:10– 9:40	6–1	6–2	6–3	6–4	6–5
3	9:50–10:20	5–1	5–2	5–3	5–4	5–5
4	10:30–10:50	1–1	2–1	2–2	2–3	2–4
5	11:00–11:25	Miscellaneous Library Work				
6	11:35–11:55	1–2	5–6	1–3	1–4	misc.
7	12:00–12:30	Lunch				
8	12:40– 1:05	3–1	3–2	3–3	3–4	1–5
9	1:15– 1:45	4–1	4–2	4–3	4–4	4–5
10	2– 3	Miscellaneous Library Work				

It will be noted from this schedule that each class has one scheduled period a week. The 29 classes in the school include five each in the sixth, fourth, and first grades, six in the fifth grade, and four each in the third and second grades. In this school, the 29 teachers have agreed to work alone in the library with their classes during one of their regularly scheduled library periods each month. This releases the librarian to visit classrooms and assist the teacher in planning class projects. It also gives the librarian time for teacher conferences. Finally, it permits the librarian to meet with committees. In this school, also, the arrangement is such that the teacher may sign up for these conferences.

High school practice favors the free library period. Pupils may use study hall or home room periods in the library. Occasionally a whole class may be scheduled for the library. Such class periods are often periods of instruction on the use of the library. More often they are reference and research periods. Pupils individually or in committees explore the center's resources for materials that help and advance the ideas of the subject under study. These exploration periods can be exploited in a number of ways.

Pupils should be encouraged to sponsor the material they like best. This may be an article in an encyclopedia or magazine, a picture discovered in the file, a filmstrip previewed in the preview room, a disk recording of national music, or a bit of manufactured goods.

Recently a fourth-grade geography unit on Mexico began in the building Materials Center in the following manner. The teacher introduced the subject in the classroom. It so happened that one of the pupils had visited in Mexico City with her parents the previous summer. She described some of the customs, costumes, sights, food, houses, music, dances, flowers, and other things she had seen, heard, tasted, smelled, and touched. From her experience and from some things the teacher told about his trip, and using the outline in the textbook, the class made up a list of the things they would like to know about Mexico. Unanimously they agreed that the Materials Center was the place to find materials and information. So it was decided to explore Mexico during the next library period in the Materials Center. The children selected their own subjects. One pupil was interested in the music of Mexico, another in the bullfights, a third in the dances, a fourth in the food, a fifth in the schools and children, a sixth in the industry, and so on. When two or more were interested in the same subject, they formed a committee. It was agreed that each subject would be presented to the class in the form of a show of any interesting materials found or made.

The class went to the Materials Center with their teacher. The librarian opened the period by saying, "I understand this class is going to begin a study of Mexico. On the basis of what we have learned about the library this year, what help do you think there is here?" One boy raised his hand and said he would go to the encyclopedia. "All right," the librarian said, "you go to an encyclopedia of your choice and find something on Mexico." The boy walked directly to the *World Book*, pulled the "M" volume off the shelf, turned in a matter of seconds to the article on Mexico, and held the volume high over his head so that the class might see it. Then the librarian asked other pupils to walk to materials that each thought would help in the study of Mexico. In succession, one pupil walked to the *Reader's Guide* and pointed to a list of articles on Mexico. Another stepped off a dozen paces, deliberately, to the vertical file and in a few seconds pulled out pamphlets and pictures. A little girl went to the recording index and discovered a disk on Mexican music and an exchange tape from Mexican children. One boy walked to the filmstrip board and found several on Mexico. Child after child went to the card catalog to locate items not yet produced.

Before the period was over, the class had discovered a wealth of materials. They agreed the next step would be to try to pick out the best materials on various aspects of Mexico they had individually and as committees chosen. So the materials were assembled and rolled into the classroom after the pupil librarians of the class had made the proper charge records.

The procedure described is neither new nor unusual. It is followed in many schools, with variations. In most instances the high degree of pupil absorption is impressive. So also is the co-operative effort of committees, the responsibility taken by the pupil librarians, and the enthusiasm with which individual items are presented and sponsored before the whole class. A high point is usually the projection of a motion picture and a comparison of details found to be similar or different from information gained in other sources. The final summary may take several forms: individual oral reports with displays of the most helpful materials; exhibits and bulletin board displays; a dramatization; opaque and transparent projection of those objects, pictures, maps, and charts that best tell the story; a diorama that employs as many of the materials used as possible.

Pupil Instruction in Materials

Library instruction by librarian or teacher or both has long been an integral part of the school curriculum. Beginning with the earliest grades, the standard library units have usually been taken as a sequence of lessons in the library, spaced over the years from grades one through twelve and varying in detail with the level and subject relationship. Library skills have also been integrated with the various school studies and taught in relation to the demands of the unit, sometimes by the teacher, at other times by the librarian, and at times together.

The standard units of library instruction usually include:

1. *The book:* its format and content, including title page, copyright notice, table of contents (contrasted with index), preface, introduction, running heads, and illustrations, how a book is made; history of the book, printing processes; some outstanding publishers.

2. *Arrangement of books:* the Dewey Decimal classification as a universal library language, and how it helps locate books; Cutter author numbers; special arrangements of fiction and biography.

3. *The card catalog:* dictionary arrangement; alphabetizing; filing rules; author, title, subject, and cross-reference cards (including "see" vs. "see also"); how to make the best use of the catalog.

4. *Periodicals and indexes:* names of the more important magazines and newspapers; importance of volume, issue, page, date; *Readers' Guide* cumulation; index entry form; how to locate the article.

5. *Dictionaries and their use:* identification of two American unabridged dictionaries, and dictionaries appropriate for given levels; definition sequence; pronunciation symbols; spelling aids; dictionary indications of preferred spelling and pronunciation; parts-of-speech abbreviations; quotations; devices for efficient use; special features.

6. *Encyclopedias:* identification of major school sets and of adult sets found in school library; whole-letter vs. split-letter volume and guide words; alphabetizing; relation of index to articles; illustrations; maps and their indexing; bibliographies; cross references and other aids.

7. *Atlases, maps and globes:* map reading; identification of major atlases; gazetteer indexes; guidebooks.

8. *Other reference books related to subject interests.*

9. *Compiling a bibliography:* form; procedure; arrangement.

To these have been added introductions to various audio-visual materials and equipment:

10. *Pictures:* posters; charts; diagrams; graphs; what to look for and how to read them.

11. *Slides and filmstrips:* care; projection; what to look for in the indexes.

12. *Motion pictures:* care; projection; what to look for in techniques, like time-lapse; how to judge a good film; indexes.

13. *Recordings:* disk and tape; care; operation; how to listen; how to record.

Classroom Housing of Materials and Equipment

To provide for both permanent and rotating classroom collections, there must be adequate housing. In the elementary school practically all instruction is carried on in the regular classroom. In the secondary school the regular classroom serves as home room and for instruction in such subjects as mathematics, social studies, and foreign languages. Special rooms and laboratories are provided for science, music, home economics, commerce, and physical education. Although these special rooms, too, should be planned for Instructional Materials use, the housing requirements for regular classrooms can be adapted.

Certain fundamentals of school architecture are of common concern in all classrooms. If Instructional Materials are to be used to best advantage, provisions must be made for physical comfort, for storage and for the accessories that make reading, viewing, and listening possible.

Physical Comfort. The basic elements of physical comfort are proper temperature, ventilation, light, and environment. Heat in winter and reasonable coolness during the warm weather will contribute to better use of Instructional Materials. Insulation and shields against the sun's rays, plus adequate ventilation, help prevent discomfort in hot weather. The introduction of air conditioning in higher-education buildings may foreshadow the day when all school construction will provide for such equipment.

Light is of vital concern to the teacher. Safeguards against strong glares and direct sun rays are now part of school architecture. It is agreed that light should be admitted to the room from both natural and artificial sources. Artificial light should be planned for the possibility of dark days and evening-class use by adults. An even intensity should be sought.

Lighting can be helped by attention to walls, ceilings, and floors. Cheerful colors brighten a room. Acoustical treatment of the walls and ceiling and a resilient floor covering will also reduce disturbing noises and help create the proper environment for Instructional Materials use. If rooms can also be so located as to be removed from noisy inside corridors and distracting outside play areas, better use of media will be assured. Nor should screening as protection against insects be overlooked.

Accessories for Instructional Materials Use. Reading, viewing, and listening require not only adequate lighting, but complementary darkening, projection, and sound provisions. There is little argument left for a separate audio-visual room in a school building. Such a special room increases cost without adding capacity. Scheduling is complicated by frustrating conflicts. The act of moving a class to a special projection center defeats some of the teaching strength of these media. Consequently, audio-visual authorities urge the equipping of all classrooms for viewing projections and listening to recordings. Such equipment, of course, should also be provided in special rooms and in the auditorium.

To handle projected and sound materials, particularly in the classroom, there must be an adequate number of electrical outlets generously distributed. The use of "electrical stripping" provides frequent outlets inexpensively. In installing electrical conduits during building construction or remodeling, the anticipated increasing use of closed-circuit television should be kept in mind.

All classrooms should be equipped for easy darkening. Seldom is complete darkness necessary. What is needed is some compromise on the overlighting that has inundated some modern school structures, plus a simple draw-curtain device. In the absence of air conditioning, an adequate ventilation device should operate during the darkening. Placement of the projection screen should insure that light does not fall on its surface.

Storage. Since every classroom will be a repository for both permanent and rotating collections of materials and equipment, storage facilities should be adequate. Thinking in terms of the Instructional Material formats reviewed thus far, shelving should meet the following standard specifications:

height: 5 ft.-6 in. elementary; 6 ft. junior high; 6 ft.-10 in. senior high
length: 36 in. is standard.
depth: 8 in. standard; 10-12 in. for magazines and picture books
shelf clearance: adjustable; if not, then 11 in. between shelves
shelf thickness: $\frac{7}{8}$ in.-$1\frac{3}{16}$ in.
shelving base: 6 in.-8 in.

The amount of shelving can be reckoned on the basis of shelves three-fourths full: per shelf foot, 12 primary books (grades one through three), eight regular books, or six reference books. Thus a 3-foot standard section (seven shelves) can be estimated to shelve (three-fourths full) 126 reference books or 168 regular books. An elementary school 3-foot section (five shelves) will accommodate 180 primary books, 120 regular books, or 90 reference books. One 3-foot section of book shelving for the permanent collection and one for the rotating collection should serve most classroom needs satisfactorily.

Storage space must be provided for maps, charts, and picture materials. Wall maps in their own mounts will be hung appropriately or kept on stands. But other maps should be stored in cabinets large enough to accommodate the largest of these materials flat, if possible, or rolled. At least one vertical file can do multiple storage duty for 8 x 11 pictures, pamphlets, maps, and other graphics. It can also be used to store temporarily that film awaiting projection, and that tape soon to be used.

A four-drawer 3 x 5 card file, primarily for indexing such classroom materials as constitute the permanent collection, but also for maintaining a request file and for compiling references, can be used to file 3¼ x 4 slides and filmstrips. There should be a vertical stand or cabinet for disk recordings. A place for the radio and television receivers, and for any projectors, recorders, and players temporarily assigned to the room, should not be omitted. Storage for graphic supplies and for completed and unfinished pupil work must also be taken into account.

Display. Along with storage facilities must come display equipment. The chalkboard is standard now, and the bulletin board almost so. But peg, flannel, and magnetic boards are still "extras" and need to be specified. Dimensions on these should be as generous as wall space will permit. Their value as teaching tools has already been indicated. Accommodation for exhibits, both on display tables and in cases, is important for the adequate use of real objects and for the exhibition of student work. Picture frames of standard sizes may be mounted on the wall to take rotated art masterpieces.

Elementary School Classrooms. Over and above these general classroom housing requirements, there are special ones that pertain to the elementary classroom. Minimum floor space of 900 square feet is specified. The contour of the classroom should be square, if possible. Ground-floor location in one-story buildings is urged to provide access to adjacent outdoor areas. Plumbing adequate to provide drinking fountain, work sink, and toilet with child-size fixtures is written into elementary classroom specifications. Furnishings should be flexible and movable so as to adjust to a variety of activities.

A few fairly fixed centers of activities aid efficient use of Instructional Materials. The reading center, for example, may group reading table and chairs around the book shelves and display. Science, homemaking, and art centers may be planned near displays of objects and graphic materials with worktables for production and demonstration.

Flexible centers may also be created for small group activities like committee meetings and search and research undertakings. But these fixed and flexible centers must in no way prevent sessions of the class as a whole involving such activities as storytelling, dramatics, rhythms, discussion, and manual work with large blocks, tools, and various simulated enterprises like a store, post office, or bank.

Secondary School Classrooms. Housing requirements that relate specifically to the regular classrooms of secondary schools suggest a minimum floor space of 750 square feet. Flexibility with movable tables, desks, and chairs, so that a variety of groupings and activities may be undertaken, is standard. Since the home room is frequently used for several subjects, adequate provision for shelving print and storing graphic material for each class is necessary. A drinking fountain combined with a work sink is always an asset.

The foregoing description of the various specifications for minimum classroom housing is no more than the skin and bones of the setting for vital multimaterials learning. More dramatic possibilities were suggested in the NEA Madison Square Garden "3-D Classroom" of tomorrow, which arranged all of the Instructional Materials and equipment into a working order plan. This model classroom of the future is still on exhibit in New York University.

THE BUILDING-LEVEL MATERIALS CENTER

In the minds of most teachers and pupils, the library or Materials Center is the special room in the building set aside to house the Instructional Materials used by the whole school. Centers at the classroom and system levels, if they are considered as libraries, are placed in a subordinate position. The term school library has usually been identified with a building-wide operation.

Looking at the building library, or Materials Center as it is now emerging, it can be described as a facility intended to house and disseminate Instructional Materials and equipment in support of the different kinds of learning that comprise the school program. Its clientele includes not only the teachers and pupils of the school but often those adults of the community who are engaged in parent-teacher activities or enrolled in adult education classes.

A corner of a building-level Materials Center. *Courtesy Houston Public Schools.*

Many activities are carried on in a Materials Center. Reading, research in groups or by individuals, storytelling, conferences, are all in the day's work. Listening, viewing, and previewing bulk larger as the Materials Center steadily enlarges its provisions for these. Production, always a part of the librarian's effort to display materials through bulletin boards, exhibits, circulars, and posters now takes on new meaning as teachers and pupils join in the effort. Finally, there are the organizational and administrative activities shared increasingly with the librarian by teachers and pupils. These activities can be grouped around procurement or accession or acquisition of materials; processing, classification, cataloging; charging, booking and circulating; maintenance and repair of both materials and equipment; housekeeping; and interpretation or dissemination or leadership in the utilization of materials and equipment.

To perform these functions, the building library or Materials Center must have adequate housing. Increasing attention to the architectural demands of the Materials Center is evident in the number of "facilities conferences" that have been held recently at state and national levels. Two good examples of guides to planning school libraries and Materials Centers are those recently issued by the Florida and Michigan departments of education. These and other conferences have produced architectural refinements that will certainly improve service.

Key points in planning the school library or Materials Center include location, size, functional units or areas, and furnishings. Since this resource center should occupy an area of maximum accessibility the location favored is near the building's center of interclass traffic. If there is a study hall, the Materials Center should be adjacent. Other requirements are that the library be away from the more noisy activities, such as music, shop, or physical education. Location on the first floor, with an entrance from the outside as well as double doors from the corridor, is another advantage in a library or Materials Center.

Specifications as to size begin with the suggestion that the Center be located where expansion will be possible. The area should be wider than the average classroom and much longer. Actual dimensions are tied to minimum seating capacity. It is suggested that the elementary school center be large enough to accommodate at one time the largest class plus 20. For the secondary school, a minimum seating capacity of 42 is established, with 12 seats or 10 to 15 per cent of every additional 100 enrollment above 300. Since the standard is to allow 25 square feet for every seated user, it is simple to calculate a reading room for 42 high school students as 1050 square feet. There are additional requirements for other activities and functions.

General-Use Area

Five functional areas of a school library or Materials Center can be distinguished. The first is the general-use area which provides for pupil reading, viewing and listening, and some storage and exhibiting. This is traditionally the part of the library where reference and research activities are carried on. Here also individual reading of books and magazines and other printed materials is concentrated. Viewing is limited to graphic materials, such as maps, pictures, posters, and diagrams. Projections of slides, filmstrips, stereographs, and other materials are limited to what can be viewed through hand equipment at a table or desk. Study of displays, exhibits, and bulletin boards is also a part of this area's activities. Such listening as is done is confined to listening posts, where earphones protect those otherwise engaged. Storage of materials used is provided in wall shelving, vertical files, cabinets, and racks.

Specifications for book shelving are the same as already given for the classroom center, except that there are many more sections. To allow for shifting and expansion, about 150 volumes are calculated for a standard 3-foot section seven shelves high. Consequently, a collection of 1500 volumes would require ten standard sections of shelving. Filing cases of legal size are recommended for the storing of pamphlets, pictures, and many other kinds of materials. At least two bulletin boards 3 x 6 are desirable, and these can be attached to the back of two sections of shelving.

Provision for users includes informal lounge chairs as well as the more formal 3- x 5-foot tables. Round tables 4 feet in diameter are used effectively in the elementary center. Stands for the larger reference books (dictionary, atlas, and other materials), and a book truck or two, complete the essentials of the general-use area.

Special-Use Areas

The special-use areas provide for activities that cannot go on in the general-use area: conferences; motion-picture viewing; still projection; record, radio, and television listening; and small group work of all kinds. Two conference rooms are desirable, one of 120 square feet, the other, 140 to 180 square feet, the latter especially for previewing motion pictures. If listening booths acoustically treated for sound can be added, recordings can be heard by small groups. Otherwise, the preview or conference rooms can be used.

Reception Area

A reception area somewhat separated from the general-use area has the advantage of removing noise and physical activity from the space reserved for concentration. Into this reception area should go all charging and booking, the public catalogs, and the inquiry or reference desk. Charging and booking desks vary in shape and size. Whether L-shaped, U-shaped, or rectangular, charging desks should provide adequate filing for records and storage of materials in transit. In schools with enrollment up to 500, catalog cabinets should contain a minimum of nine drawers. Each catalog drawer will hold about 1000 cards. In general, it is estimated that five cards per item are needed on the average to catalog materials adequately. Consequently, a cabinet of 9000 cards should handle the catalog for 1800 accessions of books, films, recordings, and other major items.

Work-Storage Area

The fourth unit in a library or Materials Center is the work-storage area. Here materials must be received, unpacked, and checked against orders and bills. Here, also, these materials will be processed and prepared for the shelves. The processes will include classification, cataloging, labeling, and treating. Special tasks for each class of materials include collating books and magazines, inspecting films and filmstrips, monitoring disks and tapes, and viewing and sampling many of these and other items. Maintenance and servicing of materials and equipment already in the collection will also be carried on here. Some of the specific tasks will include mending and binding books and magazines, cleaning and splicing films and filmstrips, oiling and inspecting equipment, and production of materials for bulletin boards and exhibits. Temporary storage for all materials in process must be provided here, and permanent storage for equipment like projectors, playbacks, recorders, screens, and public address systems.

Production Area

Finally, a production area is essential for the creation of graphic materials. In some centers this area is part of the work-storage area. But in view of the fact that teachers and students may want to use this space for instructional activity as well, a separate production area is desirable. It should be equipped with a basic supply of graphic equipment and materials.

THE SYSTEM LEVEL MATERIALS CENTER

Direction and co-ordination of the Instructional Materials program within a county or city school system is increasingly coming from a System Materials Center. Located generally in the administrative headquarters of the school system, the System Materials Center is primarily intended for teachers, librarians, and staff. It purchases centrally all materials for all of the schools, thus taking advantage of better prices that come with quantity orders. Many system centers also undertake central processing, delivering materials to the schools fully classified, cataloged, and labeled; more time is thus released for the building librarians to work with teachers and pupils. The system center by maintaining a central inventory is in a position to effect interlibrary loans of expensive or rare materials. It maintains a reservoir of materials and equipment on which the schools can draw for seasonal over-demands. In the system center is the teacher's professional library, and the collection of curriculum materials. Films owned by the school system are maintained there, and rentals for all schools are usually cleared through the system center. Productions of major proportions are undertaken in the system center. If the school system has its own radio or television station, the direction of it is in the system center.

Film maintenance in a system-level Materials Center. Here, motion-picture films are serviced on electric machines that clean, inspect, and repair approximately 400 reels a day. *Courtesy Alameda County (California) Schools Materials Center.*

Usually coordination of educational programs with the local commercial radio and television stations is the responsibility of the supervisor of Instructional Materials.

A typical system center will have several functional units. Prominent will be the professional or curriculum library with its collection of books and journals in education, psychology, and the teaching subjects. The textbook repository will also be housed in or near the center. Repositories of print, graphic, and projected materials will be sent out to supplement the schools' collections as needed. In connection with the film library, there will be preview rooms for teachers. Recording

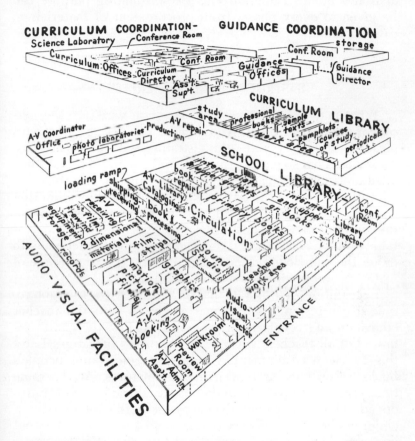

A system-level Materials Center. *Courtesy San Diego County (California) Schools.*

studios will be provided for disk and tape production. A photographic laboratory with darkroom and studio will offer opportunity for picture production. Television and radio production rooms are provided whether or not the school system operates its own stations.

There is a noticeable trend among school systems to provide a system center as a capstone for an Instructional Materials program. Under the direction of a supervisor and assistants at this headquarters, a co-ordinating purpose can be given to every phase, from procurement of materials to dissemination.

TEACHER PREPARATION IN INSTRUCTIONAL MATERIALS

What makes an Instructional Program work are the personnel responsible for it. Audio-visual experts and librarians plead for teachers and administrators who are materials-conscious. That so many principals and teachers are not, they attribute to faulty teacher education. Much of the teacher-education defect in the past is charged to the conviction that teachers can "pick up information about materials" incidentally in their methods and subject courses. But such incidental learning has not turned out a generation of teachers with either the knowledge or confidence to use the wide range of materials and equipment available today.

Recognition of this fact has in recent years brought required courses in Instructional Materials into the teacher education and certification programs. At first the course required of all teachers was one in children's literature. Later this course was augmented with units on young people's books, recordings, and even motion pictures. At the same time separate courses in audio-visual education were introduced. The most recent development is the integration of children's literature, library science, and audio-visual content into a single course in Instructional Materials. Further, since there has been an increasing trend to recruit the most interested and best-equipped teacher in Instructional Materials to assume the leadership and co-ordinator role in schools where there are not yet either librarians or libraries, teacher education institutions have tended to combine their scattered offerings in library science, children's literature, and audio-visual education into an Instructional Materials sequence.

In those institutions where at least one course is required of all students, two introductory courses in Instructional Materials are offered—one for prospective elementary teachers and the other for prospective secondary teachers. One of these courses deals with selection and utilization of Instructional Materials in grades one through six; the other covers materials for grades seven through twelve. Each course is an overview and together they include much of the content that has been covered in this book. The introductory course meets a requirement in general teacher education. But it can also be the starting point for special certification in Instructional Materials leading to school librarianship, audio-visual, specialization, and eventual supervision of a system center.

The sequence for the prospective teacher who wants to specialize in Instructional Materials may cover the following basic courses. After the first introductory course, the student takes the other introductory course so as to give him an overview of the full range, grades one through twelve. He then takes a course in materials center administration, which covers procurement, processing, housing, financing, maintenance, teacher and pupil relations, and other aspects of management.

A fourth course deals with the principles and philosophy of a materials program. It includes history of books, libraries, and other media of communications. Professional organizations, ethics, and personnel are also studied. Concepts and practices in Instructional Materials are analyzed with relationship to the curriculum and school program. It is intended in this course that the librarian or materials specialist should know his role in the learning process.

A fifth course is devoted to the reference function. Locating information and interpreting the collection to teachers and pupils are the essence of a Materials Center. Sources of information are studied in detail, and methods to help pupils find facts are examined. Teaching the use of library materials is usually incorporated in this course.

The sixth course is entirely devoted to the processing of materials. Considerable attention is devoted to classification and to the Dewey Decimal system. Almost equal attention is given to cataloging.

A seventh and final course completes the basic program. It is devoted entirely to graphic production. School-produced materials from bulletin board to filmstrip are studied. Actual laboratory opportunity to make slides, transparencies, mounted opaques, tape recordings, displays, and exhibits is a feature of the course.

These are the basic courses that lead to certification in the Instructional Materials field. Specializations are now being offered in each of the classes of materials leading to advanced degrees and supervisory certification.

Since 1955, Instructional Materials—including library science and audio-visual education—has been designated as No. 1 in the index of teacher demand. It is a teaching field with rapidly developing opportunities. In the years ahead it will require the best teaching talent this nation can produce.

Readings

DALE, EDGAR. "The Why of Audio-Visual Materials," in KINDER, J. S. and McCLUSKY, F. D. *The Audio-Visual Reader.* Dubuque, Ia.: W. C. Brown, 1954. Pp. 1–3.

DAVI. *Planning Schools for Use of Audio-Visual Materials: Classrooms.* Washington, D.C.: National Education Association, 1952. Pp. 5–28.

Dear Mr. Architect. Chicago: American Library Association, 1946.

DOUGLAS, MARY P. *Teacher-Librarian's Handbook.* Chicago: American Library Association, 1949. Pp. 1–15.

FARGO, LUCILE F. *Library in the School.* Chicago: American Library Association, 1947. Pp. 1-11.

A Functional Approach. Chicago: American Library Association, 1950.

Planning School Library Quarters. Chicago: American Library Association.

RUFSVOLD, MARGARET I. *Audio-Visual School Library Service.* Chicago: American Library Association, 1949. Pp. 69–87.

School Administrator and His Audio-Visual Program. Department of Audio-Visual Instruction, Washington, D.C.: National Education Association, 1954, Pp. 1–19.

Viewings

"Accent on Learning." Ohio State University. (Film, 30 min., sd., b & w)

"Audio Visual Aids to Learning." United States Army. (Film, 12 min., sd., b & w)

Find the Information. Coronet. (Film, 10 min., sd., b & w)

Library Organization. Coronet. (Film, 11 min., sd., b & w)

LIST OF TOOLS CITED

CHAPTER 1: GENERAL SOURCES

(1-1) *Dewey Decimal Classification and Relative Index.* Devised by MELVIN DEWEY. Abridged 7th edition. Essex County, N.Y.: Forest Press, Inc., Lake Placid Club, 1953. 315 pp. This is the small library version. The latest full edition is known as the 16th edition in two volumes.

(1-2) McCONNELL, MARIAN L., and WEST, DOROTHY HERBART (eds.). *Children's Catalog.* New York: H. W. Wilson Co., 1956. 852 pp. A classified catalog of 3204 children's books recommended for public and school libraries, with an author, title, and subject index.

(1-3) *Basic Book Collection for Elementary Grades.* Compiled by a subcommittee of the American Library Association, MIRIAM SNOW, chairman. Chicago: American Library Association, 1956. 133 pp.

(1-4) McCONNELL, MARIAN L., and WEST, DOROTHY HERBART (eds.). *Standard Catalog for High School Libraries.* New York: H. W. Wilson Co., 1957. 948 pp. A selected catalog of 3585 books.

(1-5) BERNER, ELSA R. (ed.). *Basic Book Collection for Junior High Schools.* Chicago: American Library Association, 1957. 127 pp.

(1-6) *Basic Book Collections for High Schools.* Chicago: American Library Association, 1957. 195 pp.

(1-7) *Publishers' Weekly.* New York: R. R. Bowker Co., 1872 to date. The American book trade journal, weekly.

(1-8) *Booklist and Subscription Books Bulletin.* Chicago: American Library Association. (*Booklist,* 1905–1956); *Subscription Books Bulletin,* 1930–1956; combined September 1956 to date.)

(1–9)   *Horn Book.* Boston: Horn Book, Inc., 1924 to date, bi-monthly. Magazine of books and reading for children and young people.

(1–10) *Wilson Library Bulletin.* New York: H. W. Wilson & Co. 1914 to date. September to June, monthly.

CHAPTER 2: TEXTBOOKS

(2–1)   COMENIUS, J. A. *Orbis Pictus.* Syracuse, N.Y.: C. W. Bardeen, 1887. 194 pp.

(2–2)   *New England Primer.* Albany, N.Y.: Munsell, 1875. 76 pp.

(2–3)   WEBSTER, NOAH. *Elementary Spelling Book.* New York: American Book Co., 1908. 174 pp.

(2–4)   McGUFFEY, W. H. *Old Favorites from the McGuffey Readers.* Edited by Harvey C. Minnich. New York: American Book Co., 1936. 482 pp.

(2–5)   *Textbooks in Print: the American Educational Catalog.* New York: R. R. Bowker Co., 1872 to date, annual. (Until 1956 titled *American Educational Catalog.*)

(2–6)   RUE, ELOISE. *Subject Index to Books for Primary Grades,* and supplement, *Subject Index to Books for Intermediate Grades.* Chicago: American Library Association, 1943, 1946, 1950. 236 pp., 76 pp., and 493 pp.

CHAPTER 3: REFERENCE BOOKS

Bibliographies   (*See also* Chapter 1, entries 2–10)

(3–1)   SHORES, LOUIS. *Basic Reference Sources.* Chicago: American Library Association, 1954. 378 pp.

(3–2)   WINCHELL, CONSTANCE. *Guide to Reference Books, and Supplement.* Chicago: American Library Association, 1951. 645 pp., 5500 titles, plus 1000 in supplement; classified and coded all languages; aims to be comprehensive selection "with a large general reference library in mind."

(3–3)   *Cumulative Book Index.* New York: H. W. Wilson Co.. 1898 to date, cumulated. A world list of books in the English language.

(3–4)   *Publishers' Trade List Annual,* 1873 to date; *Books in Print.* New York: R. R. Bowker Co. 1948 to date, annual. An author-title series index to the *Publishers' Trade List Annual.*

Indexes (*See also* Chapter 2, entry 6)

(3–5) *Vertical File Index.* New York: H. W. Wilson Co., 1935 to date, monthly. Service Basis. Indexes back to 1932.

(3–6) *Selected United States Government Publications.* Washington, D.C.: Government Printing Office, 1928 to date, semimonthly.

(3–7) *Bibliographic Index.* New York: H. W. Wilson Co., 1938 to date. Semiannual.

(3–8) *Essay and General Literature Index.* New York: H. W. Wilson Co., 1900–1933; *Supplements,* 1934 to date.

(3–9) *Readers' Guide to Periodical Literature.* New York: H. W. Wilson Co., 1900 to date, semimonthly, monthly July, August. *Abridged Readers' Guide,* New York: H. W. Wilson Co., 1935 to date.

(3–10) *Book Review Digest.* New York: H. W. Wilson Co., 1905 to date, monthly.

Encyclopedias

(3–11) *Compton's Pictured Encyclopedia and fact-index.* Chicago: F. E. Compton & Co., 1922 to date. 15 volumes.

(3–12) *World Book Encyclopedia.* Chicago: Field Enterprises, Inc., 1917 to date. 10 volumes.

(3–13) *Britannica Junior.* Chicago: Encyclopaedia Britannica, Inc., 1934 to date. The boys' and girls' encyclopaedia, prepared under the supervision of the editors of the *Encyclopaedia Britannica.* 15 volumes.

(3–14) *American Educator Encyclopedia.* Lake Bluff, Ill.: United Educators, Inc., 1010 to date. 10 volumes.

(3–15) *Book of Knowledge.* New York: Grolier Society, Inc., 1910 to date. 20 volumes.

(3–16) *Our Wonderful World.* Chicago: Spencer Press, Inc., 1955 to date. 18 volumes.

(3–17) *Oxford Junior Encyclopedia.* New York: Oxford University Press, 1948 to date. 13 volumes.

(3–18) *American Peoples Encyclopedia.* Chicago: Spencer Press, Inc., 1948 to date. 20 volumes.

(3–19) *Encyclopedia Americana.* New York: Americana Corp., 1829 to date. 30 volumes.

(3–20)   *Encyclopaedia Britannica.* Chicago: Encyclopaedia Britannica, Inc., 1768 to date. 24 volumes.

(3–21)   *Collier's Encyclopedia.* New York: P. F. Collier & Son Corp., 1950 to date. 20 volumes.

(3–22)   *Columbia Encyclopedia.* New York: Columbia University Press, 1935 to date. 1 volume.

(3–23)   *Lincoln Library of Essential Information.* Buffalo: Frontier Press Co., 1924 to date. 1 or 2 volumes.

Annuals

(3–24)   *Compton Yearbook.* Chicago: F. E. Compton & Co., 1958 to date.

(3–25)   *World Book Encyclopedia Annual Supplement.* Chicago: Field Enterprises, Inc., 1922 to date.

(3–26)   *World Topics Yearbook.* Lake Bluff, Ill.: United Educators, Inc., 1956 to date. (Quarterly before 1956.)

(3–27)   *Book of Knowledge Annual.* New York: Grolier Society, Inc., 1939 to date.

(3–28)   *Britannica Book of the Year.* Chicago: Encyclopaedia Britannica, 1938 to date.

(3–29)   *Americana Annual.* New York: Americana Corp., 1923 to date.

(3–30)   *American Peoples' Encyclopedia Yearbook.* Chicago: Spencer Press, Inc., 1952 to date.

(3–31)   *Collier's Yearbook.* New York: P. F. Collier & Son Corp., 1939 to date.

(3–32)   *World Almanac and Book of Facts.* New York: World-Telegram, 1868 to date.

(3–33)   *Information Please Almanac.* 1945 to date.

(3–34)   *Statesman's Yearbook.* London: The Macmillan Co., Ltd., 1864 to date.

(3–35)   *Statistical Abstract of the United States.* Washington, D.C.: Government Printing Office, 1878 to date.

Dictionaries

(3–36)   *Rainbow Dictionary,* by WENDELL W. WRIGHT; assisted by HELENE LAIRD; illustrated by JOSEPH LOW. Cleveland: World Publishing Co., 1947. 433 pp.

(3–37)   *Golden Dictionary,* words by ELEEN WALPOLE; illustrated by GERTRUDE ELLIOTT; prepared under the supervision of MARY REED. New York: Simon & Schuster, Inc., 1944. 94 pp.

(3–38) *My First Dictionary*, words by LAURA OFTEDAHL and NINA JACOBS; pictures by PELAGIE DOANE. New York: Grosset & Dunlap, 1948. 140 pp.

(3–39) *Picture Book Dictionary*, by W. D. MACBEAN. Chicago: Childrens Press, 1952.

(3–40) *Thorndike-Barnhart Beginning Dictionary*. Chicago: Scott, Foresman & Co., 1952. 645 pp.

(3–41) *Thorndike-Barnhart Junior Dictionary*, by E. L. THORNDIKE and CLARENCE L. BARNHART. Chicago: Scott, Foresman & Co., 1952. 784 pp.

(3–42) *Webster's Elementary Dictionary*. Merriam-Webster. Cincinnati: American Book Co., 1953. 740 pp.

(3–43) *Webster's: A Dictionary for Boys and Girls*. Cincinnati: American Book Co., 1956. 739 pp.

(3–44) *Funk & Wagnalls "Standard" Junior Dictionary of the English Language*, by the Funk & Wagnalls editorial staff. New York: Funk & Wagnalls Co., 1953. 768 pp.

(3–45) *Winston Dictionary for Children*. Philadelphia: The John C. Winston Co., 1953. 629 pp.

(3–46) *Thorndike-Barnhart High School Dictionary*. Chicago: Scott, Foresman & Co., 1952. 1096 pp.

(3–47) *Webster's Students Dictionary for Upper School Levels; a Merriam-Webster*. Cincinnati: American Book Co., 1953. 1002 pp.

(3–48) *Funk & Wagnalls Standard High School Dictionary*. New York: Funk & Wagnalls Co., 1955. 1024 pp.

(3–49) *Winston Dictionary for Schools*. Philadelphia: The John C. Winston Co., 1956. 950 pp.

(3–50) *American College Dictionary*. New York: Random House, Inc., 1956. 1472 pp.

(3–51) *New College Standard Dictionary*. New York: Funk & Wagnalls Co., 1956. 1424 pp.

(3–52) *Webster's New Collegiate Dictionary*. Springfield, Mass.: G. & C. Merriam & Co., 1956. 1196 pp.

(3–53) *Webster's New World Dictionary of the American Language. College Edition*. Cleveland: World Publishing Co., 1956. 1760 pp.

(3–54) *Webster's New International Dictionary of the English Language*, 2d ed. unabridged. Springfield, Mass.: G. & C. Merriam & Co., 1954. 3350 pp.

(3–55)   *Funk & Wagnalls New Standard Dictionary of the English Language.* New York: Funk & Wagnalls Co., 1947. 2895 pp.

(3–56)   *Oxford English Dictionary.* New York: Oxford University Press, 1933. 13 volumes and Supplement.

Biographical Tools

(3–57)   *Webster's Biographical Dictionary.* Springfield, Mass.: G. & C. Merriam & Co., 1943. 1697 pp.

(3–58)   DE FORD, MIRIAM. *Who was When? A Dictionary of Contemporaries.* New York: H. W. Wilson Co., 1950. Unnumbered pages.

(3–59)   *Current Biography: Who's News and Why.* New York: H. W. Wilson Co., 1940 to date, monthly.

(3–60)   *Who's Who in America. A Biographical Dictionary of Notable Living Men and Women.* Chicago: A. N. Marquis & Co., 1899 to date, biennial.

(3–61)   KUNITZ, S. D. et al. *American Authors 1600–1900; British Authors of the 19th Century; Junior Book of Authors; Twentieth Century Authors and Supplement.* New York: H. W. Wilson Co., 1936 to 1955.

(3–62)   MORGAN, JAMES. *Our Presidents. 1789–1949.* New York: The Macmillan Co., 1949. 438 pp. Brief biographies of our chief magistrates from Washington to Truman.

Additional Basic Reference Books for Schools

(3–63)   ALEXANDER, G. L. *Nicknames of American Cities, Towns, and Villages, Past and Present.* New York: Special Libraries Association, 1951. 74 pp.

(3–64)   BERREY, L. V., and VAN DEN BARK, MELVIN. *The American Thesaurus of Slang.* New York: Thomas Y. Crowell Co., 1953. 1272 pp.

(3–65)   BARTLETT, JOHN. *Familiar Quotations.* Boston: Little, Brown and Co., 1955. 1614 pp.

(3–66)   BENET, WILLIAM ROSE. *The Reader's Encyclopedia.* New York: Thomas Y. Crowell Co., 1948. 1242 pp.

(3–67)   BREWTON, JOHN EDMUND, and BREWTON, SARA WESTBROOK (comps.). *Index to Children's Poetry.* New York: H. W. Wilson Co., 1942. 965 pp.

(3–68) BREWER, EBENEZER CABHAM (comp.). *Dictionary of Phrase and Fable.* Philadelphia: J. B. Lippincott Co., 1937. 1157 pp.

(3–69) COMMAGER, HENRY STEELE (ed.). *Documents of American History.* New York: Appleton Century-Crofts, Inc., 1949. 2 volumes.

(3–70) COMMAGER, H., and NEVINS, ALLAN (eds.). *The Heritage of America.* Boston: Little, Brown and Co., 1949. 1227 pp.

(3–71) *Cushing's Manual of Parliamentary Practice.* Philadelphia: The John C. Winston Co., 1947. 267 pp.

(3–72) DOUGLAS, GEORGE WILLIAM. *American Book of Days.* New York: H. W. Wilson Co., 1948. 697 pp.

(3–73) EASTMAN, MARY HUSE. *Index to Fairy Tales, Myths, and Legends.* Boston: F. W. Faxon Co., Inc., 1952. 610 pp.

(3–74) GRANGER, EDITH (ed.). *Granger's Index to Poetry.* New York: Columbia University Press, 1953. 1832 pp.; Supplement 1951–1955.

(3–75) HISCOX, G. D. *Henley's Twentieth Century Book of Formulas, Processes and Trade Secrets.* New York: Norman W. Henley Publishing Co., 1945. 867 pp.

(3–76) HUNT, PETER. *Peter Hunt's How-To-Do-It-Book.* Englewood Cliffs, N.J.: Prentice-Hall, Inc., 1952. 294 pp.

(3–77) JACKSON, KATHRYN. *The New Golden Almanac.* New York: Simon & Schuster Co., 1952. 128 pp.

(3–78) KANE, JOSEPH NATHAN. *Famous First Facts.* New York: H. W. Wilson Co., 1950. 888 pp.

(3–79) KINGERY, ROBERT ERNEST (ed.). *How-To-Do-It-Books: A Selected Guide.* New York: R. R. Bowker Co., 1950. 293 pp.

(3–80) MEYER, J. S. *Book of Amazing Facts.* Cleveland: World Publishing Co., 1950. 186 pp.

(3–81) NORTON, D. L., and RUSHTON, PETERS. *Classical Myths in English Literature.* New York: Rinehart & Co., 1952. 444 pp.

(3–82) PARKER, BERTHA M. *Golden Treasury of Natural History.* New York: Simon & Schuster, Inc., 1952. 216 pp.

(3–83) POST, EMILY. *Etiquette.* New York: Funk & Wagnalls Co., 1950. 654 pp.

(3–84) PROCHNOW, HUBERT VICTOR. *Toastmaster's Handbook.* Englewood Cliffs, N.J.: Prentice-Hall, Inc., 1949. 374 pp.

(3–85) ROBERT, HENRY MARTYN. *Robert's Rules of Order Revised.* Chicago: Scott, Foresman & Co., 1951. 326 pp.

(3–86)   SMITH, CLEVELAND H., and TAYLOR, GERTRUDE RHODA. *Flags of All Nations.* New York: Thomas Y. Crowell Co., 1950. 168 pp.

(3–87)   SHANKLE, GEORGE EARLIE. *State Names, Flags, Seals, Songs, Birds, Flowers, and Other Symbols.* New York: H. W. Wilson Co., 1941. 522 pp.

(3–88)   ———. *American Mottoes and Slogans.* New York: H. W. Wilson Co., 1941. 183 pp.

(3–89)   ———. *American Nicknames; Their Origin and Significance.* New York: H. W. Wilson Co., 1937. 599 pp.

(3–90)   SMITH, ELSDON COLES. *Story of Our Names.* New York: Harper & Bros., 1950. 296 pp.

(3–91)   VANDERBILT, AMY. *Any Vanderbilt's Complete Book of Etiquette.* New York: Doubleday & Co., Inc., 1958. 700 pp.

(3–92)   FENWICK, MILLICENT. *Vogue's Book of Etiquette.* New York: Simon & Schuster Co., 1948. 658 pp.

(3–93)   *Who's Who; An Annual Biographical Dictionary* with which is incorporated *Men and Women of the Times.* London: The Macmillan Co., Ltd., 1904 to date, annual.

CHAPTER 4: READING BOOKS

(4–1)   MOTHER GOOSE. Many excellent editions are annotated in: McCONNELL, MARIAN L., and WEST, DOROTHY HERBART (eds.). *Childrens Catalog.* New York: H. W. Wilson Co., 1956. Pp. 45–46. Two more to look for on library shelves are: DEANGELI, MARGUERITE. *Book of Nursery and Mother Goose Rhymes.* New York: Doubleday & Co., 1954. 192 pp., and *Tall Book of Mother Goose, illustrated by* FEODOR ROJANOVSKY. New York: Harper & Bros., 1942. 120 pp.

(4–2)   McFARLAND, WILMA K. *For a Child; Great Poems Old and New.* Philadelphia: Westminster Press, 1947. 96 pp.

(4–3)   FLACK, MARJORIE. *Angus and the Ducks.* New York: Doubleday & Co., Inc., 1930. Unpaged.

(4–4)   POTTER, BEATRIX. *Tale of Peter Rabbit.* New York: Frederick Warne & Co., Ltd., 1903. 81 pp.

(4–5)   PETERSHAM, MAUD and MISKA. *Rooster Crows.* New York: The Macmillan Co., 1945. Unpaged.

(4–6)   BROWN, MARGARET WISE. *Good Night Moon.* New York: Harper & Bros., 1947. 31 pp.

(4-7) ADAMS, GEORGE A. *ABC Picture Book.* New York: Platt & Munk, Inc., 1947. Unpaged.

(4-8) TUDOR, TASHA. *A Is For Annabelle.* New York: Oxford University Press, 1954. Unpaged.

(4-9) BRUNHOFF, JEAN DE. *Story of Babar.* New York: Random House, Inc., 1933. 47 pp.

(4-10) GAG, WANDA. *Millions of Cats.* New York: Coward, McCann, Inc., 1928. Unpaged.

(4-11) DOANE, PELAGIE. *A Small Child's Bible.* New York: Oxford University Press, 1946. 142 pp.

(4-12) LEAF, MUNRO. *Manners Can Be Fun.* Philadelphia: J. B. Lippincott Co., 1936. 45 pp.

(4-13) GEISEL, THEODORE SEUSS. *And To Think That I Saw It On Mulberry Street.* New York: The Vanguard Press, 1937. Unpaged.

(4-14) McCLOSKEY, ROBERT. *Make Way for Ducklings.* New York: The Viking Press, Inc., 1941. 67 pp.

(4-15) MILNE, A. A. *When We Were Very Young.* New York: E. P. Dutton & Co., Inc., 1924. 100 pp.
———. *Now We Are Six.* New York: E. P. Dutton & Co., Inc., 1927. 103 pp.
———. *Winnie the Pooh.* New York: E. P. Dutton & Co., Inc., 1926. 32 pp.
———. *House at Pooh Corner.* New York: E. P. Dutton & Co., Inc., 1928. 17 pp.

(4-16) GRAHAME, KENNETH. *Wind in the Willows.* New York: Charles Scribner's Sons, The Heritage Press, 1907. 312 pp.

(4-17) GRAMATKY, HARDIE. *Little Toot.* New York: G. P. Putnam's Sons, 1939. Unpaged.

(4-18) BURTON, VIRGINIA LEE. *Mike Mulligan and His Steam Shovel.* Boston: Houghton Mifflin Co., 1939. Unpaged.

(4-19) LAWSON, ROBERT. *Rabbit Hill.* New York: The Viking Press, 1944. 127 pp.

(4-20) LANGSTAFF, JOHN. *Frog Went A-Courtin,* illustrated by FEODOR ROJANKOVSKY. New York: Harcourt, Brace & Co., Inc., 1955. Unpaged.

(4-21) PERRAULT, CHARLES. *Cinderella: or the Little Glass Slipper,* translated, with pictures by MARCIA BROWN. New York: Charles Scribner's Sons, 1954. Unpaged.

(4–22) HOGBEN, LANCELOT. *First Great Inventions*. New York: Lothrop, Lee & Shepard Co., 1950. 36 pp.

(4–23) SCHNEIDER, HERMAN and NINA. *Let's Find Out*. New York: Scott, Foresman & Co., 1946. 36 pp.

(4–24) LEWELLEN, JOHN. *True Book of Moon, Sun and Stars*. Chicago: Children's Press, Inc., 1954. 43 pp.

(4–25) HUNTINGTON, HARRIET E. *Let's Go Outdoors*. New York: Doubleday & Co., Inc., 1939. 88 pp.

(4–26) WEBBER, IRMA E. *Up Above and Down Below*. New York: Scott, Foresman & Co., 1943. Unpaged.

(4–27) D'AULAIRE, INGRI, and PARIN, EDGAR. *Abraham Lincoln*. New York: Doubleday & Co., Inc., 1939. Unpaged.

(4–28) DALGLIESH, ALICE. *Fourth of July Story*. New York: Charles Scribner's Sons, 1956. Unpaged.

(4–29) FITCH, FLORENCE MARY. *One God*. New York: Lothrop, Lee & Shepard Co., 1944. 143 pp.

(4–30) LANG, ANDREW. *The Blue Fairy Book*. Longmans, Green & Co., 1948.
————. *The Crimson Fairy Book*. Longmans, Green & Co., 1947.
————. *The Green Fairy Book*. Longmans, Green & Co., 1948.
————. *The Olive Fairy Book*. Longmans, Green & Co., 1949.
————. *The Orange Fairy Book*. Longmans, Green & Co. 1949.
————. *The Red Fairy Book*. Longmans, Green & Co., 1948.
————. *The Rose Fairy Book*. Longmans, Green & Co., 1948.
————. *The Violet Fairy Book*. Longmans, Green & Co., 1947.
————. *The Yellow Fairy Book*. Longmans, Green & Co., 1947.

(4–31) ANDERSEN, HANS CHRISTIAN. *Complete Andersen,* translated by JEAN HERSHOLT; illustrated in color by FRITZ KREDEL. New York: The Heritage Press, 1949. (3 volumes in 1.) There are, of course, other editions, but this is the fullest. It contains all 168 stories.

(4–32) GRIMM, JACOB and WILHELM. *Fairy Tales*. The editions are many but these are worth looking at on the shelves:
Household Stores, translated by LUCY CRANE; illustrated by JOHANNES TROYER. New York: The Macmillan Co., 1954.

Tales from Grimm and *More Tales from Grimm*. Translated and illustrated by WANDA GAG. New York: Coward-McCann Co., 1936, 1947.

House in the Woods. Drawings by L. LESLIE BROOKS. New York: Frederick Warne & Co., 1944.

(4–33) *Arabian Nights*. Some editions are:

Arabian Nights, collected and edited by ANDREW LANG; illustrated by VERA BOCK. New York: Longmans, Green & Co., 1946. 303 pp.

Arabian Nights, edited by PADRAIC COLUM; illustrated by LYND WARD. New York: The Macmillan Co., 1953. 344 pp.

Arabian Nights, edited by KATE D. WIGGINS and NORA A. SMITH; illustrated by MAXFIELD PARRISH. New York: Charles Scribner's Sons, 1937. 338 pp.

(4–34) MALORY, SIR THOMAS. *King Arthur and His Knights of the Round Table*. Editions of note are:

Boy's King Arthur, edited by SIDNEY LANIER; illustrated by N. C. WYETH. New York: Charles Scribner's Sons, 1917.

Story of King Arthur and His Knights; Story of the Champions of the Round Table; Merry Adventures of Robin Hood. New York: Charles Scribner's Sons.

(4–35) AESOP. *Fables of Aesop,* selected by JOSEPH JACOBS; illustrated by KURT WIESE. New York: The Macmillan Co., 1950.

(4–36) McSPADDEN, J. W. *Robin Hood and His Merry Outlaws,* illustrated by LOUIS SLOBODKIN. Cleveland: The World Publishing Co., 1946.

PYLE, HOWARD. *Merry Adventures of Robin Hood*. New York: Charles Scribner's Sons, 1946.

(4–37) COLLODI, C. *Adventures of Pinocchio,* translated by DELLA CHIESA; illustrated after ATTILIO MUSSINO. New York: The Macmillan Co.

(4–38) SPYRI, JOHANNA. *Heidi,* illustrated by JESSIE WILCOX SMITH. New York: David McKay Co., Inc.

———. *Heidi,* illustrated by LEONARD WEISGARD. Cleveland: The World Publishing Co., 1946. 334 pp.

(4–39) SEWELL, ANNA. *Black Beauty*. Philadelphia: MacRae, Smith Co., n.d. 295 pp.

(4–40) CARROLL, LEWIS. *Alice's Adventures in Wonderland and Through the Looking Glass*. Illustrated by JOHN TENNIEL. New York: The Macmillan Co., 1950. 177 pp.

———. *Ibid*. New York: Grosset & Dunlap. 1946. 328 pp.

(4–41) DEFOE, DANIEL. *Robinson Crusoe,* illustrated by LYND WARD. New York: Grosset & Dunlap. 1946.

———. *Ibid.,* illustrated by E. BOYD SMITH. New York: Houghton Mifflin Co., 1931. 336 pp.

———. *Ibid.,* illustrated by ROGER DUVOISIN. Cleveland: World Publishing Co., 1946. 287 pp.

These are noteworthy among the many editions of *Robinson Crusoe.*

(4–42) SWIFT, JONATHAN. *Gulliver's Travels,* illustrated by ARTHUR RACKHAM. New York: E. P. Dutton & Co.

———. *Ibid.,* illustrated by R. M. POWERS. Cleveland: World Publishing Co.

(4–43) STEVENSON, ROBERT L. *Treasure Island,* illustrated by N. C. WYETH. New York: Charles Scribner's Sons.

———. *Ibid.,* illustrated by C. B. FALLS. Cleveland: World Publishing Co.

———. *Ibid.,* illustrated by NORMAN PRICE. New York: Grosset & Dunlap.

These are three to watch for among the numerous editions of this work.

(4–44) DUMAS, ALEXANDRE. *Three Musketeers,* illustrated by MAURICE LELOIR. New York: Dodd, Mead & Co.

(4–45) CLEMENS, S. L. (Mark Twain). *Adventures of Huckleberry Finn. Adventures of Tom Sawyer,* illustrated by DONALD McKAY. New York: Grosset & Dunlap.

———. *Ibid.* New York: Harper & Bros.

(4–46) ALCOTT, LOUISA MAY. *Little Women,* illustrated by LOUIS JAMBOR and DOUGLAS W. GORSLINE. New York: Grosset & Dunlap.

———. *Ibid.,* illustrated by JESSIE WILCOX SMITH. Boston: Little, Brown & Co.

———. *Little Men,* illustrated by LOUIS JAMBOR and DOUGLAS W. GORSLINE. New York: Grosset & Dunlap.

———. *Ibid.,* illustrated by REGINALD BURCH. Boston: Little, Brown & Co.

———. *Jo's Boys,* illustrated by LOUIS JAMBOR and DOUGLAS W. GORSLINE. New York: Grosset & Dunlap.

———. *Ibid.,* illustrated by CLARA M. BURD. Boston: Little, Brown & Co.

(4–47) DODGE, MARY MAPES. *Hans Brinker: or The Silver Skates,* illustrated by GEORGE WHARTON EDWARDS. New York: Charles Scribner's Sons, 1902. 393 pp. Also available in many other editions.

(4–48)   "Landmark Books." New York: Random House. Some titles included in this series:
History:
  DAUGHTERTY, J. H. *Landing of the Pilgrims.*
  FISHER, D. F. C. *Our Independence and the Constitution.*
  KANTOR, MACKINLAY. *Lee and Grant at Appomattox.*
  LAWSON, T. W. *Thirty Seconds Over Tokyo.*
Biography:
  REYNOLDS, Q. J. *Wright Brothers.*
  SHIPPEN, K. B. *Mr. Bell Invents the Telephone.*
Social Studies:
  NATHAN, A. G. *Building of the First Trans-Continental Railroad.*

(4–49)   "All About Books." New York: Random House, include among others:
  PRATT, FLETCHER. *Rockets and Jets*
  FREEMAN, I. M. *The Atom*
  TANNEHILL, I. R *Weather*
  WHITE, A. T. *The Stars*
  BIANCO, M. W. *Pets*
  PEI, M. A. *Language*

(4–50)   "First Book" series. New York: Franklin Watts, Inc., includes *First Bible* and "First Books" of *Airplanes, Baseball, Birds, Bridges, Cats, Dolls, Electricity, Jazz, Plants,* and many more.

Professional Books for Teachers on Instructional Materials Use

(4–51)   MOTT, CAROLYN, and BAISDEN, LEO. *Children's Book on How to Use Books and Libraries.* New York: Charles Scribner's Sons, 1955. 207 pp.

(4–52)   FLEXNER, JENNIE. *Making Books Work.* New York: Simon & Schuster, Inc., 1943. 271 pp.

(4–53)   WITTICH, W. A., and SCHULLER, C. F. *Audio-Visual Materials: Their Nature and Use.* New York: Harper & Bros., 1957. 570 pp.

(4–54)   DALE, EDGAR. *Audio-Visual Methods in Teaching.* New York: Henry Holt & Co., Inc., 1954. 534 pp.

(4–55)   SANDS, L. B. *Audio-Visual Procedures in Teaching.* New York: The Ronald Press Co., 1956. 670 pp.

(4–56)   SMITH, SAMUEL. *Best Methods of Study.* New York: Barnes & Noble, Inc., 1955. 132 pp.

(4–57) WITTY, PAUL. *How to Become a Better Reader.* Chicago: Science Research Associates, 1953. 304 pp.

(4–58) FLESCH, RUDOLPH. *Why Johnny Can't Read.* New York: Harper & Bros., 1955. 222 pp.

(4–59) ARBUTHNOT, MAY H. *Children and Books.* Chicago: Scott, Foresman and Co., 1947. 626 pp.

(4–60) ROOS, JEAN. *Patterns in Reading.* Chicago: American Library Association, 1954. 138 pp.

(4–61) STEFFERUD, ALFRED. (ed.). *World of Books,* illustrated by ROBERT OSBORN. Boston: Houghton Mifflin Co.; New York: New American Library of World Literature, Inc., 1952. 319 pp.

CHAPTER 5: SERIALS—MAGAZINES, PAMPHLETS, DOCUMENTS

Lists

(5–1) *Directory of Newspapers and Periodicals.* Philadelphia: N. W. Ayer and Son, Inc., 1880 to date, an annual publication.

(5–2) ULRICH's *Periodicals Directory.* New York: R. R. Bowker Co., 1956. 740 pp. A classified guide to a selected list of current periodicals foreign and domestic.

(5–3) MARTIN, LAURA K. *Magazines for School Libraries.* New York: H. W. Wilson Co., 1950. 196 pp.

Indexes (*see also* Chapter 3, entries 5–9)

(5–4) *Subject Index to Children's Magazines.* Madison, Wisc.: Meriban Hazen, 1948 to date, monthly except June and July.

School Periodical "Chain" Publishers

(5–5) *American Education Publications,* Middlebury, Conn.

(5–6) *Civic Education Service,* Washington, D.C.

(5–7) *Scholastic Corporation,* New York, N.Y.

(5–8) *Parents Institute, Inc.,* Chicago, Ill. In addition to *Children's Digest* and *Humpty Dumpty,* also publishes *Calling All Girls* and *Compact.*

(5–9) Representative Periodicals for a Materials Center (Grades 1–12)

American Girl
American Home
American Junior Red Cross Journal
American Junior Red Cross News
Better Homes and Gardens
Booklist on Subscription Books Bulletin
Boy's Life
Child Life
Children's Activities
Children's Digest
Children's Playmates
Co ed
Coronet
Current Biography
Current Events
Explorer
Geographic School Bulletin
Good Housekeeping
Highlights for Children
Holiday
Horn Book
Humpty Dumpty's Magazine for Little Children
Jack and Jill
Jr. Natural History
Jr. Review
Jr. Scholastic
Keyboard Junior
Life
My Weekly Reader
National Geographic
New York Times
Newstime
Newsweek
Our Times
Piggity
Plays
Popular Mechanics
Popular Science
Practical English
Practical Home Economics
Read
Readers' Digest

Saturday Evening Post
Scholastic Coach
Scholastic Teacher
Science Newsletter
Senior Scholastic
Seventeen
Sport
Summertime
Time
Today's Health
Weekly News Review
World Week
Young Citizens
Young Elizabethan
Young Men

Pamphlets and Government Publications

(5–10) IRELAND, NORMA O. *The Pamphlet File*. Boston: F. W. Faxon Co., Inc., 1954. 136 pp.

(5–11) *Elementary Teachers Guide to Free Curriculum Materials.* Randolph, Wisc.: Educators Progress Service, 1944 to date, annual.

(5–12) *United States Government Publications: Monthly Catalog.* Washington, D.C.: Government Printing Office, 1895 to date.

(5–13) *Selected United States Government Publications.* July 11, 1928 to date, variously monthly, semimonthly, weekly.

(5–14) *Price Lists.* Washington, D.C.: Government Printing Office.

(5–15) LEIDY, W. P. *A Popular Guide to Government Publications.* New York: Columbia University Press, 1953. 296 pp.

(5–16) *United States Library of Congress: Monthly Checklist of State Publications.* Washington, D.C.: Government Printing Office, 1910 to date.

CHAPTER 6: PLACE MEDIA—MAPS AND GLOBES

(6–1) *Webster's Geographical Dictionary;* rev. ed. Springfield. Mass.: G. & C. Merriam Co., 1955. 1352 pp.

(6–2) *Columbia-Lippincott Gazetteer of the World.* New York: Columbia University Press, 1952. 2148 pp.

(6–3) *Rand McNally World Guide.* Chicago: Rand McNally & Co., 1953.

(6–4) WERNER, JANE. *Golden Geography.* New York: Simon & Schuster, Inc., 1952. 96 pp. A child's introduction to the world. Pictures by CORNELIUS DE WITT.

(6–5) LEAF, MUNRO. *Geography Can Be Fun.* Philadelphia: J. B. Lippincott Co., 1951. 63 pp.

(6–6) JENKINS, ELMER. *Guide to America.* Washington, D.C.: Public Affairs Press, 1953. 734 pp.

(6–7) *Goode's World Atlas.* Chicago: Rand McNally & Co., 1953. 272 pp.

(6–8) *School and Library Atlas of the World.* Rocky River, Ohio: Geographical Publishing Co., 1953. 358 pp.

(6–9) *Rand McNally Cosmopolitan World Atlas.* Chicago: Rand McNally & Co., 1956. 408 pp.

(6–10) *Hammond Complete World Atlas.* New York: C. S. Hammond & Co., Inc., 1950. 376 pp. *Hammond Library World Atlas.* New York: C. S. Hammond & Co. 332 pp. *Ambassador World Atlas.* New York: C. S. Hammond & Co. 416 pp. Some other atlases to be found in school libraries are: *Collier's World Atlas and Gazetteer.* New York: P. F. Collier & Son. 1953 to date. 480 pp. *Encyclopaedia Britannica World Atlas.* Chicago: Encyclopaedia Britannica, Inc., 1942 to date. 384 pp. *Times Atlas of the World.* Boston: Houghton Mifflin Co., 1955 to date. 5 volumes.

CHAPTER 7: PICTURES

(7–1) IRELAND, NORMA O. *The Picture File in School, College, and Public Libraries.* (Useful Reference Series, no. 81). Boston: F. W. Faxon Co., Inc., 1952. 136 pp.

(7–2) MILLER, BRUCE. *So You Want to Start a Picture File.* Riverside, Calif.: The Author, 1954. 28 pp. An aid to better teaching.

(7–3) *Standard Catalog for Public Libraries.* New York: H. W. Wilson Co., 1950. 2057 pp. Fine arts section especially helpful.

(7–4) *Art Index.* New York: H. W. Wilson Co., January 1929 to date, 1933 to date.

(7–5)   *American Library Association Portrait Index.* Washington, D.C.: Library of Congress, 1906. 1600 pp. Index to portraits contained in printed books and periodicals.

(7–6)   MONRO, ISABEL S. and KATE M. *Index to Reproductions of American Paintings.* New York: H. W. Wilson Co., 1948. 731 pp. A guide to pictures occurring in more than 800 books.

(7–7)   SHEPARD, F. J. *Index to Illustrations.* Chicago: American Library Association, 1924. Out of print.

(7–8)   MONRO, ISABEL, and COOK, DOROTHY E. *Costume Index.* New York: H. W. Wilson Co., 1937. 338 pp.

(7–9)   ELLIS, JESSIE C. *Nature and Its Applications.* Boston: F. W. Faxon Co., Inc., 1949. 861 pp. Over 20,000 selected references to nature forms and illustrations of nature as used in every way.

(7–10)   ELLIS, JESSIE C. *Travel Through Pictures.* Boston: F. W. Faxon Co., Inc., 1935. 699 pp.

(7–11)   *Selected Picture Sources*
American Iron and Steel Institute, New York, N.Y. Steel making.
United Air Lines, New York, N.Y. Aviation education.
Great Northern Railroad, St. Paul, Minn. Pictorial map.
Armour & Co., Chicago, Ill. Food sources map.
Conoco, Denver, Colo. Maps.
Travelers' Insurance, Hartford, Conn. Calendars.
National Safety Council, Chicago, Ill. Safety posters.
National Association of Manufacturers, New York, N.Y.
Informative Classroom Picture Publishers, Grand Rapids, Mich.
British Information Service, New York, N.Y.

(7–12)   *Selected Sources of Drawings and Paintings*
Artext Prints, Inc., Westport, Conn. Color prints.
Friendship Press, New York, N.Y. Pictorial maps.
Art Research Associates, New York, N.Y.

(7–13)   *Selected Sources of Professional Prints and Sets*
Creative Educational Society, Mankato, Minn.
Informative Classroom Picture Publishers, Grand Rapids, Mich.
R. R. Bowker Company, New York, N.Y.

(7–14)   *Lettering Equipment*
Keuffel and Esser Co., Chicago, Ill. Leroy Letter Scriber.
Letter Guide, Lincoln, Nebraska. Scriber.

Paratone, Chicago, Ill. "Paratype" in sheets.
Davidson Corporation, Brooklyn, N.Y. Protype electronic, photo lettering.
Embossograph Corporation of America, New York, N.Y. Embossed letters.

(7–15)   *Duplicating Equipment*
"Photo Rapid," Photorapid of America, Inc., New York, N.Y.
"Thermo-Fax," Minnesota Mining and Manufacturing Co., Minneapolis, Minn.
"Transcopy," Remington Rand, New York, N.Y.
"Verifax," Eastman Kodak Co., Rochester, N.Y.
Mimeograph, Spirit Duplicator, A. B. Dick Co., Chicago, Ill.
"Bambino," Ozalid Corporation, Johnson City, N.Y.
Silk Screen, Stationers Corporation, Los Angeles, Calif., and Active Process and Supply Co., New York, N.Y.

(7–16)   *Dry Mounting Equipment*
Seal, Inc., Shelton, Conn.

CHAPTER 8: OBJECTS

(8–1)   *Sources of Objects, Models, Displays*
Central Scientific Co., Chicago, Ill. Objects, models.
Clay-Adams Co., Inc., New York, N.Y. Cutaways
Creative Playthings, Inc., New York, N.Y. Models.
General Biological Supply House, Inc., Chicago, Ill. Specimens, exhibits.
Imitation Food Display, Brooklyn, N.Y. Food models.
The Judy Co., Minneapolis, Minn. Educational toys.
Models of Industry, Berkeley, Calif.
W. M. Welch Scientific Co., Chicago, Ill. Models, exhibits.

(8–2)   *Chalkboard Sources*
Corbett Blackboard Stencils, North Pelham, N.Y.
Ronald Eyrich, Milwaukee, Wisc.
Teaching Materials Service, Beloit, Wisc.

(8–3)   *Flannel, Magnetic, and Peg Boards*
E. J. Blosser Co., Los Angeles, Calif.
B. B. Butler Mfg. Co., Bellwood, Ill.
Demco Library Supplies, Madison, Wisc.
Judy Company, Minneapolis, Minn.
Mitten's Display Letters, Redlands, Calif.
Self-Teaching Aids, Los Angeles, Calif.
Slyd In Products, Greensboro, N.C.

CHAPTER 9: STILL PROJECTIONS—
OPAQUES, TRANSPARENCIES, FILMSTRIPS

(9–1) *Opaque Projectors*
American Optical Co., Chelsea, Mass. Delineascope.
Bausch & Lomb Optical Co., Rochester, N.Y. Baloptican.
Charles Beseler Co., East Orange, N.J., Nu Lyte.
Spencer Optical Co., New York, N.Y.
Squibb-Taylor, Inc., Dallas, Texas. Spotlight.

(9–2) *Screens*
Clearcite Screen Co., Chicago, Ill.
Da-lite Screen Co., Chicago, Ill.
Radiant Mfg. Corp., Morton Grove, Ill.
Raven Screen Corp., New York, N.Y.
Vita-Lite Screen Co., San Diego, Calif.

(9–3) *Transparency Projectors.* Filmstrip, slide, overhead.
American Optical Co., Chelsea, Mass.
Audio-Master Corp., New York, N.Y.
Bausch & Lomb Optical Co., Rochester, N.Y.
Bell & Howell Co., Chicago, Ill.
Charles Beseler Co., East Orange, N.J.
Eastman Kodak Co., Rochester, N.Y.
Keystone View Co., Meadville, Pa.
Society for Visual Education, Inc., Chicago, Ill.
Viewlex, Long Island City, N.Y.

(9–4) FALCONER, VERA M. Filmstrips: *A Descriptive Index and User's Guide.* New York: McGraw-Hill Book Co., 1948. 572 pp.

(9–5) *Filmstrip Guide.* New York: H. W. Wilson Co., September, 1948 to date. Monthly, semi-annual, annual, tri-ennial publication.

(9–6) *Educators Guide to Free Slidefilms.* Randolph, Wisc.: Educators Progress Service, 1949 to date. Annual.

(9–7) *Three-Dimensional Projectors*
Compco Corp., Chicago, Ill.
Sawyers, Inc., Portland, Oregon. Viewmaster.
Spindler & Sauppe, Los Angeles, Calif.
Three Dimension Co., Chicago, Ill.
Viewlex, Inc., Long Island City, N.Y.
Projections
Camera Services, Inc., New York, N.Y.

Deep-Vue Corp., Milwaukee, Wisc.
General Biological Supply House, Chicago, Ill.
Stereo Slide Service, Old Greenwich, Conn.
Three Dimension Photo Co., New York, N.Y.

(9–8) *Microprojectors*
American Optical Co., New York, N.Y.
Bausch & Lomb Optical Co., Rochester, N.Y.
Rayoscope Co., Delaware, Ohio.
Society for Visual Education, Inc., Chicago, Ill.
Universal Seoscope Co., Oklahoma City, Okla.
Projections
Edwards Brothers, Ann Arbor, Michigan.
Micro Facsimile Corp., New York, N.Y.
Microcard Foundation, Middletown, Conn.
Projected Books, Inc., Ann Arbor, Mich.
Readex Microprint Corp., New York, N.Y.
Recordak Corp., New York, N.Y.
Remington Rand, New York, N.Y.

(9–9) *Audio-Visual Equipment Directory.* Fairfax, Va.: National
Audio-Visual Association, 1958. 219 pp. This fourth edition
of a list prepared by the audio-visual manufacturers, groups,
lists, illustrates and describes all types of audio-visual equipment giving specifications.

CHAPTER 10: MOTION PICTURES

(10–1) *Educational Film Guide.* New York: H. W. Wilson Co.,
1936 to date. Monthly, semi-annual, annual, triennial.

(10–2) *Educators' Guide to Free Films.* Randolph, Wisc.: Educators Progress Service, 1941 to date. Annual.

(10–3) *Library of Congress Catalog: Motion Pictures and Filmstrips: A Cumulative List of Works Represented by Library
of Congress Printed Cards.* Washington, D.C.: 1953 to date.
Quarterly, annual. Now part of the *National Union Catalog.*

(10–4) *Motion Picture Projectors*
Ampro Corp., Chicago, Ill.
Bell & Howell Co., Chicago, Ill.
Eastman Kodak Co., Rochester, N.Y.
Radio Corp. of America, Camden, N.J.
Victor Animatograph Corp., Davenport, Iowa.

CHAPTER 11: RECORDINGS—DISKS AND TAPES

(11–1) EISENBERG, PHILIP, and KRASNO, HECKY. *A Guide to Children's Records.* New York: Crown Publishers, Inc., 1948. 195 pp.

(11–2) LEAVITT, A. S., and FREEMAN, M. S. *Recordings for the Elementary School.* New York: Crown Publishers, Inc., 1949.
BARBOUR, HARRIET, and FREE, W. S. *The Children's Record Book.* New York: Crown Publishers, Inc., 1947. 186 pp.

(11–3) MYERS, KURTZ. *Record Ratings.* New York: Crown Publishers, Inc., 1954. 440 pp.

(11–4) *Educators' Guide to Free Tapes, Scripts and Transcriptions.* Randolph, Wisc.: Educators' Progress Service, 1955 to date, annual.

(11–5) Other recording selection aids worthy of note are:
KOLODIN, IRVING, MILLER, PHILIP L., and SCHONBURG, HAROLD C. *The Guide to Long Playing Records.* New York: Alfred A. Knopf, Inc., 1955. 3 volumes.
TAUBMAN, HOWARD. *How to Build a Record Library.* New York: Garden City Books, 1954. 94 pp.
HASTINGS, HENRY C. *Spoken Poetry on Records and Tapes.* ACRL Monographs. Chicago: American Library Association, 1957. 51 pp.
BALDWIN, LILLIAN. *Music for Young Listeners.* New York: Silver Burdette Co., 1951. 122 pp.
Schwann Long Playing Record Catalog. 137 Newbury St., Boston, Mass. Monthly—1949 to date.

(11–6) *Sources for Disk Recordings*
Bowmar, Valhalla, N.Y.
Chesterfield Music Shop, New York, N.Y.
Children's Book Council, New York, N.Y.
Children's Reading Service, Brooklyn, N.Y.
Columbia Records, New York, N.Y.
Enrichment Materials, Inc., New York, N.Y.
Sam Goody, New York, N.Y.

(11–7) *Disk Recording Equipment*
Allied Radio, Chicago, Ill.
Audio-Master Corp., New York, N.Y.
Bell Sound Systems, Inc., Columbus, Ohio.
Califone Corp., Hollywood, Calif.

Columbia Recording Corp., New York, N.Y.
DuKane Corp., St. Charles, Ill.
Newcomb Electronics Corp., Hollywood, Calif.
RCA Victor, Div. Radio Corp. of America, Camden, N.J.
Webster-Chicago Corp., Chicago, Ill.

(11–8) *Tape Recording Equipment*
Ampex Electric Corp., Redwood City, Calif.
Ampro Corp., Chicago, Ill.
Bell & Howell, Chicago, Ill.
Bell Sound Systems, Inc., Columbus, Ohio.
DuKane Corp., St. Charles, Ill.
Magnecord, Inc., Chicago, Ill.
Tape Recorders, Inc., Chicago, Ill.
Webster-Chicago Corp., Chicago, Ill.

(11–9) *Tape Recording Libraries*
A-V Tape Libraries, New York, N.Y.
EMC Recordings Corp., St. Paul, Minn.
International Communications Association, Cleveland, Ohio.
Kent State University, Kent, Ohio.
Phonotapes, Inc., New York, N.Y.
Shakespeare Tape Library, Washington, D.C.
A number of universities and state departments of education offer tape recording services.

(11–10) *National Tape Recording Catalog*
Kent, Ohio: Kent State University, 1957. 76 pp.

CHAPTER 12: RADIO AND TELEVISION

(12–1) *Sources of Advance Information About Radio and TV Programs Billboard.* Cincinnati: Billboard Publications Co., 1894 to date. Weekly.
Broadcast News. Camden, N.J.: Radio Corporation of America, 1931 to date, 5 times yearly.
Broadcasting-Telecasting. Washington, D.C.: Broadcasting Publications, Inc., 1931 to date, weekly; annual broadcasting, telecasting and marketing yearbooks. The News Weekly of Radio and Television.
Cue. New York: Cue Publishing Co., 1932 to date, weekly. The magazine of New York living.
International Television Almanac. New York: Quigley, 1956 to date, annual. Lists continuing network programs.
Listener. London: BBC, 1929 to date, weekly.

Newsweek. New York: Weekly Publications, 1933 to date, weekly.

Networks provide information through various media, such as ABC's *Advance Program Information,* NBC's *Program Information,* CBS's ditto form release, and *Mutual Program Folio.*

Radio and Television Weekly. New York: John Riesenfeld, 1916 to date.

Radio-Television Daily. New York: Radio Daily Corp., 5 times weekly.

Radio Times. London: British Broadcasting Corp., 1925 to date, monthly.

Television Magazine. New York: Frederick Kugel Co., Inc., 1944 to date, monthly; annual data book.

TV Guide. Philadelphia: Triangle Publications, Inc., 1948 to date, weekly.

TV-Radio Life. Hollywood, Calif., 1940 to date, weekly.

Variety. New York: Variety, Inc., 1905 to date, weekly.

(12–2) *Radio and Television Equipment*
Dage Television Co., Michigan City, Ind.
DuKane Corp., St. Charles, Ill.
Fairchild (Freed-Eisemann), Syosset, Long Island, N.Y.
General Electric Co., Syracuse, N.Y.
Magnavox, Fort Wayne, Ind.
Philco, Philadelphia, Pa.
RCA-Victor, New York, N.Y.
Zenith, Chicago, Ill.

CHAPTER 13: THE MATERIALS CENTER

(13–1) *American Library Association. Dear Mr. Architect.* Chicago: American Library Association, 1946.
American Library Association. Planning School Library Quarters: A Functional Approach. Chicago: American Library Association, 1950.

(13–2) DeBernardis, Amo. "An Instructional Materials Center." *Education,* LXXVII (January, 1957), 306–9.

(13–3) Douglas, Mary P. *The Teacher-Librarian's Handbook.* Chicago: American Library Association, 1949.

(13–4) *Florida State Department of Education. The Materials Center.* Tallahassee: 1955. 136 pp. Prepared under direction of Sara Krentzman Srygley.

(13–5)   *National Education Association. Department of Audio-Visual Instruction, Planning Schools for Use of Audio-Visual Instruction. No. 1, Classrooms; No. 2, Auditoriums; No. 3, AV Instructional Material Centers.* Washington, D.C.: National Education Association, 1954–54. 3 volumes.

(13–6)   RUFSVOLD, MARGARET. *Audio-Visual School Library Service.* Chicago: American Library Association, 1949.

(13–7)   SHORES, LOUIS. "Enter the Materials Center." American Library Association Bulletin, XLIX (June, 1955), 285–88.
————. SPEARS, HAROLD, and BUSHONG, JAMES W. "Library and AV Center—Combined or Separate?" National Education Association Journal, XLVII (May, 1958), 342–44.

NAME INDEX

SUBJECT INDEX